Theology for a Scientific Age

Signposts in Theology

Theology for a Scientific Age

Being and Becoming – Natural and Divine

ARTHUR PEACOCKE

Basil Blackwell

1990

First published 1990

Basil Blackwell Ltd
108 Cowley Road, Oxford, OX4 1JF, UK

Basil Blackwell, Inc.
3 Cambridge Center
Cambridge, Massachusetts 02142, USA

British Library Cataloguing in Publication Data

A CIP catalogue record for this book is available from the British Library.

Library of Congress Cataloging in Publication Data
Peacocke, A. R. (Arthur Robert)
     Theology for a scientific age : being and becoming –
natural and divine / Arthur Peacocke
        p.   cm.
     ISBN 0–631–15426–4
     1. Religion and science–1946-   I. Title.
BL240.2.P352   1991   90–31368
261.5′5–dc20   CIP

Typeset in 10½pt on 12½pt Century Schoolbook by Vera Reyes
Printed in Great Britain by Billing & Sons Ltd, Worcester

To fellow members
of the
Society of Ordained Scientists

CONTENTS

PREFACE

Anyone who has been at all concerned with the history of the interaction between Christian theology and the natural sciences cannot but view current controversies between the self-appointed 'conservatives' and the pejoratively labelled 'liberals' with an acute sense of *déjà vu*. For again and again Christian theology has had to face up to the challenge of new knowledge about the natural world – and indeed about its historical origins and sacred scriptures – and the heresies of one generation have become the orthodoxies of the next. So much so that, even when the traditional words are used in creeds and worship by a twentieth-century Christian, the content of their belief often bears only a distant genetic relation to what was believed in the context of the thought-world centuries, or even a millennium, ago. For the whole framework in which affirmations of belief about nature, humanity and God are set have changed radically over the centuries, and never more rapidly than in the twentieth.

It is no use pretending that these recent changes have been at all helpful to membership of the mainline churches in the West which have usually been associated with the conservation of past beliefs rather than with intelligent, open inquiry into new modes of expression of commitment to God in Christ through the Holy Spirit, to use traditional terms. The current resuscitation of very conservative positions, both in and outside these churches, is a sign not so much of a recovery of faith as of a loss of nerve before the onslaught of new perceptions of the world.

The understanding of the world which is evoked by the contemporary natural sciences is commonly taken in the West to be inimical to, or at least subversive of, religious belief in general and Christian belief in particular. I am convinced that this widely accepted view is mistaken and that the myth of the gulf between Christian theology and the natural sciences is debilitating to our culture while impoverishing the spiritual and personal life of the generations who have come to believe it. Study of this interaction, as expressed in my earlier writings* (some of them listed on p. 189), has impelled me to evolve a theology that has been refined, as far as it lay within my powers, in the fires of the new perceptions of the world that the natural sciences have irreversibly established. Such a theology needs to be consonant and coherent with, though far from being derived from, scientific perspectives on the world.

In the compass of the volumes on this series, it is not possible to present a fully systematic theology. What has been attempted is the discernment and working out of the consequences for our concept of God and of God's interaction with the world of the comprehensive perspectives of the sciences. (I hope in a later extension of this work to turn to more specifically Christian doctrines concerned with 'Human being and becoming', to follow Part II of this volume, 'Divine being and becoming'). I offer these reflections not in any spirit of wishing to disturb those for whom fully traditional formulations and interpretations still have meaning, but to those who would like to follow in the Christian 'Way' but have thought they could not do so with intellectual integrity.

Arthur Peacocke
Oxford, February, 1990

Note 'God' is neither male nor female, and I have earlier (in *Creation and the World of Science*, Clarendon Press, Oxford, 1979, pp. 141–4) been quite explicit concerning the need to recover and extend the use of both feminine attributes of God and feminine models of God's relation to the world. So I have tried to avoid the use of male pronouns in sentences about 'God'. Sometimes, however, the exigencies of English syntax and euphony have defeated me. I ask the reader to be indulgent to me in these unavoidable lapses and not to attribute any theological significance to them.

---

* The Introduction to this volume incorporates ideas, and some actual text, drawn from lectures by the author in part published in: *Religion and Intellectual Life*, 2 (1985), pp. 7–26; ibid., 5 (1988), pp. 45–58; *Religion, Science and Public Policy*, ed. F. T. Birtel (Crossroad, New York, 1987), pp. 3–29; *Cosmos as Creation*, ed. Ted Peters (Abingdon Press, Nashville, 1989), pp. 28–43.

The Theological and Scientific Enterprises

1 'SCIENCE AND RELIGION'

There are many indications that the understanding of the world which is evoked by contemporary science is seen in the West as inimical to, or at least subversive of, religious belief – mainly Christian belief. That this impression is induced early on in life was well substantiated, just to take one example, in a report in 1977 on the beliefs of young people:

> Childhood belief is breached with incredible ease on the basis of a simplistic scientism...
>
> In general... what we find... is an uncritical acceptance of a vocabulary of natural science which is... out of date... and is capable of enshrining new myths within itself... Instead of religion our young people have a mild form of science fiction...
>
> [We are]... left with a growing suspicion that one of the crucial processes at work in our modern world is, or has been, the imperialistic advance of a *vocabulary* of rationality, science and individualism... what has got crowded out is a *language* which modern society will regard as valid in which symbols and rituals can be described and expressed.[1]

In a wider context, Lesslie Newbigin, with his long missionary experience in the Third World, has recently reflected upon the shrinking influence of the churches in modern Western culture – which now includes not only the peoples of Europe and North America but also their former colonial and cultural offshoots and those parts of the Third World that are undergoing 'modernization' under the influence of education, the media and invading industries. No-one concerned with the future of the Christian, or indeed any other religion, can avoid facing up to the impact of science on faith.

This encounter is identified by Newbigin as the crucial point at which the gospel is failing to have any impact on 'Western' men and women.[2]

The general level of discussion of issues which involve any relating of scientific knowledge to received Christian belief, or rather to what is widely assumed to be such, remains at a depressingly low level – witness the controversies surrounding so-called 'creationism' in the United States and the relation of a fertilized human ovum to the human 'soul', not to mention the welcoming by even the 'serious' press in the English-speaking world of any controversy among evolutionary biologists as somehow casting doubt on 'Darwinism' and thereby implicitly vindicating 'religion'. Every year when the British Association for the Advancement of Science meets, some journalist or other inevitably resuscitates the myth (and 'myth', in the popular sense of 'untrue story', the historians are now showing it to be) of how the Saint George of science in the person of T. H. Huxley slew the dragon of religious bigotry in the person of the then Bishop of Oxford, Samuel Wilberforce, at its 1860 Oxford meeting.

In a more serious vein, I would hazard the guess that leading Western intellectuals, and particularly the scientists who have this century set the pace for the others, would concur that the natural sciences were *par excellence* the manifestation of the human search for intelligibility. I would also guess that they would recognize too the validity of the human search for the meaning of existence, and some might even concur that religion was one of the fundamental manifestations of the existence of this unfulfilled human longing – along with the arts and non-religious rituals. For in spite of many prophecies, religion has not withered away entirely, even in Western societies, and in many parts of the world it is positively flourishing. The human need to discern meaning and significance for the individual in the universe as understood and experienced has, if anything, been sharpened and the appetite for it quickened by the widening vistas opened up by the sciences. For the perennial challenges of our sense of mortality within the joyful vitalities of existence, of human suffering and yet also of human joy and exaltation in achievement, of our inner transcendence over that on which we reflect and of our vulnerability to the fragility of the fantastically complex organization of our evolved bodies – all these experiences, and much else, continue to fire in us humans longings and aspirations that appear incapable of satisfaction from within the resources vouchsafed to us by the too-monochrome scientific descriptions of our world. So it is perhaps not so surprising, after all, that the investigations of, for example, the Alister Hardy Research Centre at Oxford, have uncovered how widespread in highly secularized late twentieth-century Britain are experiences of awareness of a benevolent non-physical power that appears to be partly or wholly beyond, and far greater than, the individual self. Such experiences are properly designated as 'religious', whatever the official allegiance, or lack of it, of those reporting them to any religious institution.

The form of religion with which the greater proportion of those nurtured in Western societies, in the narrow sense, is acquainted is Christianity. It has shaped our art, music, architecture, customs, laws and inbuilt social assumptions, and through our use of symbols and language still does so shape the inner pattern of our thinking in incalculable ways, even that of those who overtly repudiate it. We may perhaps, after a lifetime's study and immersion in another (for example, Buddhist) culture become sufficiently indigenized that 'God', if there is one, can speak to us through the resources of that culture – but it is extremely unlikely that we shall achieve such a degree of re-enculturation in an average lifetime, and there are very few who actually do so. A shrewd appraisal of what might be a fruitful use of time and energy would suggest that a Western writer seeking to interpret the religious experience of human beings to a Western readership could best do so with reference to their common Christian inheritance, even if it is no longer appreciated by the majority. This is the policy pursued in this book, but in no way is this meant to imply that other non-Christian religions cannot be a path to that reality which is, as I shall argue, God.

Moreover, since the aim of this work is to rethink our 'religious' conceptualizations in the light of the perspective on the world afforded by the sciences, there are at least two further reasons, in addition to the cultural one just proposed, why the relation of Christianity to that perspective has a special significance for all forms of religious experience and cultures.

The first is that Western Christianity in its Catholic, Protestant and Anglican forms (Eastern Orthodox Christianity constitutes a different experience) was the first major religion to encounter the full impact of the natural sciences on important features of the received content of its beliefs. Their systems of Christian belief incorporated many basic affirmations about the relation of God, humanity and nature within a matrix of assumptions concerning the natural world that had accumulated over many centuries of 'natural philosophy', later called 'natural science', or just 'science'. Since it was in England that Newton and Darwin first propounded their ideas, the Church of England in particular had, a little earlier than some other churches, to take the full brunt of the revolution in our thinking about the natural world initiated by these key figures. In this context, it is interesting to note how the relatively conservative reformation of the Church in England was viewed in that formative period for the rise of science, the seventeenth century, by a contemporary historian – Thomas Sprat, the first historian of the Royal Society of London:

> we behold the agreement that is between the present *Design* of the *Royal Society*, and that of our *Church* in its beginning. They both may lay equal claim to the word *Reformation*; the one having compassed it in *Religion*, the other purposing it in *Philosophy* . . . They both suppose alike, that their *Ancestors* might err; and yet retain a sufficient reverence for them . . .[3]

In fact it was on a church of this kind, in a society in which the church, though influential, could and did have its beliefs subjected to wide and open criticism, that the scientific revolution had such a major impact. In fact, the reaction to Darwin in nineteenth-century England was very mixed and recent historical studies show that there was much less antagonism on the part of theologians and more on the part of scientists than the current mythology allows.[4] There is indeed much that can be learnt concerning the interaction between the theological and scientific enterprises from the careful and objective historical study of such interactions between scientists ('natural philosophers') and theologians. Although such historical analysis is not the focus of this study, what follows has, I hope, been informed by it.

The second reason why the Christian religion merits special attention as a paradigm case of a religion operating in the new cultural climate associated with the rise of science is that the Christian religion has had to take up the gauntlet thrown down by what is loosely called the 'Enlightenment'. It, almost alone among the major world religions, has been subject within its own culture to critical, historical, linguistic and literary analysis of its sacred literature and its sources; has had its beliefs exposed to sceptical philosophical critique; its attitudes to psychological examination; and its structures to sociological inquiry. All this has occurred in the course of barely three centuries during which the immense economic upheavals of industrialization have, along with increased freedom and education, entirely altered people's lives and outlooks.

It is one of the ironic features of this culture in the last decade or so of the twentieth century that after more than 300 years of a fecund natural science – one of the supreme achievements of human reason and curiosity – the search for intelligibility concerning the nature and origin of the cosmos has plunged human beings irrevocably, and for some unwillingly, into the darker stream of the search for meaning. An irony it is – for did not this selfsame science, according to popular mythology, only acquire its freedom even to seek intelligibility by unshackling itself from the stifling embrace of a Christianity too much concerned with meaning and too little concerned with what came to be called the evidence? But the irony is compounded, for Christian civilization itself, having given birth to its child of science[5] and having seen that growing infant cut its umbilical cord, has resorted more and more to an emphasis on subjective personal experience ('meaning for me') as its basis, only to find that twentieth-century human beings cannot find such a resource of meaning in the Christian religion (or in anything else) unless it is consonant with their understanding of the world which is itself moulded by that same science.

So after two centuries or more of bickering, or of sullen silence with demarcation of spheres of interest, these two fundamental activities, the search for intelligibility and the search for meaning, that characterize respectively, but not exclusively, science and religion, find themselves inextricably interlocked with each other in the common human enterprise of seeking *both* intelligibility *and* meaning. Each now provides the other with challenges to and resources for an interaction gradually becoming more fruitful and wholesome. This judgement on the contemporary scene could be illustrated from many spheres: the understanding of the human person as a psychosomatic unity in both science and religion; the integration of biological evolutionary ideas with the sense of God as an immanent, ever-working Creator; or reflections on the origins of the cosmos induced both by astrophysics and cosmology, on the one hand, and clarification of the Judeo-Christian doctrine of creation on the other.

The last trumpet in the so-called warfare of science and religion has long since become silent and those engaged in both enterprises have today, I think, acquired a new humility – not least because they have come to recognize both the limitations of their presumed knowledge and the dire, indeed evil, social consequences of ultra-dogmatic, over-confident, imperialistic applications of half-truths about their respective quests. For example, the intellectual descendants of the Enlightenment have long castigated religion, with justification, for the wars fought in its name, only to find themselves to have sired in twentieth-century nuclear physics the possibility of global, rather than local, holocaust.

Implicit in this study is the assumption of the significance of the relationship between 'science' and 'religion', not only for the health of each enterprise but also for the future of humanity. For the relationship between these two claimants on human loyalty is probably the most fundamental challenge that faces the mind and spirit of human beings today. It is necessary to be more precise about these terms. By 'science' I shall mean the *natural* sciences, including not only the physical and biological sciences but also the 'human sciences' (psychology, sociology, etc.). That is, by 'science' I shall be referring to *naturwissenschaften* rather than to *geisteswissenschaften* (the 'humanities'[6]). Furthermore, I shall be concerned principally with 'theology' rather than with the more widely ranging area of 'religion'. The distinction is difficult to make precise, but broadly I shall take 'theology' to refer to the reflective and intellectual analysis of the experience of God[7] and, for the reasons mentioned above, principally the Christian forms of that experience, though this inevitably includes much of the Jewish experience too, since this shares the same roots. Such analysis of the Christian experience of God that is the concern of theology necessarily involves a careful consideration of the content of Christian belief, for Christianity, more than most of the major world religions, makes cognitive claims. It affirms, in some sense, the reality of that to which it refers. The sense in which this is so will be discussed later in this chapter.

It is also apparent that scientists, and the general public who utilize the fruits of their claimed knowledge, believe even more strongly that science affirms the reality of that to which it refers. Hence, there is a strong *prima facie* case for re-examining the claimed cognitive content of Christian theology in the light of the new knowledge derivable from the sciences, since both enterprises purport to be dealing with what they regard as realities. If such an exercise is not continually undertaken theology will operate in a cultural ghetto quite cut off from most of those in Western cultures who have good grounds for thinking that science describes what is going on in the processes of the world at all levels. The turbulent history of the relation of science and theology bears witness to the impossibility of theology seeking a peaceful haven, protected from the science of its times, if it is going to be believable. Indeed, theology has been most creative and long-lasting when it has responded most positively to the challenges of its times, as when the Cappadocian Fathers used Greek philosophy to express the categories of Christian theology and when St Thomas Aquinas faced up to and triumphantly utilized the then overwhelming intellectual resources of Aristotelianism to reshape that same theology into a form that endured for centuries. It is in this spirit that we set out on the journey to attempt to shape a contemporary expression of the Christian experience of God in terms – metaphors, models, analogies and symbols – that might be believable and usable by a 'Western' humanity now deeply and irreversibly, and quite properly, influenced by the sciences.

2 ATTITUDES TO SCIENCE AND THEOLOGY

Before going further it is worth reflecting a little on the respective standings of both the scientific and theological enterprises in our Western societies today. Let us take science first.

The standing of science has changed abruptly in the 1970s and 1980s from a general glow of public approval, which was translated politically into generous provision for scientific research, through an increasing hesitation about the long-term social value of science, to a current downright suspicion on the part of many ordinary citizens, who nevertheless continue to reap its benefits in terms of the ease, health and longevity of their lives. This tarnishing of the image of science can be traced back to a succession of public disasters generated by a scientifically-based technology – the thalidomide tragedies, oil spills (of which the *Torrey Canyon* and *Amoco Cadiz* were to prove to be only the first of a long line), acid rain, and the nuclear industry accidents at Long Island and Chernobyl, to mention only a few of the more publicized. Everyone can give their own accounts of more local and personal incidents in which it has seemed that the previously worshipped idol of science, and its offspring, technology, were proving to have feet of clay. The tendency of science to imperiousness in our intellectual and cultural life has been dubbed 'scientism' – the attitude that the *only* kind of reliable knowledge is that provided by science, coupled with a conviction that all our personal and social problems are 'soluble' by enough science. Many popularizers of science – more rarely those most engaged at the frontiers of scientific investigation of the mysteries of the natural world – appear, implicitly at least, to acquiesce in such 'scientistic' attitudes.

These and many other factors have led to a recent increase in anti-scientific attitudes. These are actually not new in Western cultures, for there has been quite a long history of profound dissatisfaction with purported scientific 'explanations' that do not answer the questions human beings actually ask, despite the acknowledgement of many committed scientists that science could not answer them. The Australian philosopher, John Passmore, has studied the development of both scientistic and anti-scientific attitudes with some care. He has some scathing comments on, for example, that presumed pecking order in the prestige of scientists which puts mathematical physicists, dealing with the most abstract entities, at the top (the 'aristoscientists'), followed by those who work with entities (such as molecules and genes) that are a little less abstract to the non-scientist, down to those concerned with obviously accessible phenomena like butterflies and the weather, and finishing with those concerned with people – anthropologists and sociologists, only doubtfully admitted into the club at all. Passmore judged that this hierarchical view generated attitudes of mind that are socially dangerous, even affirming, not irrelevantly to our present themes, that 'the resemblance between the aristoscientist and the mediaeval theologian daily becomes more striking.'[8]

Such attitudes have understandably provoked anti-scientific attitudes. Nevertheless Passmore concludes that

> many of the major charges which have been brought against science cannot be sustained ... I have not pretended that all is for the best in the best of all possible worlds, or denied that science has encouraged, even when it did not generate, attitudes of mind which can have adverse consequences. We are all of us, I think, coming to recognize that fact, scientists along with the rest. Science needed an injection of humility, and has had it ... When it touches on human affairs, science is no longer accorded automatic respect.[9]

Yet in spite of all this scepticism about its social value and antipathy to excessively arrogant claims on its behalf, science still seems to most people, both intellectuals and others, to be the paradigm of what constitutes reliable knowledge. For allowing, as it does, prediction and control in many simple and complex circumstances involving the natural world, what it refers to is seen by most people simply to be 'real' – they cannot afford to ignore it in their dealings with nature. Such a 'naive realism' regards scientific concepts, theories and mechanisms as literal descriptions of the natural world. In this vein Henry Harris, a practising medical scientist, could stress that, although it is true that in physics Einstein's equations superseded those of Newton, yet this

> is no argument at all for the notion that all scientific conclusions are similarly bound eventually to be displaced. I do not believe that it will ever be shown that the blood of animals does not circulate; that anthrax is not caused by a bacterium; that proteins are not chains of amino acids. Human beings may indeed make mistakes, but I see no merit in the idea that they can make nothing but mistakes.[10]

Hence it is not surprising – such is the influence of the media and of some exceptionally good popular presentations of science on television in recent years – that scientific accounts of the world are taken as literally descriptive and as constituting for most people the framework, or stage, of the 'reality' in which they believe their lives to be set and enacted. However, this constitutes a naive philosophy of science and we need to examine the relation between scientific knowledge and the 'reality' it purports to describe. Therefore, before embarking on an inquiry into a believable theology for a scientific age, we must first establish what kind of knowing and what kind of knowledge of 'reality' actually prevails in the sciences. As a working definition, we shall take 'reality' to mean that to which we find we cannot avoid relating in our experiments and experience.

Now the world described by some parts of modern physics, to take just one area, is a very strange one indeed, far removed from any world to which it is possible to extrapolate from our senses, including as it does apparently obscure entities such as electron holes, black holes, gravitational waves, anti-matter, and so on. So we shall have to consider to what it is that scientific terms actually refer. Do they depict reality? This question will be taken up later, in discussing science and theology today (p. 11).

Let us turn now to theology. Almost the only usage of the word 'theology' with which the general public is now familiar is that of politicians who employ it to refer pejoratively to the views of their opponents, thereby intending to characterize them as 'theoretical', 'abstract', 'utopian', 'unrealistic' – all thought to be highly undesirable features – while at the same time signalling that their own opinions and policies are 'realistic', 'practical' and, of course, 'relevant'. Even within the membership of the Christian churches, 'theology' is frequently regarded as the activity of intellectuals of doubtful Christian commitment, pontificating from remote academic ivory towers and isolated from the realities and tensions of the religious experience of 'ordinary' believers living in the 'real world'. This gap between the pew and the study has been much in evidence in recent years in relation to a number of controversies, at least in England, surrounding the doctrines of the incarnation and resurrection. The gulf shows no signs of narrowing, such is the general appallingly low standard of lay adult education in the churches. Yet the content of what 'ordinary' Christians believe is inevitably 'theology', even when it is relatively uninformed. One of the principal causes of the weakness of the churches' mission to Western humanity must be their failure to find a convincing way of expressing their beliefs, that is, of having a theology which is capable of coping with the contemporary cultural and intellectual situation and of out-thinking it. But the unfortunate theologian has to fight on at least one other front – that of his fellow scholars and intellectuals. For in spite of the universality of religious experience amongst human beings,[11] the academic study of the philosophy, history and tradition of such experiences – namely, theology – is still looked at askance by the Western intellectual world, despite massive attempts by many Christian theologians to be in genuine dialogue with new knowledge and social developments.

Furthermore, within theology itself there has been a crisis of authority in the Christian religion which will just as surely overtake other religions as critical education becomes more widespread. The effects of the Enlightenment are, quite rightly, irreversible, and no sacred writings and no sacred tradition can ever again be self-authenticating in the sense of itself validating its own claims to truth. Some fulcrum, some point of leverage, of assessment from outside the written sacred word or the sacred tradition, is needed to assess the truth of their affirmations and the reality of that to which the adherent of a religion commits him- or herself. So theistic religions have to face sharp questions today: Is talk about God valid? Do theological terms refer to reality? These and related questions

are of the same kind as those generated about the status of theoretical terms and theories in science and, in a parallel manner, press
us into making an assessment of the nature of religious language
and its ability, if any, to depict reality. For both science and theology
have only the resources of human language to explicate the significance of their experiments and experience. It is this shared necessity that we must now explore a little further in the conviction that
examination of the relation between the languages of, and so the
status of assertions in, science and theology is no mere 'academic'
exercise, but a vital component in the clarification of their relationship. Only so can there be established that *modus vivendi* between
science and theology, the lack of which is already proving so
debilitating to the moral and spiritual health of late twentieth-
century humanity.

3 SCIENCE AND THEOLOGY TODAY: A CRITICAL-REALIST PERSPECTIVE

There have been a variety of philosophies of science in the twentieth
century, ranging from the widespread and popular naive realism
already mentioned, which was inherited from the last century and
was rapidly discredited by the revolutions in physics in the first few
decades of this; through instrumentalism and decades dominated by
positivism; to a variety of views in the last decade which range from
a socially-contextualized view of scientific knowledge through non-
sociological but anti-realist positions to the critical realism which is
the view espoused here. It is moreover, I believe, also the implicit,
though often not articulated, working philosophy of practising
scientists who aim to depict reality but know only too well their
fallibility in doing so. The arguments for critical realism as a valid
and coherent philosophy of science have been widely rehearsed
elsewhere.[12] All I propose to do here is to summarize this view,
without any attempt at a detailed justification.

This is less easy than might at first appear, for there are many
forms of 'realism' concerning science which are all non-naive and so
could be described as 'critical' or, at least, as 'qualified'. For, as has
been justly observed, 'Like the Equal Rights Movement, scientific
realism is a majority position whose advocates are so divided as to
appear a minority.'[13] However, the fine distinctions between different forms of non-naive scientific realism (meaning realism with
respect to scientific knowledge) are less important for the purposes

of our present exercise than its principal, general stance which distinguishes it from earlier, other philosophies of science of this century and also from very socially-contextualized interpretations of the content of science as an almost purely social construct. In spite of the variety of adjectives that may qualify 'realism' as a philosophy of science, there is a common core which I shall, in company with others, denote as 'critical realism'. The position may be summarized thus, in the words of J. Leplin, 'What realists do share in common are the convictions that scientific change is, on balance, progressive and that science makes possible knowledge of the world beyond its accessible, empirical manifestations.'[14] It is aiming to depict reality. For the basic claim made by such a critical scientific realism is that it is the long-term success of a scientific theory that warrants the belief that 'something like the entities and structure postulated by the theory actually exists.'[15] A formidable case for such a critical scientific realism as 'a quite limited claim that purports to explain why certain ways of proceeding in science have worked out as well as they (contingently) have'[16] can, in my view, be mounted, based on the histories of, for example, geology, cell biology and chemistry. During the last two centuries, these sciences have progressively and continuously discovered hidden structures in the entities of the natural world that account causally for ob-served phenomena.

Critical realism recognizes that it is still only the *aim* of science to depict reality and that this allows gradations in acceptance of the 'truth' of scientific theories. It is a 'critical' realism about entities, structures and processes which figure in scientific theories (the 'terms' of the theories), rather than about theories as such. For the 'reality' of what theories describe is more problematic, since they are concerned principally with the relations between its constitutive terms – and such relations are an aspect of the causal nexus which itself serves to characterize those terms and thereby to justify that reference to them which is the basis of any attribution of reality to them. Only gradually does confidence in theories (and models, see below) increase, as a result of success in explanation, eventually to the point where the entities, structures and processes referred to in them are ascribed some degree of reality. Critical realism recognizes that it is the aim of science to depict reality as best it may – and since this can be only an aim, the critical realist has to accept that this purpose may well be achieved by scientists with but varying degrees of success. So such a critical realism might more correctly be regarded as a programme for the natural sciences, and the extent to which the aim is achieved should be regarded as open to assessment in any particular case. It must never be forgotten that the realism is always qualified as 'critical' since the language of science is, as we shall shortly see, fundamentally metaphorical and revisable, while nevertheless referring.

This last remark reminds us that this position of critical realism as regards the status of scientific propositions inevitably involves some theory of reference.[17] At the very least, what is required is a 'causal' theory of reference to the effect that the referent of a term in a theory is 'that which causes' particular effects or phenomena, or 'that magnitude responsible for the effect or effects' which the experimentalist observes.[18] The new postulated 'particles', 'electrons', say, in J. J. Thomson's Cavendish Laboratory cathode ray tube experiment, were 'that which caused' the spot of light to appear at the end of the tube and to be deflected by electric and magnetic fields. It was, say, the double helical structure of the DNA molecule in M. H. F. Wilkins's X-ray diffraction experiments on DNA fibres that caused the diffraction pattern to have its characteristic diagonal cross form.

Often, a historical sequence can be traced in the use of a theoretical term back to the terminus of a historical-causal chain, the original act of introducing the term into the language, its 'baptism' or dubbing. For the whole process of referring to scientifically postulated entities, structures and processes is often both social and historical, depending on an unbroken history of reference in a continuous linguistic community that stretches back to the initiating experiment or theorizing in which the entities, etc., were first dubbed or, as it is often said, 'discovered'. Such a continuity of reference is entirely consistent with changes in the concepts concerning that which is referred to, as, for example, when the beams of 'electrons', up to this point regarded as particles, gave rise to a diffraction pattern on being passed through a crystal of nickel, and so were then seen also to partake of wavelike properties. In such cases the theory of reference on which a critical realism rests will include an overt social perspective, for this enhances our understanding of the way in which the reality of a referent persists through change in theory and is gradually established in a community by a critical winnowing process. The basic essential for such social reference is adequately provided by the 'causal' links in each experiment – the postulate that there *is* a cause of the phenomena observed, that there is a 'that which causes' the observed effects. Thus it is that science can often be confident of the realities to which its theories refer, but accepting that its language and models concerning these realities are always revisable and subject to change.

It is in this context that we have to be reminded of the use of models and metaphor in science. In general, 'an object or state of affairs is a model when it is viewed in terms of its resemblance, real or hypothetical, to some other object or state of affairs.'[19] Or, with particular reference to science, 'a model in science is a systematic analogy postulated between a phenomenon whose laws are already known and the one under investigation.'[20] Models, which need not be linguistic at all, and metaphors, which are strictly speaking figures of speech, are closely linked, for metaphors arise when we speak on the basis of models.[21] The use of models is fundamental to any developing science and has been widely investigated. The deeply and irrevocably metaphorical character of scientific language does not detract from the aim of such language to refer to realities. Moreover, recognition of the metaphorical nature of scientific language entails an acceptance of its revisability in seeking to explore a world only partially and imperfectly understood – and whose ultimate reality is bound to be elusive since we ourselves are structures in the selfsame world we study.

We have seen that the status of models in science covers the spectrum from naive realism via positivism and instrumentalism to a critical realism. Theology also employs models that may be similarly classified. I urge that a critical realism is also the most appropriate and adequate philosophy concerning religious language and theological propositions.[22] Critical realism in theology would maintain that theological concepts and models should be regarded as partial and inadequate, but necessary and, indeed, the only ways of refer- ring to the reality that is named as 'God' and to God's relation with humanity. Metaphor obviously plays an even wider role in religious language than in scientific. Thus God is variously described, just to take the Judeo-Christian tradition, as Father, King, Judge, etc.; in that same tradition, Jesus is described as the Anointed (Christ), Son of God, Second Adam, the Good Shepherd, etc.; and the third *persona* of the Trinity as Holy Spirit, Paraclete (Advocate, Comforter).

One major difference between the way models are deployed in science and theology is that in the latter models have a strong affective function evoking moral and spiritual response. However, the models stir the will and emotions because of their implied cognitive reference to that which makes demands on our wills and evokes our emotions. But how can such an intuition cope with the philosophical pressure to show how theological propositions actually *refer*, that theological models depict reality?

We have to distinguish between referring to God and describing him; this is crucial to a critical-realist stance in theology. It is at this juncture that, in all religions, *negative* theology and *positive* theology meet. The former (the *via negativa*) recognizes that, having referred to God, whatever we say will be fallible and revisable and *ex hypothesi* inadequate; and sometimes goes so far as to say that nothing can positively be said about God. However, this too easily becomes a slippery slope to atheism, so positive theology (the *via positiva*) affirms that to say nothing about God is more misleading than to say something – and that then we have to speak in metaphors. The metaphors of theological models that explicate religious experience can refer to and can depict reality without at the same time being naively and unrevisably descriptive, and they share this character with scientific models of the natural world. We may reasonably hope to speak realistically of God through revisable metaphor and model.

Fortunately there certainly have been, and still are, individuals and communities who affirm they have experienced God. Moreover, it is as justifiable in theology as it is in science with respect to its own focus of inquiry, that one can have grounds for affirming that 'God' is 'that which is causing, or has caused, this particular experience now (or in the past) in me (or in others)'. Rather, since we wish to avoid describing 'God' as an entity within the causal nexus (not even as the 'First Cause'), and since we shall eventually be recognizing that 'God' is at least personal in some sense, we would be wiser to say that God is 'the One who is encountered in this particular experience now (or in the past) in me (or in others)'. How, in theology, 'that which, the One who, is encountered' in any particular experience is to be identified with what the tradition has named as 'God' is by inferring to the best explanation by application of the criteria of reasonableness that are used generally to assess ideas and, in particular, in appraising scientific models and theories – namely, fit with the data, internal coherence, comprehensiveness, fruitfulness and general cogency.[23]

This kind of critical theological realism takes as central the past and present religious experience of one's own and of others, so that there is also a continuous community and interpretative tradition, in comparison and in contrast with which one's own experience can be both enriched and checked. In that community and tradition, the seminal, initiating experiences of particular individuals, small groups of individuals, and sometimes even whole communities, when God was encountered, will be recalled, especially in liturgical contexts. Using our previous terminology, we would have to say that in the initiating, 'dubbing' experiences, reference was being made to 'God' and since then the community has continuously provided by recapitulation links of referential usage in and through repeated experiences of the same kind. This process enables us today to refer to that which the initiators referred to, even though we may well have revised the models and metaphors which we use to refer to the same reality, namely God. Not all such claimed experiences of God will be perpetuated in a community, but some over the centuries become widely available as a resource and come to enrich the lives of others in the community who have not participated directly in the original seminal experience. Some even become what in Christianity is called 'catholic' in the classical Vincentian sense of what has been believed everywhere, always and by all – although, formulated as propositions, the number that meet such exacting criteria is inevitably small.

This approach to theology recognizes that both the mediated, positive way, through the world and the revelation transmitted by the community, and the direct, 'negative' way of contemplation and silence, are ways to the reality that is 'God'. The language used eventually to articulate the 'positive' way can be said to depict the reality of God but not in any unrevisable fashion. It has to allow what the 'negative way' stresses, namely, our incapacity ever to express in human language the nature of that ultimate Being who is called 'God'. It is the aim of theology to tell as true a story as possible. Like science, it too must allow gradations in the degree of acceptance, in the belief in the 'truth', of theological propositions and that there is a hierarchy of truths – some more focal and central (and defensible) than others. The whole theological enterprise has often been criticized because it has been said to have no way comparable in rigour to that of science in the sifting and testing of its 'data', in this case the content of religious experience and tradition and the scriptures that preserve some of them. However, some philosophers of religion have in fact been able to mount what seems to me to be an effective defence of the warranty of religious belief as expressed theologically.[24] For theology, like science, also attempts to make inferences to the best explanation – or, rather, it *should* be attempting to do so. In order to do this it should use the criteria of reasonableness already mentioned, for these are criteria which at least have the potentiality of leading to an inter-subjective consensus. Some signs that this is not an entirely forlorn hope are provided by the changes that were initiated in the Roman Catholic Church by Vatican II, with its moves towards a greater collegiality in its deliberations, so that we might hope that the constituency of the *sensus fidelium* will eventually be wider than its current hierarchical concentration; and by the development during this century of the World Council of (non-Roman) Churches, which has generated the remarkable Lima document on *Baptism, the Eucharist and the Ministry*, the fruits of a convergence unthinkable even a few decades ago. Furthermore, dialogue between the world's major religions is only just beginning as movements of population have brought them into closer contact in free societies. In all this it must be remembered that consensus is, of course, not a reason for believing a theological statement to be depicting reality: that can come only from successful application of the criteria of reasonableness which warrant inferences to the best explanation. But at least parallels to inter-subjectivity in the scientific and religious communities seem to be emerging with regard to their respective models.

The need now is for theology to develop the application of its criteria of reasonableness in a community in which no authority would be automatic (for example, of the form 'the Church says', 'the Bible says', etc.) but would have to be authenticated inter-subjectively to the point of consensus by inference to the best explanation. This needs to be combined with an openness to development as human knowledge expands and experience is further enriched. When I urge this kind of critically realist aim and programme on Christians, and indeed on the adherents of all religions, I cannot help feeling a little like William Temple who is reputed to have said: 'I pray daily for Christ's one holy, catholic and apostolic Church – and that it may yet come into existence.'[25] That could also be said of the present situation of a critical-realist theology. It has broadly the same intentions as that described by Hans Kung[26] as 'truthful', 'free', 'critical' and 'ecumenical' (both inwardly among the churches and outwardly towards other religions, ideologies and the sciences) – a theology which deals with and interprets the realities of all that constitutes the world, especially human beings and our own inner selves.[27]

There is no hope of obtaining an inter-subjective consensus, even within Christianity, on the basis of an appeal to authority, since there have been, and still are, classical, and entrenched, disagreements between the Protestant, Anglican, Orthodox and Roman Catholic churches about the mode, scope and location of authority for the Christian believer – and no independent way of adjudicating between these positions, if the appeal is only to 'authority'. More importantly for the future of Christianity, an appeal to the 'authority' favoured by any one of these groups of churches cannot hope, in a post-Enlightenment culture, to foster any conviction on the part of even sympathetic inquirers into the truth of Christian affirmations.[28] For any theology to be believable it will have to satisfy the criteria of reasonableness that lead us to infer the best explanation of the broader features of the natural world ('natural theology', traditionally), and of what men and women believe to be their experiences of 'God'. Truths that are claimed to be revealed or are the promulgations of ecclesiastical authority cannot avoid running the gauntlet of these criteria of reasonableness, for they cannot be at the same time both self-warranting and convincing. Any belief system resulting from such a sifting process would inevitably involve a 'hierarchy of truths'; that is, it would explicitly recognize that some beliefs were integral to Christian identity, others less so, and yet others held simply to be not inconsistent with the core of belief but mainly of devotional value for those brought up in certain church traditions.

In spite of what the 'cultured despisers' of Christianity might say, there are 'data' available to the theological enterprise, just as there are to the scientific. These latter are constituted by the broad features of the entities, structures and processes that science is demonstrating as characteristic of the natural world.[29] For theology, the 'data' are constituted by the well-winnowed traditions of the major world religions, among them Christianity which provides our principal source in the West of tested wisdom about how to refer to that which is encountered in those experiences initially dubbed as experiences of God. As John Bowker has put it: 'Religions are a consequence of successive generations testing, correcting, confirming, extending, changing, the accumulating wisdoms of experience.'[30] In this book we are attempting to reflect on some of the principal aspects of the 'accumulating wisdom' of the Christian religion in the light of and in relation to the realities in the world that are referred to and depicted in the natural sciences.

4 THE RELATION BETWEEN SCIENCE AND THEOLOGY

From a critical-realist perspective both science and theology are engaging with realities that may be referred to and pointed at, but which are both beyond the range of any completely literal description. Both employ metaphorical language and describe reality in terms of models, which may eventually be combined into higher conceptual schemes (theories or doctrines). Within such a perspective, it is therefore entirely appropriate to ask how the respective claimed cognitive contents of science and theology might, or should be, related.

Before doing so, however, it is pertinent to point out that this way of asking the question about the relationship between science and theology has itself already been sharpened and made more explicit by the adoption of a critical-realist standpoint. For example, one might adopt the point of view of what is often called the 'strong' programme in the sociology of scientific knowledge, whereby the actual content of scientific cognitive claims is regarded as predominantly socially conditioned.[31] Those having this view would adopt *a fortiori* a similar view of the cognitive claims of theology and then the exercise of relating science and theology would be reduced to that of relating two ideologies and so would itself become a purely sociological inquiry or exercise in the history of ideas. No cognitive claims of either science or theology would be countenanced and the whole question of the relation of science and theology, and even more so that of science and religion, would have been relativized into non-existence. To adopt a critical-realist view of science and of theology is to reject this position, and I think there are good grounds for doing so.[32] However, this does not mean to say that at any one stage in their respective histories the cognitive claims of science and theology are so insulated from society that the cluster of metaphors, models, theories and doctrines that they employ are a 'truth' determined only by 'reality'. That would be entirely inconsistent with the known histories of the two disciplines. Nevertheless, I think it to be the case in science and, I would urge, it *should* be the case also for theology, that any particular state of the discipline can be shown to have been subjected to a critical winnowing process by application of the criteria of reasonableness I have described.

I mention the 'strong programme' in the sociology of scientific knowledge as a somewhat extreme example, inconsistent as it is with the experience of practising scientists and religious believers, because it illustrates that any individual's view of the relation of science and theology is closely dependent on his or her view of their epistemology and of the ontological status of that to which they respectively refer. I have delineated elsewhere[33] at least eight putative relations between science and theology, apart from the social dimension. Thus science and theology may be regarded as non-interacting approaches to reality; as constituting two different language systems; as generated by quite different attitudes; as each subservient to its own 'object' of study and defined only in relation to it ('nature' for science and 'God' for theology). As R. J. Russell[34] has pointed out, these positions may be differentiated with respect to four 'dimensions' of the science–theology relationship, namely: *approaches, languages, attitudes* and *objects*. In each of these four 'dimensions', the relation between science and theology can be construed as either positive and reconciling and so as mutually interacting, or as negative and non-interacting. This makes a total of eight ($=4\times2$) different, conceivable relationships between science and theology. It is the first of the four 'positive' relationships which is the outcome of a critical-realist philosophy of both science and theology – namely, that *science and theology are seen as interacting approaches to reality.* To this we will revert below, but for the moment it is worth pursuing a little further this inquiry into the general character of the relationships between science and theology.

In addition to these eight possible relationships, support has been given by some authors to seeing science and theology as referring to two distinct 'realms': for example, the natural/supernatural; the spatio-temporal/eternal; the order of nature/the realm of faith; the physical-and-biological/mind-and-spirit; and so on. This view, which is contrary to that adopted here, takes a negative non-interacting position with respect to all four 'dimensions'.

Instead of allowing only two alternatives in each of the four 'dimensions' (approaches, languages, attitudes and objects) of the possible relationship between science and theology, it might be better, Russell has suggested,[35] to envisage a continuum of possibilities in each 'dimension', now conceived as more like axes in a four-dimensional space. The extrema of the axes would have to be designated as the most positive and the most negative positions with respect to each dimension ('positive' in the sense of 'consonant and reconciling'; 'negative' in the sense of 'non-interacting'). Various constellations of perspectives on the relation between science and theology would then occupy different locations in this four-dimensional 'space'. This model serves, at least, to emphasize the richness and complexity of the possibilities of interaction between two disciplines whose epistemologies are themselves subject to such differing interpretations.

I have chosen to steer a path based on a critical-realist appraisal of both science and theology and this brings us back to our earlier question: how are the claimed cognitive contents of science and theology to be related? Might it not be simply that 'theology and science deal for the most part with different domains of the same reality',[36] so that, as the same author continues, 'Science has no access to God in its explanations; theology has nothing to say about the specifics of the natural world.' However, to say the least, the history of theology shows that its development is intimately related to the understanding of the natural, including the human, world that has prevailed at different periods.[37] More pertinently to the present context, since the aim of a critical-realist theology is to articulate intellectually and to formulate, by means of metaphor and model, experiences of God, then it behooves such a theology to take seriously the critical-realist perspective of the sciences on the natural, including the human, world. For on that theology's own presuppositions, God himself has given the world the kind of being it has and it must be in some respects, to be ascertained, revelatory of God's nature and purposes. So theology should seek to be at least consonant with scientific perspectives on the natural world.

Correspondingly, the sciences should not be surprised if their perspectives are seen to be partial and incomplete and to raise questions not answerable from within their own purview and by their own methods, since there are other realities – there is a Reality – to be taken into account which is not discernible by the sciences as such. A critical-realist science and theology cannot but regard themselves as mutually interacting approaches to reality. But we need to examine further the relations between the 'realities' to which each refers. This is the principal objective of the present work.

With an increasing richness and articulation of its various levels, the expansion of our scientific knowledge of the natural world has more and more shown it to consist of a hierarchy of systems in levels of organization, each successive member of which is a whole constituted of parts, often preceding it historically in the series. As we shall see in chapter 2,[38] the science pertinent to each level may well develop non-reducible concepts of its own appropriate and relevant to the specific behaviours, relations and properties that can be seen only at that level. This has the important consequence *inter alia* that we have no basis for any favoured attribution of 'reality' to the different levels in the hierarchy of complexity. Knowledge of each level, or (perhaps better), along each 'vector' of inquiry, has to be regarded as a kind of slice through the totality of reality.

Now human beings are natural parts of the universe and among their characteristic experiences are those of reaching out to God and of God coming towards them: theology is the intellectual analysis of such experiences in which this traffic is experienced as being in both directions between God and humanity. When human beings are thus experiencing the presence and activity of God, whether or not engaged in explicitly 'religious' and worshipping activities, they are operating at a level in, or 'vector' of, the hierarchy of complexity that is more integrative than any of the levels or 'vectors' studied by the individual natural, human and social sciences. In such human 'religious' activities, whole persons believe themselves to be interacting with each other, with the natural world, and with the transcendent, yet immanent, Creator as the source of all that is – the One who gives them and the world meaning and significance. No higher level or more significant 'vector' of integrated relationships in the hierarchy of the natural could be claimed or envisaged. Theology, we have seen, is about the requisite conceptual schemes (doctrines) and models and associated metaphors that articulate the content of these experiences of God of both the individual and of a historical community.

There appear to be two ways in which this fundamental, integrative, role of theology, the study of humanity-nature-God, might be expressed – ways that correspond to the two modalities of God's relation to all-that-is (both humanity and nature), namely the transcendent and the immanent.[39] If one emphasizes the transcendence of God, the activity and language of the theological enterprise can be regarded as reflecting on that specifically and uniquely human activity, the 'religious', which involves nature, humanity and God in its total integrating purview. This activity then stands at the summit of conceivable integrative complexity and wholeness (and, note, nearest to the level of the human and personal). From this perspective, theology, albeit no longer the medieval 'queen of the sciences', might still possibly be accorded the position of a constitutional monarch. This may indeed be the proper placement for theology when we consider ultimate ontological relationships, the relation of the Being of God to all other derived being.

But when we contemplate God's activity in the world, and so God's Becoming, rather than God's ultimate Being, we also (as we shall see later) have to predicate immanence of God as Creator and to emphasize God's presence to, in, with, under and through all natural events. Thus it may well be that theology should be regarded as an exploration of the ultimate meaning of all levels[40] – that is, as an attempt at interpreting the significance of the various levels of natural reality in the total scheme of things. Any particular levels would be viewed in relation to God's continuous creative activity at all levels through all space and time. We encounter here that difficult requirement of a fusion of the concepts of transcendence and immanence, in this instance, in relation to the role of theology and its relation to science, which will lead us in the Postscript to speak rather of 'transcendence-in-immanence' and of the 'immanence-of-the-transcendent' to articulate our understanding both of the human person[41] and of God's relation to the world.[42]

All of this implies that, before proceeding with further theological reflection, we must look carefully at the broad characteristics and features of the entities, structures and processes of the world that the sciences are postulating as the currently best explanations of their observations.

PART I

Natural Being and Becoming

CHAPTER 1

Introduction

It has become a commonplace to observe that the last three centuries have witnessed an unparalleled transformation in the way human beings have come to regard the natural world and their relation to it; yet from time to time we need to be reminded of this. One needs only, say, in the English-speaking world, to reread a play of Shakespeare to be reminded of the enormous gulf that separates us from a pre-scientific culture in terms of what it believes is actually in the world and is actually going on in it. As historians such as Herbert Butterfield have amply demonstrated, the advent of the scientific culture 'outshines everything since the rise of Christianity and reduces the Renaissance and Reformation to the rank of mere episodes, mere internal displacements, within the system of mediaeval Christendom.'[1]

Even as a purely social phenomenon, any community of religious believers, in order to communicate at all with their contemporaries, would have to take account of this fundamental displacement, in what Butterfield called human 'habitual mental operations even in the conduct of the non-material sciences'.[2] More significantly, this shift in human 'habitual mental operations' constitutes a challenge to the conceptual schemes whereby the principal theistic religions organize their reflections on their characteristic experiences, that is, their experiences of God. This challenge is particularly cogent for Christianity, which takes with utmost seriousness the reality and nature of the natural world, both because of its doctrine of creation, which it basically shares with Judaism and Islam, but more particularly because of its belief that the Creator God was present in and was manifested through an historical human person, himself part of nature and human history. So the now scientifically observed and understood character of the natural world, including humanity, is today of immense *theological* significance. For what nature is like, what God is like, indeed whether or not God exists, have become interlocked questions that cannot be considered in isolation – in

spite of the tendency of much contemporary theologizing nevertheless to do just this.

However, necessary though the attempt is to work out the relations between nature, humanity and God in the light of the staggeringly new understanding of the world afforded by the natural,
human and social sciences, it is also necessary to enter a word of
caution. For, as has often been remarked, a theology which marries
the science of today is liable to find itself a widow tomorrow, such is
the rapidity with which science changes. There is wisdom in this
charge, but as we have seen, H. Harris has sharply affirmed that
because some, indeed many, scientific ideas become obsolete and
are superseded, this 'is no argument at all for the notion that all
scientific conclusions are similarly bound to be displaced ... Human
beings may indeed make mistakes, but I see no merit in the idea that
they make nothing but mistakes.'[3]

As I hope became clear in making the case for a critical-realist
view of science, there are solid grounds in many wide areas of the
natural sciences for believing that these sciences are giving us a
reasonably assured account of what the natural world is like and
what has been going on in it. We have to recognize that scientific
language is metaphorical but is none the worse for that in its
attempt to depict reality, and that it does increasingly succeed in
referring to aspects of natural reality, as evidenced by its success in
prediction and control. Even so, the caveat entered concerning the
ephemeral nature of many currently countenanced scientific proposals is a proper one. It warns us that it should be only with the
best-established general features of the scientific accounts of the
world that we should be concerned in our reflections on the relation
of nature, humanity and God.

The rest of Part I will be devoted to delineating certain features of
the accounts of the world afforded by a range of sciences for
consideration later as we come to attempt a formulation of what
might constitute a contemporary and defensible understanding of
nature, humanity and God. Inevitably, the discussion will take place
at a level of generalization which it will be impossible to substantiate in a work of this compass. I can but refer the reader to some of
the works listed in the notes and assure him or her that the broad
features and characteristics of the world of science I attempt to
collate are ones which seem to be widely recognized by authors of
many different philosophical positions and religious beliefs.

CHAPTER 2

What's There?

We are accustomed to looking at the world around us and attempting to identify its furniture. We ask 'What's there in the world? Of what is the world made up? In what does the world consist?' In raising such questions we inevitably reveal a conception of the world in which, as it were, objects are inserted into space at a particular time and all that human beings need to do is to look around and see what 'is there', even though such a looking at the world may now involve the experimentally and theoretically sophisticated methods of the sciences. For a very wide range of the sciences – from chemistry, concerned with the atomic and molecular, to ecology, concerned with ecosystems – this attempt to discern the entities, structures, and processes in the world has been remarkably successful. The presupposition that such questions in such a form may be addressed, as it were, to the world turns out to be not only legitimate but even capable of being answered through experimental science combined with human ratiocination.

1 SPACE, TIME, MATTER AND ENERGY

In the Newtonian perspective, which dominated the mind of the West for two and a half centuries – and still prevails in the general intellectual climate since it corresponds so well with intuitions derived from our senses – the stuff of the world, *matter*, possesses *energy*, and is located in *space* at a particular *time*. Even though by the end of the nineteenth century there had been a profound enrichment and enlargement of our understanding of both matter and energy, these two concepts were still quite distinct and absolute space and time still provided the basic framework in which they were deemed to exist. The concepts of space, time, matter and energy continued to appear to be 'given', self-evident features of the world, *a priori* concepts essential to our thinking. Although, as we shall see, this understanding has been fundamentally overthrown in modern physics, the fact is that it still provides the basic conceptual framework for most of the sciences from the molecular to the ecological. But though the intuitions derived from our sense experience are still useful in these ranges, they cease to be so in the range of the very small, the very large, and the very fast – that is at the sub-atomic particle level, at the cosmological level and for anything moving at speeds close to that of light. The relation between these different ranges and regimes of phenomena is well understood. It may be roughly characterized by the assertion that the understandings of space, time, matter and energy of the 'classical' perspective turn out to be approximations (in most of the sciences concerned with the not very small, not very large and not very fast) of more subtle, and often unpicturable, concepts and entities which are related in ways that were unthinkable before the first few decades of this century. For during that period relativity theory, in its special and general forms, and, even more iconoclastically, quantum theory, together caused a complete revolution in human understanding of the physical world, the consequences of which are still being to be absorbed into philosophy – and hardly yet into theology.

In Newtonian physics *space* was held to be uniform and three-dimensional, obeying the geometrical laws of Euclid. It was physically inert, infinite in extent, continuous and infinitely divisible. For Newton it had an absoluteness which he thought of as God-given. These premises were overthrown by Einstein, with the possible exception of its infinity and infinite divisibility. Certainly the commonsense notion of juxtaposition cannot be understood coherently when absolute simultaneity is also denied, as it was by Einstein. Indeed, our intuitively separate concepts of space and time become inextricably interwoven and mutually defined in relativity theory, now completely accepted in modern physics. Not only do the space measurements in one system determined by an observer moving relative to it depend on time differences, but also *mutatis mutandis* the time measurements made by such an observer on the same system involve space measurements. So modern relativistic physics adds to our intuitive spatialization of time a dynamization of space.

Time was also a fundamental concept in the classical physical picture of the world – the single dimension in which instants followed each other. Like space, it too was homogeneous, independent of any objects or events 'in' it, inert, infinite, continuous. In the special theory of relativity, absolute simultaneity exists only for events occurring at the same location. Consequently the concept of a great three-dimensional 'now', of world-wide instants, loses all physical significance. However, the succession of events which form causal chains is independent of the choice of frame of reference and, indeed, the concept of *causality* is affected by this initial theory of Einstein only to the extent that we now have to recognize that causal influences can never be transmitted through the universe at a speed greater than that of light. Although the metrical scale of time intervals (the 'dilatation of time') depends on the frame of reference, this is a distortion only from the perspective of the relative motion of the observer. In Einstein's later general theory of relativity, the concept of time is more fundamentally transformed and loses its classical features of homogeneity and uniformity (its dilatation in a gravitational field is not merely related to a particular frame of reference), and its independence of physical content.

In fact, physicists concerned with events on a cosmic scale, or with velocities significantly close to that of light, measure intervals between events in terms of a combined function, 'space-time'. Fortunately, for the greater part of the range of natural events which are the concern of most of the sciences ranging from chemistry to ecology, and much even of astronomy, these considerations do not arise and the natural intuitions we have of an actual 'now' at a particular point in space suffice adequately. However, this does not detract at all from the fundamental reassessment of our concepts of space and time that relativity theory has necessitated; they turn out to be mutually interlocking concepts and, as we shall see, not at all independent of the concepts of matter and energy.

There is another aspect of the reassessment of time that the sciences have forced upon us during the last century and a half. That we experience time as having a direction is not only a part of our psychology, it is also built into our organization as a biological system proceeding from birth to death, and this itself is, in the long run, but a manifestation of the wider irreversibility of all natural processes in the observable universe. Whether or not this experienced directionality is a necessary aspect of the concept of time, or is only a feature of our experience and therefore interpretation of it, has been much, and inconclusively, debated.

Hawking has argued[1] that storage of information in an entity must always involve the expenditure of energy and its consequential partial dissipation as heat, and always involves a net increase in disorder, and so of entropy. So our subjective sense of time (our memories are of the past) runs parallel with the thermodynamic arrow of time, the net increase of disorder (entropy) in all natural processes. He reports calculations that suggest that this increase in disorder (the thermodynamic arrow of time) points in the same direction as the cosmological arrow of time not only in an expanding universe such as ours appears to be, but also (and this is what had to be calculated) in the future universe, if it eventually contracts. Disorder will continue to increase during the contraction – but it is only in the expanding phase, in which we now are, that intelligent beings could exist. This well-defined thermodynamic arrow of time is in fact necessary for intelligent life to operate, since living organisms have to consume food to maintain their organization and convert it into heat, a more disordered form of energy. So, Hawking argues, the thermodynamic, psychological and cosmological arrows of time point in the same direction.

It suffices for our present purposes, namely, discernment of the meaning and significance of such intelligibility as the world yields, to stress that the direction of time in which our lives move, from birth to death, is the same on the cosmic scale as that in which physical and biological forms develop. As is well known,[2] there is very good evidence for the 'hot, big, bang' account of cosmic history, according to which our universe has been expanding to the present time from a highly condensed, extremely hot and compacted state, of dimensions of the atomic order, for about $10-20 \times 10^9$ years. (Speculations which modify the validity of such an extrapolation over the first 'instants' of this supposed range of physical time will be discussed later.) So there appears to be a *direction in time* from the sub-nuclear to galaxies and the many forms of matter that constitute them and exist in the space between; and also, on the Earth, a direction in time towards increasing complexity and variety of biological forms up to the myriad intricacies of human society. Time, far from flowing equably and leaving everything much the same (as in the classical Newtonian perspective) is now seen from the perspective of an impressive number of the sciences (thermodynamics, cosmology, astronomy, geology, biology) to be the 'carrier or locus of innovative change'.[3] Over far longer timescales than that of any individual biological life, science now bears formidable witness that new entities, structures and processes come into being that did not previously exist; that is, there is a coming into being of that which was not, as well as changes in, and often the disappearance of, that which is.

Even before the full blossoming of quantum mechanics, with its many anti-intuitive and paradoxical insights into the nature of matter, Einstein's special theory of relativity had rendered impossible the classical notion of *matter* as something impenetrable that fills space. For the interconvertibility, initially required as a mathematical consequence of the theory, and now verified by the electricity coming from any nuclear power station, of mass and energy (the famous $E=mc^2$) also blurred the distinction between space and mass. Furthermore, if a 'particle' of matter is but a certain local configuration of space-time, as it is according to the general theory of relativity, how can it be said to 'move in' a 'space' that itself constitutes its own nature? Einstein's theory undermined the natural distinction between motion and that which moves, a distinction that seems so natural to our ordinary sense perception, and one whose obliteration was completed by subsequent developments in quantum mechanics.

Yet this intuitive, natural distinction, limited though it is by the above considerations, served well enough as the basis for a highly successful methodologically reductionist development in science until well into the twentieth century, whereby the observable structures and entities of the natural world were successively, and successfully, broken down into smaller and smaller component units – first molecules, then atoms, then protons and neutrons. The limit of attainable divisibility continually became smaller and for a long time the units so unveiled could still be conceived of as just small bits of the world – admittedly very small bits but nevertheless essentially tiny particles, easily imaginable by extrapolation downwards from our ordinary sense experience of the macroscopic world. However, as larger and larger energies had, by the nature of the case, to be deployed to penetrate deeper and deeper into the substructure of the world, the interchangeability of matter and energy required by relativity theory became more and more significant.

The other great discovery of the early decades of this century, namely that energy is quantized, that it is transmitted and absorbed in finite, irreducibly small units, had to be incorporated into the perceptions of what was being discovered, 'uncovered' rather, at these deep levels of natural reality. The 'fundamental particles' that emerged had to be thought of, paradoxically, at first as having a wave-like character as well as being particulate. This anomaly was then transcended by quantum field theory at the cost of a loss of naive picturability but with the gain of the discovery of a profounder

rationality, now expressible only in the language of mathematics –
the only adequate way of dealing with the 'quarks' and 'gluons' and
other entities that the physicists postulate. The simple idea of their
being a kind of accessible bedrock to the physical world (and so to
the biological too), that could be visualized in terms of the categories used to interpret our human sense experience, has proved to be
not only naive and simplistic but downright misleading. There is a
genuine limitation in the ability of our minds to depict the nature of
matter at this fundamental level; there is a mystery about what
matter is 'in itself', for at the deepest level to which human beings
can penetrate they are faced with a mode of existence describable
only in terms of abstract, mathematical concepts that are the products of human ratiocination. It seems likely that this increase in
abstractness and unpicturability will never stop as physicists delve
deeper into matter and further and further back into the early
universe, when the energies pertaining far exceed any achievable in
principle on earth (so that the early universe becomes the only
available 'laboratory' for such studies). Certainly the experience of
science has been always that of finding new conceptual frontiers to
cross as each territory yields its secrets.

In the early classical Newtonian world of physics *energy* was at
first a concept whose formulation was closely interlocked with what
were regarded as the basic categories of space, time and mass, this
latter being linked with classical concepts of matter itself. The
kinetic energy of a body in motion was proportional to the square of
its velocity (change of position in space per unit time) multiplied by
its mass, which was supposed to be calculable by summing a
property of each of the body's components. But other forms of
energy had early to be recognized, such as that possessed by a body
in virtue of its location in a gravitational field with the concomitant
recognition that the energy of a system could be increased by 'work'
(force × distance) being done upon it. Gradually, and especially
during the nineteenth century, other forms of energy came to be
recognized as interchangeable with these mechanical, kinetic and
gravitational forms, namely, electrical, chemical and magnetic forms
of energy storage. With Einstein's equating of energy with mass it
came also to be recognized that the mass of a body was actually
dependent on the binding energies of its components and therefore
not a simple sum of quantities characteristic of each component
taken separately.

So during the twentieth century we have been witnessing a process in which the previously absolute and distinct concepts of space, time, matter and energy have come to be seen as closely and mutually interlocked with each other – so much so that even the modification of our thinking to being prepared to envisage 'what is there' as consisting of matter-energy in space-time has to be superseded by more inclusive concepts of fields and other notions no longer picturable and expressible only mathematically. Fortunately at the low energies, low velocities and small time and space scales ('low' relative to those needed to penetrate the sub-atomic world and 'small' relative to the velocity of light and to the scale of the cosmos), the classical concepts continue to be adequate to account for our experimental observations and our experience. More significantly for our present purposes, these classical concepts are broadly those operative in a wide range of the sciences – though, of course, even certain macroscopic phenomena only find their explanation in terms of quantum theory (for example, many features of computer hardware) and even relativity theory (for example, the electrical energy from nuclear power stations). However, this should not delude us into thinking that when we pursue the question 'What is there?' to its ultimately accessible limits we are going to come up with answers that are at all picturable and intelligible in terms of our 'common-sense' experience of the world. Even so, this intermediate level, if we may call it that, between the ultra-microscopic and the ultra-macroscopic still constitutes the vast bulk of the natural world and the great majority of the natural sciences concerned with investigating it. The multiple and diverse pictures and features of the natural world so provided are of immense significance for our understanding the content of its structures, entities and processes, and, needless to say, of immense significance also for human beings in interpreting their own world, which itself falls between these extremes. So let us now take, as it were, a 'cut' through space-time 'at' our own time, for we are not moving with a velocity approaching that of light; and let us examine what are the general features which have been discerned in the material entities and structures to be found in the contemporary world through the intensive investigation it has undergone by the natural sciences up to our own day. The processes by which it reached the condition so discerned will be examined in chapter 3.

2 Structures and Entities

What would undoubtedly first strike any intelligent being from Mars or any other planet – were there any such, since all the observable planets seem to lack life, certainly in any developed form – would be the enormous diversity in the *structures* and *entities* that exist on our planet, especially in the millions of species of living organisms living at present, not to mention the probably hundredfold greater number that have existed in the past and are now extinct. Moreover, this terrestrial diversity is, as it were, only the surface layer of an underlying diversity of 'fundamental' particles, atoms, molecules and the various manifestations of energy that are dispersed throughout the universe. Such a visitor could be forgiven, were he/she/it innocent of terrestrial science, for concluding that there was no such thing as nature-as-a-whole, that there exists only a multitude of individual 'natures' according to place and time. Even a denizen of this planet accustomed to the flora and fauna of a temperate zone can still be overwhelmed by the sheer fecundity and kaleidoscopic variety of life in more tropical climes. The briefest view of the teeming marine life in, say, coral reefs cannot but generate a sense of wonder at the luxurious and multiform proliferation that has occurred on this planet alone, let alone elsewhere in the immensity of space with its 10^9 galaxies each containing 10^8 to 10^{11} stars (remembering that our Sun with its planetary system qualifies as one star in these reckonings).

Such a spontaneous sense of wonder is enhanced and heightened when this great diversity is seen through the lenses of the natural sciences, for these explicate in increasing detail and comprehensiveness the contemporary interlocking relationships and the mutually involved histories that characterize this daunting diversity. This complexity comes increasingly to be seen through the natural sciences as a diversity-in-unity wherein relatively simple laws, principles and relationships weave, through their operation over periods staggeringly long for the human imagination, the almost extravagantly rich tapestry of the world we now observe. The world has a simplicity that is sophisticated and subtle in its outworkings and manifestations through both cosmic and, more locally, terrestrial space and time. How this rich complexity emanates from simplicity has been well expounded both on our television screens and in elegant books by scientific authors of both theistic and non-theistic persuasions – for the vista of the sciences is capable of evoking a sense of wonder among scientists whatever their religious convictions or otherwise.[4]

This cornucopian diversity stems from the givenness of certain basic parameters, such as the speed of light, the mass and charge of the electron, certain interaction constants, Planck's constant, etc., combined with the operation of only four fundamental forces. These forces are those of gravity and electromagnetism, the effects of which are comparatively familiar to us in ordinary life in a technological society, and the less obvious, but nevertheless basic, weak and strong nuclear forces which operate within the short ranges characteristic of the atomic nucleus. Physicists have already been able to unify two of these in one mathematical description (the electromagnetic and weak nuclear forces) and there are increasing hopes of uniting with these also the strong nuclear forces in a Grand Unified Theory (GUT) – the ultimate prize being the unification of gravity with these other three forces and the bringing of all this into unity with general relativity and particle theory, into what some call TOE, a 'theory of everything'. This prize may prove to be beyond human reach but the fact that it is even sought is a significant testimony to the underlying unity beneath the complexity of the observed, and to the increasingly warranted convictions of scientists that it is and will be more and more successfully discerned, as it has been over the last few centuries.

This underlying unity has only been wrested from the diversity of visible objects by application of the most abstract powers of thinking of which the human mind is capable, not to mention the extremely sophisticated (and often large and very expensive) equipment required to penetrate the mysteries of the sub-atomic world. From the levels of the atomic through to that of biological populations and ecosystems, the corresponding sciences fortunately afford knowledge of the entities with which they deal that is much more readily picturable, even though the subtleties of what holds these entities together as units and the processes by which they change are still only fully comprehensible with the help of sophisticated mathematical concepts. So it is worth while to take, as it were, a section or slice through space-time at a contemporary instant, confident that the velocities of all observers on the planet Earth relative to each other are sufficiently far from that of light to allow one to speak of 'now' with no need of any relativistic qualifications.

In their accelerating expansion the natural sciences have been giving us a picture of the world as consisting of a complex hierarchy

– a series of levels of organization of matter in which each successive member of the series is a 'whole' constituted of 'parts' preceding it in the series, frequently said (as a convention, with no implication of value judgements) to run from 'lower' to 'higher' as the complexity increases. These 'wholes' are organized systems of parts that are dynamically and spatially interrelated. Such a sequence is particularly well illustrated in the various levels of organization of living systems, namely the sequence (incompletely) represented by: atom – molecule – macromolecule – subcellular organelle – cell – multicellular functioning organ – whole living organism – populations of living organisms – ecosystems – the biosphere. Usually the interactions among subsystems (the 'parts') are relatively weak compared with the interactions within the subsystems themselves, a property which helps to simplify their identification and description. The strength of the additional forces which holds the sub-units together progressively diminishes as one goes up the scale of complexity, while the forces operative at lower levels of complexity also continue to be deployed in holding the more complex structures together. The gravitational forces between the atoms in a molecule are 10^{35} to 10^{39} times smaller than the net electrostatic interactions between them, and the energies of binding of atoms in a molecule are themselves 10 to 100 times smaller than the energies by which electrons are held by the nuclei within atoms, which in turn are 100,000 to a million times smaller than the energies of binding of the 'particles' in the nucleus. It takes much less energy to break a cell wall than it does to atomize a molecule, and to smash atoms needs tens of thousands of 'electron volts' (the energy acquired by an electron in dropping down a potential gradient of one volt per centimetre); to penetrate a nucleus millions of electron volts are deployed – and this increase continues the deeper one goes, for the deeper energy levels are separated by larger energy gaps than the higher, 'surface' ones.

It is tempting to visualize the natural hierarchy of levels as nested in the spatial sense, rather like a series of Russian dolls, with smaller and smaller systems packed inside one another, the smallest being that of the physico-chemical level and the largest being at least that of the biosphere of the planet Earth – which is itself, of course, only a minute speck relative to cosmic scales. However, although this picture would be satisfactory for envisaging the relation between some levels, this kind of spatial inclusion is not adequate for depicting the relation between other kinds of functional complexity, since some of the most elaborate and sophisticated are often relatively small in total physical volume – for example, the human central nervous system. Moreover, each level in the hierarchy is often characterized by a distinctive internal logical structure of its own, its properties describable in terms of a distinctive and logically consistent system of concepts, different from those invoked for adjacent levels 'above' and 'below' or 'inside' or 'outside' of it.

When the hierarchy of complexity is also, in fact, a hierarchy of increasing size (as in the 'biological' sequence described above) then, concomitantly and consistently with this, the larger entities usually also exhibit slower and slower response times to external changes. Furthermore, the sequence of biological evolutionary development in time is, as we shall see in the next section, also a sequence of increased complexity evoked by environmental pressures, and not necessarily following any neat logical prescriptions other than those imposed by the need for one function and structure to precede another as its necessary historical precondition.

3 REDUCTIONISM

Since we are adopting a critical-realist stance, we have to take seriously this picture from the natural sciences of the world as a hierarchy of complexities of the kinds just indicated. Corresponding to the different levels in these hierarchies of the natural world there exist the appropriate sciences which study a particular level – though there are, of course, sciences which cut across a number of disciplines, in the way that, for example, genetics is significant for the whole of biology. Clarification of the relationship between the depictions of reality that the sciences afford at their own distinctive levels of operation is of very great significance in our estimate of the relevance of such knowledge to the wider concerns of humanity and, in particular, with respect to its relation to theology, as mentioned in the previous chapter.

It is a natural transition for a molecular biologist, say, who is accustomed to breaking down complex (biological) entities into units small enough to be examined by the techniques in which they are trained (in this case those of physics, chemistry and biochemistry), to transform this practical, methodological 'philosophy' into a more general, now genuinely philosophical, belief that (in this instance) biological organisms *are* 'nothing but' the bits into which they have analyzed them, 'nothing but molecules and atoms'. Many practising molecular biologists are, because of this transition, implicit 'reductionists'. Some, indeed, are quite explicit; for example, Francis Crick has affirmed that 'the ultimate aim of the modern movement in biology is in fact to explain *all* biology in terms of physics and chemistry.'[5] Whether explicitly or implicitly embraced, such a reductionist interpretation of the relation between the different sciences can limit and determine any understanding of the nature of the levels of the natural world under consideration – in this instance, living organisms including human beings. The issue[6] here is whether or not the theories, experimental laws and theoretical terms and concepts formulated in one science operating at its own level can be shown to be but special cases of, that is 'reduced to', the theories, etc., formulated in some other branch of science operating at a lower level of the natural hierarchies. It is what is often being urged upon us when we are told that 'scientific study X is nothing but scientific study Y' – hence the label 'nothing-but-ery' for this kind of assertion.

There is wide agreement on the need, indeed necessity, to break down unintelligible, complex wholes into their component units and then to see how they fit together, but this does not preclude more holistic methodologies. However, some reductionists, while recognizing this, nevertheless do so only as a kind of concession to the present incompleteness of our knowledge and still believe, however vaguely, that all the sciences will one day be reduced to physics and chemistry. On this view, complex wholes (for example, biological organisms) *are* 'nothing but' their component parts.

There are two forms of this view. The first asserts simply that the laws of physics and chemistry apply to all processes (for instance, biological ones) at the atomic and molecular levels; this excludes, for example, all 'vitalist' views concerning biological organisms. On this there would be wide agreement. A second, and stronger, form of such reductionism asserts that higher complexes *are* 'nothing but' atoms and molecules in the sense that a physico-chemical account of their atomic and molecular processes is all there is to be said about them.

Now it is true that the answer to 'What else is there (other than atoms and molecules) in, say, a living organism?' is 'no-thing at all', but this does not mean that describing its molecular constituents and their properties is all there is to be said, that there is nothing more to be said by way of description of the individuality of a particular living organism, especially if it is a human one.

As we have seen, the expansion of our knowledge of the natural world which has occurred particularly in the twentieth century has shown it to consist of a complex hierarchy of systems, with a science appropriate to each level. At each level distinctive kinds of interlocking relationships occur and these require distinctive concepts to order them and render them coherent. Very often these concepts cannot be envisaged or translated into those appropriate at lower levels of organization; that is, they are not reducible. Because of widely pervasive reductionist pre-suppositions, there has been a tendency to regard the level of atoms and molecules as alone 'real'. However, there are good grounds for not affirming any special priority to the physical and chemical levels of description and for believing that what is real is what the various levels of description actually refer to. There is no sense in which subatomic particles are to be graded as 'more real' than, say, a bacterial cell or a human person or a social fact. Each level has to be regarded as a slice through the totality of reality, in the sense that we have to take account of its mode of operation at that level.

In particular, terms such as 'consciousness', 'person', 'social fact' and, in general, the languages of the humanities, ethics, the arts and theology, to name but a few, are not prematurely to be dismissed from the vocabulary used to describe the human condition, since in all these instances a strong case can be made for the distinctiveness and non-reducibility of the concepts they deploy. The languages, for example, that human beings have developed to articulate and express, as in music and poetry and religion, their states of consciousness and their interactions with each other and with God, many would say, have a genuine *ab initio* claim to be taken as seriously at their own level of reference as the languages of the sciences at theirs.

4 INTERCONNECTEDNESS AND WHOLENESS

The diversity which we, or those extra-terrestrial visitors, see on our planet Earth is real enough, for at the various levels at which particular patterns of organization of matter can be distinguished they certainly exhibit that variety I have been describing. The different structures are presented to us as distinctive and distinct. We have recognized that this variety is the result of the joint operation of surprisingly few forces, basic laws and fundamental constants, and is thereby constitutive of that degree of underlying unity we have already remarked upon. In doing so, we have also recognized the role of the natural sciences in explicating and explaining this diversity-in-unity, both as it is now observed and how it has developed and changed in the course of time, as we shall see in chapter 3.

However, the underlying unity of the world is not only a matter of derivation from common underlying principles, laws and constants, but extends also to a common interrelatedness and interconnectedness. This is manifest at two different levels.

In quantum theory, the amplitude of the wave function that represents the extension in space of any particular 'particle' declines only slowly with distance, and never quite to zero, as the distance from its most probable location increases. Since the square (roughly speaking) of this amplitude at any point in space is proportional to the probability of finding the particle at this point, there is no point in the actual universe at which it is totally impossible to find the particle – no point at which the amplitude of the wave function actually becomes zero. In practice, the values decline so rapidly away from the atom or molecule, or whatever, in which the particle is normally regarded as residing, that for almost all purposes it may be ignored. However, this must not detract from the 'spread-out' character of all matter, so that in a very real sense every fundamental particle, or structure constituted of them (which means every*thing*), is interacting to some extent with everything else in the universe. For example, it has been calculated[7] that, even on the basis of classical physics, the detailed motions (that is, directions and velocities) of a set of billiard balls, colliding with only a negligible loss of energy, would, as we shall discuss in more detail in chapter 3, be affected by an effect as minute as the gravitational attraction of an electron at the edge of the galaxy. Of course, for most practical purposes, and this includes those of science itself, only a very few local interactions amount to anything significant. However, that these minuscule, universal interactions occur at all suggests that we must not take a too excessively fragmented view of the world and its apparently discrete contents. Indeed in certain situations at the subatomic level, it becomes imperative not to consider particles as discrete entities but only conjointly together as total systems (for example, as in the systems that are the concern of J. S. Bell's theorem and its tests[8]).

There is another quite different level at which the interconnectedness and interrelatedness of the diverse, apparently discrete, structures and entities of the world is a dominant feature. All living organisms live in intricate systems consisting of many cross-flows and exchanges of energy and matter that constitute labyrinths of sometimes baffling complexity. These biological ecosystems themselves are incorporated into the much larger inorganic systems of the flows of energy and matter through the seas, in the atmosphere and over the land. This macro-perspective therefore also serves to correct any excessively fragmented understanding of the world, convenient though it often is for clarity of thought and precision in the use of language, which inevitably fragments by naming.

CHAPTER 3

What's Going On?

Up to this point we have deliberately been taking a static view of the world, as if one could take a slice through space-time at a particular time and could then hope to identify meaningfully entities in space at that time which merited analysis and description. Because human observers of the universe are not moving with velocities at all comparable with that of light, relativistic distortions of our perspective of most entities in our observed world are not significant and so in the last section of chapter 2 we were able to give a broad account of the general features of these entities as observed by the natural sciences. However, the world is, almost notoriously, in a state of continuous flux, and it has, not surprisingly, been one of the major preoccupations of science to understand the changes that occur at all levels of the natural world. It has asked 'What is going on?' and 'How did these entities and structures we now observe get here and come to be the way they are?'

Because almost all observable entities and structures are subject to change, though on widely disparate timescales, so that all 'being' is in fact in process of 'becoming', some have argued that the fundamental units of the world are not so much entities or structures constituted of units, as 'events' – trajectories in space-time. There is no such thing, in this perspective, as 'inert stuff'; only, as it were, 'goings on'. But since we can, in fact, discriminate discrete entities and structures, along the lines of the preceding section, it is for the most part not misleading to think that the question of 'What's going on?' can be responded to in terms of accounts of the changes in time of entities and structures observed at particular times, past and present. The object of our curiosity is both causal explanation of past changes in order to understand the present and also prediction of the future course of 'events', of changes in the entities and structures with which we are concerned.

1 Predictability, Causality and 'Top-Down' Causation

The notions of explanation of the past and present and predictability of the future are closely interlocked with the concept of causality. For detection of a causal sequence in which, say, A causes B, which causes C, and so on, is frequently taken to be an explanation of the present in terms of the past (i.e., an historical explanation) and also predictive of the future, insofar that observation of A gives one grounds for inferring that B and C will follow as time elapses, since the original A–B–C ... sequence was itself a succession in time.

There has, of course, been a long and intricate debate over the centuries about the extent to which observation of a 'constant conjunction' of events can be logically predictive of the future – the 'problem of induction'. Common though such inductive reasoning is, however, it has been widely recognized that causality in scientific accounts of natural sequences of events is only reliably attributable when some underlying relationships of an intelligible kind between the successive forms of the entities have been discovered, over and beyond mere conjunction as such. These explanatory relationships often involve an understanding of how the constituent units of any entity give it the form it has and how changes in such 'internal' relationships can manifest themselves in observations on the system as a whole – though such a generalization is far from capturing the enormous variety of explanations of change that the sciences afford across the vast range of their operation. Nevertheless, it serves to emphasize this fundamental concern of the sciences with the explanation of change and so with predictability and causality. It transpires that various degrees of predictability pertain to different kinds of natural systems and that the accounts of causality that are pertinent are correspondingly different. It must be recalled that although absolute simultaneity is lost in the theory of relativity, the succession of events which occur at a given location and which form causal chains is independent of the choice of frame of reference. (The only type of succession whose order depends on the frame of reference is that of causally *un*related events.) Indeed the concept of causality is affected by Einstein's theory of relativity only to the extent that we now have to recognize that causal influences can never be transmitted through the universe at a speed greater than that of light. Let us now examine some natural systems which differ with respect to the predictability of their development in time and with respect to the account we have to give of their causal connectedness.

a Predictability and Causality in Relatively Simple, Dynamic, Law-obeying Systems

Science began to gain its great ascendancy in Western culture through the succession of intellectual pioneers in mathematics, mechanics and astronomy which led to the triumph of the Newtonian system with its explanation not only of many of the relationships in certain terrestrial systems but, more particularly, of the geometrical orbits and periods of planetary motions in the solar system. These orbits and periods obeyed precise mathematical relations and the future states of the systems (with certain notable deviations which were later explained by postulating the existence of previously undetected planets) were predictable from these relationships, which naturally were then regarded as 'laws'. This led, not surprisingly considering the sheer intellectual power and beauty of the Newtonian scheme, to the domination of the criterion of predictability in the perception of what science should, at its best, always aim to provide – even though such single-level systems, we now realize, are comparatively rare. It also reinforced the notion that science proceeded, indeed *should* proceed, by breaking down the world in general, and any investigated system in particular, into their constituent entities. Its procedure was, it was assumed, to determine the relations between these entities, so distinguished, and such modifications with time as they underwent. These relations, if well established, eventually qualified as the laws that, given the initial conditions, determined the future course of events, which were thus predictable. Such procedures naturally gave rise to a view of the world as mechanical and deterministic and the ability to make predictions almost came to be regarded as the necessary criterion of a successful scientific explanation. As we shall see, the dominance of this criterion has had to be qualified but it has, even so, been applicable to a wide variety of other systems less simple than the planetary one.

The concept of causality in such systems can be broadly subsumed into that of intelligible relations with their implication of the existence of something analogous to an underlying mechanism that generates these relationships (the 'generative mechanism').[1]

*b Predictability and Causality of Certain Statistical Properties
of Assemblies (In Spite of the Intractability of Micro-prediction)*

Certain properties of a total assembly can sometimes be predicted
in more complex systems. For example, it was the application of
essentially the idea of an assembly of gas molecules as behaving like
colliding Newtonian bodies which led to a successful derivation, in
broad principle, of the gas laws (e.g., pressure times volume is
proportional to temperature) from the collisional behaviour and
properties of the individual molecules constituting a gas. This statistical calculation is not vitiated by our lack of knowledge of the
direction and velocities of individual molecules. The macroscopic
behaviour of the whole gas (e.g., obeying the 'gas laws') can still be
attributed to that of the individual molecules and the latter can
justifiably be said to be the 'cause' of the former.

As is, of course, notorious, the predictability of events at the
atomic and sub-atomic level has been radically modified by the
realization that accurate determinations of the values of certain
pairs of quantities (momentum/position and energy/time) are mutually exclusive; that is, the uncertainty in the value of one of the pair
times the uncertainty in the value of the other is a constant. This
constant is very small so that the real uncertainty in the values of
these quantities is of numerical significance only for small particles
of the sub-atomic order: however, it is not eliminable in practice or,
it now seems, in principle and introduces a fundamental uncertainty
into the quantitative description of events at this micro-level. This
reinforces the unpredictability in all respects, though not in some
significant ones (e.g., the gas laws), of such macro-systems. We are
here referring, of course, to the famous Uncertainty Principle of
Heisenberg, one of the fundamental pillars of quantum theory.
Other, related, kinds of unpredictability are now also accepted with
reference to other systems at the sub-atomic level. Thus, in a
collection of radioactive atoms it is never possible to predict at what
instant the nucleus of any particular atom will disintegrate; all that is
known is the probability of it breaking up in a given time interval.
However, with a given particular kind of atom (e.g., radium) it is
perfectly possible to predict with complete accuracy how long it will
take for a given fraction, say, one half, to disintegrate, on the basis of
earlier observations. Here then is an instance of relative unpredictability (or, better, only probabilistic predictability) at the micro-level
in conjunction with statistical predictability at the macro-level. It

exemplifies the current state of quantum theory which allows only for the dependence on each other of the *probabilities* of elementary events and so to a looser form of causal coupling at this micro-level than had been taken for granted in classical physics. But note that causality, as such, is not eliminated, for physical situations at this micro-level still depend on each other, if only now in a probabilistic fashion.

c Predictability and Causality in Newtonian Systems
Deterministic Yet Not Totally Predictable at the Micro-level of Description

That there are such systems has been a time-bomb ticking away under the edifice of the deterministic/predictable paradigm of what constitutes the world-view of science from at least as long ago as the 1900s. The French mathematician Henri Poincaré then pointed out[2] that, since the ability of the (essentially Newtonian) theory of dynamical systems to make predictions depended not only on knowing the rules for describing how the system will change with time, but also on knowing the initial conditions of the system, such predictability was extremely sensitive to the accuracy of our knowledge of the parameters characterizing those initial conditions. Thus it can be shown that even in assemblies of bodies obeying Newtonian mechanics there is a real limit to the degree of predictability. Indeed, beyond quite restricted limits such systems can become totally unpredictable, in spite of the deterministic character of the laws of Newton, on account of our inability ever to determine sufficiently precisely the values of the initial 'determining' parameters.

For example, in a game of billiards suppose that, after the first shot, the balls are sent in a continuous series of collisions, that there are a very large number of balls (so collisions with any edges can be ignored) and that collisions occur with a negligible loss of energy. One might assume that the ordinary laws of collisions in Newtonian mechanics would allow one to predict indefinitely which balls were moving and with what velocities and in what directions. This was the assumption on which Laplace based his famous assertion that, given knowledge of all the forces controlling nature and of the values of all relevant parameters at any instant, then all future states of the universe would be predictable to a powerful enough intelligence.

However, the results of collisions between convex bodies are exquisitely sensitive to errors in the angle of their impact. If the average distance between the balls is ten times their radius, then it can be shown[3] that an error of one decimal digit at the nth place of decimals in the angle of impact of the first collision leads to the conclusion that after n collisions all certainty in the directions of the balls is lost – it will not be known whether any particular ball is moving in any given direction or one at right angles to it.

For example, an error of one in the 1000th decimal place in the angle of the first impact means that all predictability is lost after 1000 collisions. Clearly infinite accuracy is needed for the total predictability that Laplace assured us was possible. The uncertainty of movement grows with each impact as the originally minute uncertainty becomes amplified and there is an exponential amplification of the uncertainty in the directions of movement after each impact. Even quite small effects quickly reach macroscopic proportions. So, although the system is deterministic at the micro-level – the constituent entities obey Newtonian mechanics – it is never totally predictable in practice at this level.

But it is not predictable for another reason, for even if *per impossibile* the error in our knowledge of the angle of the first impact were zero, unpredictability still enters because no such system can ever be located away from the effects of the gravitational fields exerted by everything else that exists – it cannot be outside the universe. Thus, suppose our ensemble of colliding bodies were actually a gas of billiard-ball-like molecules colliding elastically (the assumption of the quite successful kinetic theory of gases). Then it turns out that the gravitational force exerted by one electron at the observable limit of the universe would render the molecular motion unpredictable (direction uncertain by a right angle, as above) after only 50 collisions, that is, after about only 10^{-10} seconds for such an assembly – or after a minute for a set of actual billiard balls.[4] So, in practice, deterministic 'laws' often still do not allow predictability, even in the mechanistic world of Newtonian mechanics, of all the descriptive parameters of a system, namely the exact description of the velocity and direction of movement of each individual molecule.

Now, attempts to specify more and more finely the initial conditions will eventually come up against the barrier of 'Heisenberg' uncertainty, mentioned above, and this is in principle unsurmountable, according to the most widely agreed interpretation of the Heisenberg Uncertainty Principle, the one that rejects the existence of 'hidden variables'. So even this kind of Newtonian system can be described as unpredictable in principle with respect to any detailed description of its microscopic properties (velocities and positions of individual bodies in such a system). On a critical-realist account of scientific knowledge, this means we can say that such systems *are* indeterminate with respect to these microscopic properties (if not with respect to macroscopic properties of the assembly; see b above).

It should be noted that, as with all smaller entities that are part of larger wholes, the velocity of the whole relative to some frame of reference external to the system is superimposed on that of each molecule relative to the others. To this extent, the movement of the system as a whole (for example, if a box containing gas is dropped) is a causal factor in the movement of the individual molecules – and this constitutes a basic kind of 'top-down' causation, more subtle forms of which will be discussed below.

d Predictability and Causality in Non-linear Dynamical Systems

One of the striking developments in science in recent years has been the increasing recognition that many dynamical systems – physical, chemical, biological and indeed neurological – that are governed by non-linear dynamical equations can become unpredictable in their macroscopically observable behaviour. (In certain cases – in which there is dissipation of free energy in open systems far from equilibrium – they may manifest new levels and kinds of organization and then the non-linearity resides in the relation between certain key variables of the dissipative system, for example the fluxes of material or energy and the 'forces' controlling them.) Examples of such time-dependence include: turbulent flow in liquids; predator-prey patterns; reactor systems that involve autocatalytic relations; yearly variation in insect and other populations in nature; and the weather. The last-mentioned involves what has been called the 'butterfly effect' (Edward Lorenz), whereby a butterfly disturbing the air here today could affect what weather occurs on the other side of the world in a month's time through amplifications cascading through a chain of complex interactions.

It is now realized that the time-sequence of complex dynamical systems can take many forms. Those that have 'closed' solutions to the relevant differential equations can settle down either to one particular state or oscillate, in a 'limit cycle', between a sequence of states that are traversed periodically, such as the solar system (cf.

Section a above) or the pendulum of a grandfather clock. Or, consider chemical reaction systems: normally these are taken to come eventually to the resting state of chemical equilibrium. But there are chemical systems, including some significant biochemical ones, that involve positive and negative feedback and, under particular initial conditions, settle down to regular oscillations in time and space with respect to the concentrations of key constituents. The same applies to biological populations of predators and prey. In both cases the mechanism involves particular values for the parameters that control formation/destruction of the units in question and their rate of movement through space. These are very striking phenomena to observe – startling even – and they are of particular significance in relation to living systems, for they indicate the way patterns can emerge.[5]

What has transpired is that the mathematicians find that when they build up piecemeal, usually with the help of modern computers, the kind of solutions that are given by the non-linear equations governing many natural complex dynamical systems, they find that they do not have such 'closed' solutions and that the following can occur. Variation of a key controlling parameter (or parameters, in some cases) can at first lead to a single unique solution and all seems quite 'normal' and well-behaved from a determinist viewpoint; all is still predictable. But at a certain critical value of this key parameter, the solutions bifurcate into two possibilities, either of which may occur first as this critical point is passed – but *which* one is not predictable. As time proceeds, the system can 'flip' between these two alternative allowed states and, under some circumstances, these interchanges can constitute regular oscillations. As the key parameter increases all kinds of further complexities can occur: successive bifurcations; periods of entirely erratic behaviour, mathematically 'chaotic'; and yet further bifurcations. Finer and finer numerical subdivisions of the key parameters keep on repeating such sequences.[6] It is important to stress that in these cases this unpredictability is an ineradicable one, because of the irreducible limit to precision with respect to initial conditions that is prescribed by the Heisenberg Uncertainty Principle. Such systems may therefore be said to be truly unpredictable, which means, on the critical-realist account of scientific knowledge that we are espousing, that such systems *are* genuinely indeterminate.

In the real world most systems do not conserve energy: they are usually *dissipative systems* through which energy and matter flow, and so are also 'open' in the thermodynamic sense. Such systems can often give rise to the kind of sequence just mentioned. At one set of values of a controlling parameter the system at first settles down to an equilibrium or near-to-equilibrium steady state in which typical characteristics of the system (e.g., reactant concentrations) do not vary with time. At somewhat higher values of this same system parameter, the solutions bifurcate and seemingly stable behaviour occurs, patterned in space and/or time (e.g., limit cycles). This may be succeeded at still higher values of the controlling parameter by mathematically 'chaotic' behaviour. Many examples of these kinds of system are now known: the formation of vertical hexagonal cells of convecting fluids in liquids heated from below (the Bénard phenomenon); the transition to both irregular and periodic fluctuations in space and time of the concentrations of reactants in a chemical systems that exhibit positive and negative feedback with diffusion; pattern formation in developing tissues through which both activators and inhibitors diffuse; the distribution of predators and prey in a particular territory; and so on.

In the change-over to temporal and spatial patterns of system behaviour, we have examples of what Ilya Prigogine and his colleagues at Brussels have called 'order through fluctuations'.[7] For in these systems, at the critical points of bifurcation an arbitrary fluctuation has been amplified to such an extent that its scale becomes comparable in magnitude to that of the whole system and effectively takes it over, as it were, with a consequent transformation of the system's properties. A new regime emerges. In the last two decades, the Brussels school has studied the thermodynamics of such irreversible processes in open, dissipative systems that are a long way from equilibrium and are non-linear (with respect to the relation between controlling fluxes and forces). Thermodynamics, one of the greatest scientific achievements of the last century and a half, embodies its famous Second Law to the effect that, in isolated systems undergoing natural irreversible processes, the entropy and 'disorder' (appropriately defined) always increase. Ilya Prigogine and his colleagues were able to demonstrate that the emergence of new more 'ordered', or rather 'organized', regimes were in fact required by the thermodynamics of such systems.

Explicit awareness of all this is only relatively recent in science and necessitates a reassessment of the potentialities of the stuff of the world, pattern formation in which had previously been thought to be confined only to the macroscopically static, equilibrium state – so that special, somewhat esoteric and conjectural, 'forces' or 'fields' were often (and still sometimes are, even today) postulated to account for the ability of the natural world to engender new patterns and forms of organization. In these far-from-equilibrium, non-linear, open systems, matter displays its potential to be self-organizing and thereby to bring into existence new forms entirely by the operation of forces and the manifestation of properties we already understand – but operating now under the constraints and with the potentialities afforded by their being incorporated into systems the properties of which, as a whole, now have to be taken into account. As Crutchfield *et al.* put it: 'a system can have complicated behaviour that emerges as a consequence of simple, nonlinear interaction of only a few components... Through amplification of small fluctuations it [nature] can provide natural systems with access to novelty.'[8]

e 'Top-down' Causation

Apart from the very simple instance (see section b above) of the effects of the general movement of a whole system on that of its constituent units, the notion of causality, when applied to systems, has usually been assumed to describe 'bottom-up' causation – that is, the effect on the properties and behaviour of the whole system of the properties and behaviour of its constituent units. However, in the case of these dissipative systems which manifest 'order through fluctuations', an influence on the state of the system as a whole on the behaviour of its components units – a constraint exercised by the whole on its parts – has to be recognized. Following D. T. Campbell[9] and R. W. Sperry,[10] we may call this 'top-down' causation. For, to take the example of the Bénard phenomenon, beyond the critical point, individual molecules in a hexagonal 'cell', over a wide range in the fluid, move with a common component of velocity in a coordinated way, having previously manifested only entirely random motions with respect to each other. Or, in reaction systems which display rhythmic temporal and spatial patterns in the concentrations of the reactants, thousands of molecules in a particular region at a particular time suddenly all change to another form, whereas previously the probability of change was quite independent of their location. In both these instances,[11] the changes at the micro-level, that of the constituent units, are what they are because of their incorporation into the system as a whole, which is exerting specific constraints on its units, making them behave otherwise than they would in isolation.

It is important to emphasize again that recognition of the role of such 'top-down' causation in no way derogates from that of 'bottom-up' causation. But the need for recognition of the former is greater because hardly anyone since the rise of reductionist scientific methodologies doubts the significance of the latter. Indeed, this lack of a proper recognition of the former has unfortunately often inhibited the development of concepts appropriate to the more complex levels of the hierarchy of natural systems. The dual character of the directions in which 'causality' operates in such complex systems is further indicated by the recognition that epistemological analyses of many complex systems and situations also necessitate the distinguishing of a 'top-down' from a 'bottom-up' process. Thus Michael Arbib and Mary Hesse advocate what they call a 'two-way reductionism' as 'a more realistic view of the relation between two sciences, such as those of mind and brain', and go on to expound what they mean by this as follows: 'We use "top-down" and "bottom-up" analysis to refer to the two-way process of modifying and extending, respectively, the lower-level science to explain the higher level, and the higher level in the light of the implication of the lower level.'[12]

Their description of this two-way process as a 'reductionism' is somewhat misleading, since this term has generally been confined to the process whereby 'the theories and experimental laws formulated in one field of science can be shown to be special cases of theories and laws formulated in some other branch of science. If such is the case, the former branch of science is said to have been reduced to the latter.'[13] The direction of this reduction has invariably been that of the putative 'higher' level science to the 'lower', for example of biology to physics and chemistry. But the terminology is less important than what they are referring to, namely the two-way character of the process of epistemological analysis that is required in the natural sciences.

On the critical-realist view of the epistemology of the sciences, this has the further implication that the entities to which the 'theories and experimental laws' refer in our epistemological analyses correspond, however inadequately and provisionally, to realities which must be deemed to exist at the various levels being studied – that is, they also have an ontological reference, however elusive. As

Arbib and Hesse put it, 'there is no question of any of the properties being shown to be unreal', for they, rightly in my view, wish to anchor their epistemology 'in the reality of everyday experience'. There are indeed 'all manner of levels of reality',[14] as we have persistently affirmed in this work. So it is legitimate to describe the realities postulated as existing at the higher levels (the wholes, the 'top' of the 'top-down' terminology) to be causally interactive, in both directions, with the realities postulated as existing at the lower ones (the parts, the 'bottom') – while continuing, of course, to recognize the often provisional nature of our attempted depictions of realities at both levels. For this reason I do not share Arbib's and Hesse's reservations[15] concerning, in particular, R. W. Sperry's emphasis on the causative efficacy of higher level states,[16] since there need be no implication that either 'bottom-up' analyses or the discerning of 'bottom-up' causation is thereby ruled out. For all such 'fundamental and interesting'[17] systems there is indeed, as Arbib and Hesse agree, never likely to be a time when both methods of analysis are not going to be needed and so, I would add, the need to recognize the joint operation of 'causation' in both directions. We shall see that this kind of 'top-down' causation has increasing significance in those kinds of complex systems that are living.

2 THE LIVING WORLD

a *The Origin of Life*

However else living organisms may be described, there is no doubt that they are, at least, constituted of atoms of kinds widely distributed in the inorganic world. These atoms make up the structures of molecules of a wide range of sizes, almost all of which are engaged in a complex network of reactions also involving molecules entering the organisms from outside – through breathing the atmosphere, or taking in and expelling water (as fishes) and through ingestion of food. Living organisms also have the special characteristic of being able to self-reproduce their whole interlocking structure from one generation to another, and this is a necessary, if not sufficient, requirement for any material system to qualify as 'living'.

The studies on dissipative systems (see pp. 52–3 above) have shown how interlocking systems of reactions involving feedback can, entirely in accord with thermodynamics (and not precluded by its Second Law), undergo transitions to more organized and more complex forms, provided such systems are open, non-linear and far from equilibrium. All these conditions would have been satisfied by many systems of chemical reactions present on the Earth during its first 1,000 million years of existence. Furthermore, with our increasing knowledge of how molecular patterns can be copied in present living systems – the story of the translation of information in nucleic acids to sequences of amino-acids constituting distinctive proteins – it is now possible to make plausible hypotheses concerning the way in which early forms of nucleic acids and proteins might have formed a self-replicating macromolecular system, such as the 'hypercycle' of Eigen and Schuster. Such systems can be shown to multiply at the expense of less efficient rival ones.[18] What these studies indicate is the inevitability of the appearance of more organized, self-replicating systems, the properties of atoms and molecules being what they are; but what form of organization would be adopted is not strictly predictable since it depends on fluctuations.[19] In *retro*spect, the form of molecular organization that is self-reproducing is now intelligible, after three decades of 'molecular biology', but in *pro*spect, even with our present knowledge, it would not have been strictly predictable. So there is an openness and flexibility in the development of life even at this critical juncture which has to be reckoned with as a feature of our world.

b Evolution

The forms of living matter, that is, of living organisms, evolve – as we now know – through those changes in the genetic controlling material (DNA) that result in changes in the organism that increase the chance of its having surviving progeny. This is, of course, simply neo-Darwinian evolution which may be summed up in two propositions:[20] all organisms, past, present and future, descend from earlier living systems, the first of which arose spontaneously (according to the principles discussed above); and species are derived from one another by natural selection of the best procreators. The changes in the genetic macromolecule DNA are produced by a variety of agents – for example, the absorption of a quantum of energy from ultraviolet light which thereby changes the chemical structure in one of the units in the DNA chains. This alters or, more often, destroys the genetic information it is conveying at that point in the chain, and thus changes the organism in some respect, however slight, and so the chance, for better or for worse, of its producing progeny in its ecological niche. The significant point for our present purposes is that the changes in the DNA itself are scattered along the read-out sequences of its immensely long chains in a way that is random with respect to the ultimate effects of these changes on the ability of the organism to have progeny. For the effect of any particular DNA change depends on quite other factors, especially the environment of the organism in the widest sense – that is, including not only food resources, but also the nature and number of its predators, the 'social' organization of like organisms, and so on, in an ever-widening network of connections.

The possibility of science being predictive of such a process is vitiated on at least two counts. First, the original molecular event which alters, or destroys, a constituent unit in the DNA comes within the range of unpredictability through the operation of the 'Heisenberg' uncertainty of quantum-scale events. Second, the eventual effect on the ability of the organism to procreate is the result of the intersection of two independent causal chains – that producing changes in the DNA and the interaction between the thus-changed organism (especially in its ability to procreate) and its environment. The requisite knowledge to predict such an intersection is never likely to be forthcoming, as we observe (if only hypothetically) any particular organism in a particular environment; so, on this ground too, the sequence of events is not in practice predictable, though entirely intelligible afterwards. It is this combination of continuous random changes in the genetically controlling material with the 'accidental' filtering out of changes favourable to the production of progeny that gives to the evolutionary process its apparently opportunistic character and its dependence on actual historical situations. Even so, the process does display trends and certain generalizable features which we shall come to.

What concerns us more particularly here is the pattern of 'causal' relationships in this process. We are dealing with a process in which a selective system 'edits', as it were, the products of direct physico-chemical causation over periods of time covering several reproductive generations. Let us take an example from Donald Campbell to illustrate this:[21] the surfaces and muscle attachments of the jaws of a worker termite are mechanically highly efficient, entirely conforming with the best engineering and physical principles, and their operation depends on the combination of properties of the particular proteins of which the jaws are made. Selection has optimized viability at the level of the organism gnawing wood, picking up seeds, etc. So we need the principles operative at this level (laws of

levers, relations between protein structures and mechanical properties of their aggregates, and so on) to explain the structure and
distribution of the proteins in the jaws and hence to account for the
presence in the organism's DNA of the particular sequences it
contains that control the production of these particular proteins. So,
from the perspective of the whole organism's activity and its being
only one in a series of generations of termites, it is the efficacy of the
proteins in constituting jaws, that has been monitored by natural
selection, which is here apparently determining the sequences of the
DNA units – even though when one looks at the development of a
single organism, one observes only, with the molecular biologists,
the biochemical processes whereby protein sequences, and so structures, are 'read out' from the DNA sequences.

Hence there is a sense in which the network of relationships that
constitute the evolutionary development and the behaviour pattern
of the whole organism is determining what particular DNA sequence
is present at the controlling point in its genetic material in the
evolved organism. This consideration becomes even more striking if
one instances those species in which the evolution of division of
labour within it has led to specialization in function and the development of different types of jaws in different sub-groups. Here the laws
of sociological organization are determining the DNA sequences, it
seems. Campbell called this 'downward' or 'top-down' causation,
insofar as specification of the higher levels of organization is necessary for explaining the lower level – in this case, the sequence in a
DNA molecule. Where there is selection of the whole organism at
the higher level, the higher level laws are necessary for a complete
explanation and specification of the lower. The part of the DNA that
controls the jaw protein sequences is constrained to be there and be
what it is by virtue of its presence within the whole system of an
organism-with-an-evolutionary-history.

As Elisabeth Vrba has said, this kind of downward causation is
really a commonsense notion; for instance, 'as natural selection
sorts among organisms it willy-nilly "downward causes" the sorting
of all included lower entities, be they non-coding DNA sequences,
genes, cells, chromosomes, etc.'[22] But, as she also goes on to remark,

> There is also a more subtle form of downward causation. The struc-
> tural or organizational aspects of a particular higher individual may

downward determine the introduction and sorting of variation among lower level entities included in its 'body'... [for example] the structural group character of group size may downward cause the sorting of variation among included phenotypes (e.g., the spread of altruistic phenotypes by random drift, against the force of natural selection, which requires small population size).[23]

Some biologists have stressed furthermore that what happens, evolutionarily speaking, to organisms are consequences of themselves – that is, of their state at any given moment, with all its dependence on historical accidents – as well as of their genotype and environment.[24] Thus innovative behaviour on the part of a living creature in its environment can be a major factor in subsequent change, and so in its evolution,[25] and this introduces another imponderable limiting predictability in evolutionary change in addition to those already discussed.[26]

Description of such complex interlocking networks of events and changes operating at different levels does not seem adequately to be captured by their description as *causally* connected, with its often hidden assumption that some kind of force is operative in a sequential constant conjunction of events. The word 'causal' is more normally used for the linkage of different events at the same level of explanation (physical, informational, or even psychological). We seem to have here a determination of form through *a flow of information*, rather than through a transmission of energy, where 'information' is conceived of in a broad enough sense to include the input from the environment whereby molecular mechanisms are selected, including, for example, the DNA sequences in the termite jaw example. In this kind of determinative relation, 'causal' explanations are in terms of non-physical categories, like 'information', but real enough, nevertheless – as any computer engineer would testify with respect to the programme controlling the electronic changes in a computer. Such determinative relations may operate between two different kinds of 'level' in nature. One can continue to use the 'top-down' terminology of Campbell, provided one does not thereby assume that such 'causation' can be described only in terms of forces operating to transmit energy or of the movement of matter, as is often true of causality operating at only one level. The determination of form by form requires a flow of information, in this case, between levels.[27]

c   *The Brain, Mental Events and Consciousness*

It is in terms such as those just mentioned that some neuro-scientists and philosophers have come to speak of the relation between mental events and the physico-chemical changes at neur-ones, which are the triggers of observable actions in living organ-isms that possess brains sufficiently developed for it to be appropriate to attribute to them some kind of consciousness. As John Searle has recently put it:

> Consciousness . . . is a real property of the brain that can cause things to happen. My conscious attempt to perform an action such as raising my arm causes the movement of the arm. At the higher level of description, the intention to raise my arm causes the movement of the arm. At the lower level of description, a series of neuron firings starts a chain of events that results in the contraction of the muscles . . . the same sequence of events has two levels of description. Both of them are causally real, and the higher level causal features are both caused by and realised in the structure of the lower level elements.[28]

This view of consciousness as causal, and as an emergent in evol-ution, has also been espoused by certain neuroscientists, in particu-lar, Roger Sperry, though with a somewhat different terminology concerning causation. (Here, as indicated above, we prefer to follow a usage as clarified by Mackay.)[29] For them, 'mental events' in human beings are the internal descriptions we offer of an actual total state of the brain itself and are not events in some entity called the 'mind' which exists in some other non-physical mode that is ontologically distinct from matter and 'interacts' (mysteriously, one would have to say) with the brain as a physical entity. So this is a monist and not a dualist view of the 'body-mind problem'. The point which has to be emphasized in the present context is that this whole state of the brain (or possibly some parts of it in certain instances) acts as a constraint on what happens at the more specific level of the individual, constituent neurones, so that what occurs at this lower level is what it is because of the prevailing state of the whole. In other words, there is operative here a top-down causation between the level of the brain state as a whole and of the individual neurones. Descriptions of the total brain state in purely neurological terms would be exceedingly complex – and, indeed, considering the com-plexity of the brain, may never be forthcoming in anything other that broad terms. But we do have available the language of ordinary experience to refer accurately, sometimes surprisingly so, to our mental events in a communicable fashion, so that the language of mental events may be taken as genuinely referring to realities that *are* brain states, which are in themselves aspects of the total action that expresses the intention of the agent (cf. the earlier discussion in chapter 2 section 3 of reductionism in relation to the language used to explicate consciousness). The language we use concerning the connections between our mental experiences – the language of reasons, intentions, and so forth – really does, on this view, refer to actual causal linkages between whole brain states. The causal effectiveness of the whole brain state on the actual states of its component nerves and neurones is probably better conceived of in terms of the transfer of information rather than of energy, in the way a programme representing a certain equation, say, controls the chips in a computer – but this whole area of investigation is still very much *sub judice*.

It seems that with the evolution of brains, the significance of this kind of 'top-down' causation has become more and more significant in the evolutionary development as the whole state and behaviour of the individual organism itself plays an increasing role. As we saw, this has introduced a further element of unpredictability into a process which is in principle, at least, intelligible *post hoc*. Furthermore, since the brain-in-the-body is a highly dissipative system, one has to raise the question of whether or not its future states are irreducibly unpredictable and whether this might not, at the level of consciousness, be the physical situation corresponding to the experience of freedom in human beings.

3 THE HISTORY OF NATURE

Our earlier examination of 'what's there' in the natural world led us to emphasize that it contained hierarchies of levels of complexity, often related like a series of nested Chinese boxes – though other forms of hierarchical relation are also manifest in the world, especially within the control mechanisms of living organisms. It is now time for us to take account of the *dynamic* character of these relationships, to recognize that the world in all its aspects, as explicated especially by the natural sciences of the last two centuries (that is, since the 'discovery of time' by the eighteenth-century pioneers of geology), has come to be seen as always in process, a nexus of evolving forms, some changing rapidly, others over immensely long time-scales, but never static. Our accounts of the observed structures of the world ('what's there') can never be separated from our understanding of the way they came to be the way they are, from our accounts of the processes whereby they came into existence. For the 'being' of the world is always also a 'becoming' and there is always a story to be told, especially as matter becomes living and then conscious and, eventually, social too. 'Evolution' in the general sense can be said to occur cosmologically, inorganically, geologically, biologically, socially and culturally. There occurs a continuous, almost kaleidoscopic, recombination of the component units of the universe into an increasing diversity of new forms, which last for a time only to be re-formed out of the same simpler entities into new and different patterns. The process never stops and our accounts of it all are irreducibly narrative.

a Features and Trends

Features and trends in the history of nature which the sciences now bring to our attention include the following.[30] History is a seamless web, a *continuity* which is increasingly *intelligible* as the sciences with more and more success explicate the nature of the transitions between natural forms. The process can be characterized as one of *emergence*, for new forms of matter, and a hierarchy of organization of these forms themselves, appear in the course of time and these new forms have new properties, behaviours and networks of relations which necessitate the development of new epistemologically irreducible concepts in order accurately to describe and refer to them. At each level of analysis, trends can be detected in the history of nature which are significant for eventual theological reflection – though one must always be cautious not to transfer generalizations about trends at one level to other levels without further warrant.

New patterns can only come into existence in a finite universe ('finite' in the sense of the conservation of matter-energy) if old patterns dissolve to make place for them. This is a condition of the creativity of the process – that is, of its ability to produce the new – which at the biological level we observe as new forms of life only through death of the old. For the death of individuals is essential for release of food resources for new arrivals, and species simply die out by being ousted from biological 'niches' by new ones better adapted to survive and reproduce in them. Biological death of the individual is the prerequisite of the creativity of the biological order, that creativity which eventually led to the emergence of human beings. At this biological level we discover the process to be that of 'natural selection', but it is possible to discern cognate processes occurring also at other levels.

Complex living structures can only have a finite chance of coming into existence if they are not assembled *de novo*, as it were, from their basic sub-units, but emerge through the accumulation of changes in a simpler forms, as demonstrated by H. A. Simon in a classic paper (discussed further on p. 67). Having come on to the scene, they can then survive, because of the finitude of their life spans, only by building pre-formed complex chemical structures into their fabric through imbibing the materials of other living organisms. For the chemist and biochemist there is the same kind of difficulty in conceiving how complex material structures, especially those of the intricacy of living organisms, could be assembled otherwise than from less complex units, as there is for the mathematician of conceiving of a universe in which the analytic laws of arithmetic were inapplicable. So there is a kind of 'structural' logic about the inevitability of living organisms dying and of preying on each other – for we cannot conceive, in a lawful, non-magical universe, of any way whereby the immense variety of developing, biological, structural complexity might appear, except by utilizing structures already existing, either by way of modification (as in biological evolution) or of incorporation (as in feeding).[31] The statistical logic is inescapable: *new forms of matter arise only through the dissolution of the old; new life only through death of the old.*

One of the most general and widely agreed trends in nature – indeed, it constitutes one of the pillars of modern physical science – is that there is always an *increase* in the quantity (entropy) which measures *disorderliness* in natural processes in isolated systems, systems across whose boundaries no matter or energy passes. The 'disorderliness', or 'randomness', referred to here is a precisely defined quantity (the entropy) which is related to the number of possible dispositions of matter over the available energy states. It is the converse of the kind of 'order' to be seen in the arrangements of atoms or molecules in a perfect crystal, or in a perfect wallpaper pattern. It is to be distinguished from 'organization', for example that of a biological system, though clearly an increase in 'disorder' is inimical to the presence of biological organization. This trend towards disorder in individual isolated systems, the famous Second Law of Thermodynamics, has frequently been generalized and applied to the universe as a whole, assuming that, almost by definition, it is an 'isolated system' in the sense required by the Second Law. But such a generalization has always been of dubious validity. Perhaps the most that may be said is that the Second Law leads one to expect that over increasingly wide tracts of the universe there will a tendency to reach thermal equilibrium (the so-called 'heat death'). But how long fluctuations will persist in any given region is extremely difficult to estimate, so that ebbs and flows of matter and energy may continue long beyond the period of existence of anything like the universe we now observe.

Many regions of the universe will continue to behave as open systems through which matter and energy are flowing. But in such regions, if any systems are non-linear and far from equilibrium, then dissipative structures can arise and new forms of ordering of matter and energy can occur, in fact *will* do so, as we have already discussed – 'order through fluctuations'. This is the explanation we now have of the anomaly that puzzled nineteenth-century scientists of how, in a universe that was increasingly 'disordered', biological *evolution towards increased 'organization'* could occur – the apparent discrepancy between two of that century's most significant scientific discoveries, Darwinian evolution and the Second Law of Thermodynamics.[32]

In our earlier discussion of predictability, it became clear that although many processes and sequences of events are afterwards intelligible, there is often an irreducible element of unpredictability about their future states. That is, there is an *open-endedness* about the course of many natural events. Indeed, only relatively simple dynamic lawlike systems, having closed solutions to the equations that govern their trajectories, could be said to be entirely predictable, and only then in respect to certain well-defined parameters. But in other systems predictability, although possible at the macro-level, is impossible at the micro-level; and dissipative systems are unpredictable even at the macro-level. This open-endedness of such natural systems is compounded when they are living.

Furthermore, the course of biological evolution on the surface of the Earth has a contingent, historical character consequent upon evolutionary changes being dependent on the crossing of independent causal chains.[33] This open-ended character of biological events is enhanced as living organisms manifest increasingly individual characters and behaviour patterns. It is a tendency that reaches its apogee in the human experience of freedom, which may itself, as we have hinted, be rooted in a fundamental open-endedness and unpredictability of brain states.

However, this open-endedness is not just a confused jumble, in the usual non-technical sense, for what we call 'chance', whether at the micro- or the macro-level, operates within a law-like framework which constrains and delimits the possible outcomes. As in many games, the consequences of the fall of the dice depend very much on the rules of the game.[34] During the last decade it has become increasingly apparent that it is chance operating within a lawlike framework that is the basis of the inherent creativity of the natural order, its ability to generate new forms, patterns and organizations of matter and energy. If all were governed by rigid law, a repetitive and uncreative order would prevail: if chance alone ruled, no forms, patterns or organizations would persist long enough for them to have any identity or real existence and the universe could never be a cosmos and susceptible to rational inquiry. It is the combination of the two which makes possible an ordered universe capable of developing within itself new modes of existence.[35] *The interplay of chance and law is creative.*

In those parts of the universe where the temperature is low enough for molecules to exist in sufficient proximity to interact, there is a tendency for more and more complex molecular systems to come into existence and this process is actually driven, in the case of reactions that involve association of molecules to more complex forms, by the tendency to greater overall randomization, that is, as a manifestation of the Second Law.[36] Such systems, if open and if they also exhibit feedback properties, can, as we saw, become 'dissipative' and undergo sharp changes of regime with the appearance of new patterns in space and time. In other words, even in these non-living systems, there is an increase in complexity in the entities involved in certain kinds of natural process. This appears to be an example of what Karl Popper has called a 'propensity' in nature.[37] Popper argued that a greater frequency of occurrence of a particular kind of event may be used as a test of whether or not there is inherent in the sequence of events (equivalent to throws of a die) a tendency or propensity to realize the event in question, in this instance an increase in complexity. 'There exist weighted possibilities which are more than *mere possibilities*, but tendencies or propensities to become real: tendencies or propensities to realize themselves.' Such propensities, he argues, 'are not mere possibilities, but are physical realities'.

But this *propensity for increased complexity* is also manifest in the history of living organisms. What significance is to be attributed to this? Is it simply, as W. McCoy has put it,[38] that biological 'evolution is a process of divergence and wandering rather than an inexorable progression towards increasing complexity', so that evolution '*permits* the emergence of new complexity, but does not in any particular case necessitate it'. Certainly, as J. Maynard Smith has pointed out:

> All one can say is that since the first living organisms were presumably very simple, then if any large change in complexity has occurred in any evolutionary lineage, it must have been in the direction of increasing complexity ... 'Nowhere to go but up' ... Intuitively one feels that the answer to this is that life soon became differentiated into various forms, living in different ways, and that within such a complex ecosystem there would always be *some* way of life open which called for a more complex phenotype. This would be a self-perpetuating process. With the evolution of new species, further ecological niches would open up, and the complexity of the most complex species would increase.[39]

But this is, as Maynard Smith goes on to admit, 'intuition, not reason'. Nevertheless, the fact is that there *has* been, taking biological evolution as a whole, an emergence of increasingly complex organisms, even if in some evolutionary lines there has been a loss of complexity and so of organization. So, on Popper's criterion enunciated above, we would be correct in saying that there is a propensity towards increased complexity in the evolution of living organisms.

Saunders and Ho in a (disputed) interpretation[40] identify the basis of this tendency to be the process by which a self-organizing system optimizes its organization with respect to locally defined requirements for fitness. They argue that the random removal of a component from a system which is at or near to a local peak of fitness must tend to make the system less fit than before; whereas the random addition of a component allows the possibility of an increase. So such systems will tend to permit the addition of components more readily than their removal and this, Saunders and Ho suggest, is the chief cause of the observed increase in complexity during biological evolution. This sounds plausible enough but, in the nature of the case, is difficult to substantiate. In any case, the fact is that, even if it cannot be judged as inevitable in any particular evolutionary line, there has over biological evolution as a whole been an overall trend towards and an increase in complexity, so that it is right to speak of a propensity for this to occur.

By 'complexity' in this context we have been meaning simply the number of different types of components that are present in the systems in question. This must be distinguished from the 'organization' which such a system needs in order to survive, with complexity as the necessary but not sufficient condition for organization.[41] The need for organization for survival was beautifully demonstrated by H. A. Simon,[42] who showed that the simplest modular organization of, say, the structure of a watch, so that each module had a limited stability, led to an enormous increase in survivability during manufacture in the face of random destructive events.

So the increases we observe in complexity and organization (subsumed under 'complexity' from now on) in the natural world are entirely intelligible and not at all mysterious in the sense of requiring some non-naturalistic explanation. It is important to emphasize this, since a link has been proposed between this natural increase in complexity and the *increasing levels of consciousness* in biological evolution, for instance by Teilhard de Chardin. Certainly consciousness depends on the coming into existence of certain forms of very complex organizations of matter – nervous systems and brains – but these are particular forms of complexity and it is misleading simply to correlate consciousness with 'complexity' without further qualification.

Indeed, biologists are usually rather cautious about postulating trends in biological evolution and mostly prefer to limit themselves to describing the emergent features of later products of the evolutionary process.[43] These include not only the increase in complexity we have remarked upon already but also an increase in the general energy or maintained level of vital processes, protected reproduction, care of the young, and either an increase in specialization and adaptation or, as in the case of *homo sapiens*, an increase in flexibility and adaptability to an increasing range of environments.

It is from this standpoint that one should appraise the emergence of more and more complex, not necessarily larger, brains in the evolutionary development. The more capable an organism is of recording, analysing and making predictions from information about its environment, the better chance it will have of surviving in a wide variety of habitats. This sensitivity to, this sentience of, its surroundings inevitably involves an increase in its ability to experience pain, which constitutes the necessary biological warning signals of danger and disease, so that it is impossible readily to envisage an *increase of information-processing ability* without an increase in the sensitivity of the signal system of the organism to its environment. In other words, an increase in 'informational' capacity cannot but have as its corollary an increase, not only in the level of consciousness, but also in the experience of pain. Insulation from the surrounding world in the biological equivalent of three-inch nickel steel would be a sure recipe for preventing the development of consciousness.

Each increase in sensitivity, and eventually of consciousness, as evolution proceeds, inevitably heightens and accentuates awareness both of the beneficent, life-enhancing elements and of the inimical, life-diminishing elements in the world in which the organism finds itself. The stakes for joy and pain are, as it were, continuously being raised, and the living organism learns to discriminate between them. So *pain and suffering*, on the one hand, and *consciousness of pleasure and well-being*, on the other, *are emergents* in the world. The presence of the latter never causes any surprise (why not?) and it is the presence of the former which, as is well known, is usually taken to constitute a problem for belief in a creating God. Be that as it may, what it is important to emphasize at this point is that, from a purely naturalistic viewpoint, the emergence of pain and its compounding as suffering as consciousness increases seem to be inevitable aspects of any conceivable developmental process that would be characterized by a continuous increase in ability to process information coming from the environment. For this entails an increase in sensitivity, hence in vulnerability, and consequently in suffering as consciousness ramifies. In the context of natural selection, pain has an energizing effect and suffering is a goad to action: they both have survival value for creatures continually faced with new problematic situations challenging their survival.[44] In relation to our later theological reflections, it must be emphasized that pain, suffering and death are present in biological evolution, as a necessary condition for survival of the individual and transition to new forms long before the appearance of human beings on the scene. So the presence of pain, suffering and death cannot be the result of any particular human actions, though undoubtedly human beings experience them with a heightened sensitivity and, more than any other creatures, inflict them on each other.

b The Limits of Time

The foregoing emphasis on the historicity of nature has taken for granted our ordinary, commonsense awareness of time, even if quantified in science and everyday life by measuring devices of various degrees of sophistication. However, as we saw, the nature of time in modern relativistic physics is very different from this commonsense understanding of time as an endless dimension along which entities proceed and change. Modern physics and cosmology have raised again, in a new form, earlier discussions in theology concerning the relation of time and eternity, now more in the form of the question 'Does time have a beginning and end?'.

The concept of time is now seen to be but a component of the more inclusive concept of space-time, the curvature of which is dependent on the distribution of mass, energy and pressure of whatever matter is present. So it is not surprising that, when physicists and cosmologists try to understand that state of the early universe 10–20 thousand million years ago when it was compressed into a space of atomic dimensions, or even less, they find themselves questioning the very nature of 'time' itself. They are able to extrapolate back to a few seconds after the singularity of the 'hot big bang' without having to make any fundamental modifications of the concept of 'time' they have used in relativistic physics, or, for that matter, in ordinary life.

However, recently they have become particularly aware that close to the point from which the history of the universe in classical, ordinary 'time' can be taken forward, and to which it is extrapolated backwards from the present, very surprising events might have occurred in which there was an expansion of the universe by a factor of 10^{50} during the first 10^{-35} to 10^{-30} seconds of the universe's existence. This 'inflationary' period – which, be it noted, is still within classical, ordinary time – allows explanation of certain otherwise baffling features of the universe as it later expands. The state leading to this inflationary period can be understood only by a combination of quantum and relativity theory which involves a radical reformulation of our perception of time in a way not hitherto necessary.

For the concept 'space-time' in general relativity 'only has an unambiguous meaning within the framework of non-quantum physics',[45] whereas the idea of three-dimensional 'space' can be applied in quantum theory, as well as in classical theory. As one goes back in real 'time' (as dimensionally conceived, even in relativity theory) to that original exceedingly small and unimaginably dense early in universe, the distinction between 'space' and 'time' breaks down and they acquire a converging status, according to the recent speculations of J. B. Hartle and S. W. Hawking.[46] C. Isham expounds their ideas as follows:

> it becomes harder to sustain an interpretation of an evolution with respect to a genuine time variable. Basically, as the underlying equality of space and time directions starts to assert itself, the phenomenological time [ordinary, physical dimension time] begins to pick up an imaginary part ['imaginary' in the mathematician's sense of including a factor of i, the square root of -1] with its associated non-physical features. By this means, the problem of the 'beginning of time' is adroitly averted.[47]

In this proposal of Hartle and Hawking (still, be it noted, very much a matter for debate among theoretical physicists) there is no singularity at which phenomenological, physical time 'begins', together with three-dimensional space including matter-energy, and at which the universe could be said to have 'begun'. Rather the universe of space-time-matter-energy appears as the result of a 'quantum tunnelling' effect whereby absolutely nothing (=no space, no time) gives rise to something in (mathematically) imaginary time. From this point on, 'imaginary time' merges more and more into phenomenological, physical time – and the expansion of the universe proceeds in *that* time in the ways the physicists and cosmologists have made familiar.

Many people, like this author, soon find themselves out of their depth in this conceptual abyss – but the significant point is clear enough. Time as we know and record it, in science as in history and ordinary life, is a necessary concept for interpreting all we see in nature and history and life. But we now have to accept that physicists and cosmologists are beginning to question whether time can be naively extrapolated back to the 'beginning' of the universe without a profound modification of the whole concept.

But what about the 'end' of the universe in time? Does it *have* an end? At the moment the evidence is not adequate to decide between two possible fates of the universe as we know it.[48] According to one, the universe will go on expanding, the galaxies moving further and further apart, with a continual drop in temperature, the formation of 'black holes' and the eventual heat death of the universe – though fluctuations and flows of matter and energy might persist for a large proportion of these unimaginably long times, so that dissipative, ordered systems might not be precluded from forming. How long would life persist? Freeman Dyson has suggested that even human life might survive by interstellar migration well beyond the demise of our own solar system.[49] But this is pure speculation; certainly life on planet Earth has a terminus when the energy of the Sun becomes exhausted.

The other possible fate is that, if there is enough matter in the universe, its gravitational attractions will eventually, acting like a long piece of elastic, draw the galaxies back together and the universe will end in a big crunch – from which it may or may not expand again. Nobody knows which of these possible scenarios is the most likely. However, despite Freeman Dyson's speculations, all have the consequence that human life on the planet Earth will disappear, and this is something that any theology must reckon with. Personally I find this no more daunting a problem than facing up to the disappearance from the face of the Earth of that constituent of it with which we are most familiar – our individual selves. For the possible fates of the universe raise the question of whether or not, whatever religious believers may say, its whole history is not, after all, futile.

CHAPTER 4

Who's There?

The most striking feature of the universe is one that is so obvious that we often overlook it – namely the fact that we are here to ask questions about it at all. That the regular laws of nature acting upon and in the entities we have described in chapter 2 should have generated the processes (chapter 3) that in the course of time culminated in an entity, humanity, which can know the route by which it has arrived on the scene, is an astonishing outcome of that highly condensed system of matter-energy enfolded in the tight knot of space-time with which the universe began. What the best explanation is of this well-established feature of the universe must always be a major consideration in any reflection (such as will be undertaken in Part II) upon the meaning and intelligibility of all-that-is. But we need now to be more explicit about what it is that is distinctive about us.

Undoubtedly many of the characteristics of *homo sapiens* which we think are special to us are in fact developments of, extrapolations of, even exaggerations of, features and abilities to be observed in the higher mammals: our ability to expand into a wide variety of environments; our flexibility and adaptability; our long-extended care of our young; our strong individualization; our highly developed and complex brains and the concomitant intelligence which has proved to be such a selective advantage through its ability to monitor and alter our environment for our own purposes; and, dependent on our cerebral capacities, our use of language and the consequent elaborate socialization which we have thus been able to develop.[1] But let us now look a little harder at ourselves and our special peculiarities. For there is no doubt that in humanity there emerge new kinds of behaviour and experiences which demand new non-reducible, autonomous concepts for their description and analysis – as is recognized in calling the human individual a 'person'.[2]

1 HUMAN PERSONHOOD

Evolutionary biology can trace the steps in which a succession of organisms have acquired nervous systems and brains whereby they obtain, store, retrieve and utilize information about their environments in a way that furthers their survival. That this information so successfully utilized must be accurate enough for their survival has led to the notion of 'evolutionary epistemology'. This finds a warrant for the reality of reference of the content of such awareness of living organisms, especially human beings, in their actual successful survival of the naturally selective processes. Awareness and exploration of the external world reach a peak in *homo sapiens* who, through the use of language, primarily, visual imagery and, later, mathematics, is able to formulate concepts interpreting the environment. The role of language is especially apparent in growing children, and observation shows that their abstract concepts and their acquisition of language are developed through their experience and their interactions with adults.

The natural environment, both physical and social, is experienced and becomes a possible object of what we then call 'knowledge' – that which is reliable enough to facilitate prediction and control of the environment, and so survival. Our sense impressions must be broadly trustworthy, and so must the cognitive structures whereby we know the world – otherwise we would not have survived.[3]

The capacity for abstract thought appears to be distinctively human and the acquisition of language is so closely linked with it that many think the latter is necessary for the former. In these parallel processes discrimination occurs within the content of cognitive awareness of the person as 'subject' and the natural environment that is experienced as 'object'. Minimally, and in purely functional terms, 'consciousness' may be defined as that power of the human brain to form internal representations of its physical and social environment (including the body of any particular brain), of its relations to that environment and of itself forming those representations; and this power pertains to both actual and possible (putatively future) representations of the environment, the self and their mutual relations. However clear, though, our awareness of the content of our consciousness is to ourselves, it is obscure and certainly not widely agreed how that same conscious activity may be described in terms of brain activity. Moreover, any such description is itself only articulable, and mutually and reciprocally defined, through its relation to some defensible hypothesis concerning the evolution of consciousness as a facet of brain activity – and there is no agreement on this either.[4]

What also seems to be uniquely characteristic of human beings is their ability as 'subjects' to treat the content of consciousness as putative 'objects', that is, to be self-aware. Human beings develop language that contains concepts of themselves as the subject of experiences and in their use of language they transcend themselves. We may say that human beings are 'self-transcendent'. So self-awareness and self-consciousness, coupled with our intelligence and imagination, generate a capacity for self-transcendence which is the root from which stems the possibility of a sense of the numinous – and so of the divine, we shall be suggesting in due course.

Human beings have a sense of inwardness which is reflected in language in the semantically peculiar ways in which they use 'I' of themselves. This sense is only gradually acquired by the growing child as its self-knowledge, and indeed its self-image, flowers and fructifies, or is withered and stunted, by its interactions with its environment and especially with other persons close to it. For there is considerable evidence that this distinguishing of part of the environment as consisting of persons and the formation of relationships with them is essential to the growing child's sense of personhood. The extent to which these relationships are, or are not, affectionate is, it appears, crucial for the self-image of the child and of the adult it becomes. Thus does the growing child become the centre of a network of relationships which are constitutive of being a person. This has social and, indeed, legal consequences when human beings consider each other as bearers of rights so that, although each is unique, the 'other' is someone with whom the individual self can imagine changing places. This becomes the source both of compassion and of the more legal concept of 'person' continuously transformed, as it has been historically, by changing apprehensions and sensitivities.[5]

As self-awareness, cognition and the conceptual resources for representing other people and the environment develop in the individual, and indeed in the species, human beings become capable of exercising their imaginations and so of choice and intended action. They become agents capable of bringing about one state of affairs rather than another. Since they have, or believe themselves to have, reasons for so acting, human beings may be described as rational agents, making choices for what appear to them to be

'reasons' – even though these are often the complex net sum of
other motivations. In any case, the ordinary causal laws operative in
the external world are not operative – at least in any obvious way –
in making such choices. So human agents have the experience of a
sense of freedom, of being able to choose their own thoughts in, for
example, making moral choices and aesthetic judgements and in
choosing between beliefs. We regard ourselves as having 'free will',
so we say, and this enables us to act with creative novelty: it is the
basis of that creativity which characterizes our self-awareness and
sense of inwardness. Paradoxically, such 'free will' is only possible
at all in a milieu in which natural processes follow 'lawlike' regularities so that 'free' choices have broadly predictable outcomes. Choice
would be illusory if all were totally unpredictable. Hence a regular
environment is the prerequisite for the exercise of freedom and so
of moral choices by persons. Furthermore, in making choices persons irreversibly shape their own lives as they bring about their own
intentions and thereby transcend the processes of individual development and of the evolution of species which characterize all other
living organisms.

A primary characteristic of being a person is a sense of purpose
and intentionality and these generate biological and social adaptability. But this thread of intentionality and purpose which runs
through a self-conscious human life becomes increasingly coloured
by awareness of the inevitable termination of its continuity in death.
Human beings – uniquely, it seems, among living organisms – have to
come consciously to terms with anticipation of their own demise.
Homo sapiens has, from the evidence of the earliest traces of its
existence on earth, buried its dead with rituals indicative of reflection on this *terminus ad quem*. Such reflections seem to have been
linked with the sense of the numinous in relation to the natural
world and to the individual's own creative self-transcendence and
sense of worth, as evidenced by wall paintings and other artifacts.
Here we have to recognize the ancient beginnings of another distinctive feature of human persons – the propensity to worship and
prayer to another order of Being conceived as the source of all other
lesser being.

The continuities of human beings with their evolutionary pre-
decessors are obvious enough, – in anatomy, biochemistry, physiology, for example, and even, and more clearly perceived than
formerly, in activities involved in tool-making, exploring the environment and counting. However, these last-named 'mental' activi-

ties occur only partially in other creatures and the features of *homo sapiens* to which attention has been drawn above in fact represent a genuine discontinuity in the evolutionary process.

In human beings a number of cognitive functions, that are also to be found in animals and that individually make their own contribution to survival, are 'integrated into a system of higher order', to use a phrase of Konrad Lorenz.[6] Lorenz has identified these functions as: the perception of form which then constitutes a mechanism of both abstraction and objectivization; the central representation of space, especially through sight; locomotion, following on from visual orientation; memory, storing of information, as the learnt basis of insight-controlled behaviour; voluntary movement in conjunction with the feedback it produces; exploratory behaviour; imitation, the basis for the learning of verbal language; and tradition, the transmission of individually acquired knowledge from one generation to another.

In the integrated unity of the human being, so emerging, there arise the new characteristics of the faculty of language and abstract conceptual thought, the power to foresee the consequences of one's own actions and the ability to accumulate knowledge transmitted non-genetically via a cultural tradition utilizing words and symbols. Human beings in developing language and society create artifacts such as libraries, tapes, music, pictures, sculptures, buildings, diagrams, computer records, etc., which transmit knowledge and experience from one generation to another, thereby outstripping the processes of natural selection through which humanity first emerged and which are still operative in other creatures. Something new has emerged in humanity which requires autonomous concepts for its description and elaboration. In humanity 'biology' has become 'history' and a new kind of interaction – that of humanity with the rest of the natural order – arises in which the organism, *homo sapiens*, shapes its own environment, and so its future evolution, by its own choices through utilizing its acquired knowledge and social organization. The root of human inter-subjectivity manifest in culture is the evolved capacity for self-awareness which arises *pari passu* with that higher-order functioning that integrates all these other functions into one

'distinctive activity, distinctive in being owned, localized, personalized. The unity of personality ... is to be found in an integrating activity, an activity expressed, embodied and scientifically understood in terms of its genetic, biochemical, [etc. . . .] manifestations. What we call human behaviour is an expression of that effective, integrating activity which is peculiarly and distinctively ourselves.[7]

Yet, oddly enough, there are signs of a kind of misfit between human beings, persons, and their environment which is not apparent in other creatures. We alone in the biological world, it seems, individually commit suicide; we alone by our burial rituals evidence the sense of another dimension to existence; we alone go through our biological lives with that sense of incomplete fulfilment evidenced by the contemporary quests for 'self-realization' and 'personal growth'. We have aspirations and what appear to us as needs which go far beyond basic biological requirements for food, rest, shelter, sex, and an environment in which procreation and care of the young is possible. Human beings seek to come to terms with death, pain and suffering and they need to realize their own potentialities and learn how to steer their paths through life. The natural environment is not capable of satisfying such aspirations – nor can the natural sciences describe, accurately discern or satisfy them. So our presence in the biological world raises questions outside the scope of the natural sciences to answer. For we are capable of happinesses and miseries quite unknown to other creatures, thereby evidencing a dis-ease with our evolved state, a lack of fit which calls for explanation and, if possible, cure. 'Has something gone wrong?' we cannot help asking, as we contemplate human history and the ravaging of this planet by human activity.

2 CONDITIONS FOR THE EMERGENCE OF PERSONS

One of the remarkable features of recent reflections, informed by modern astro-physics, particle physics and cosmology, on the relation of humanity to the rest of the universe has been a reversal of the effect of the Copernican Revolution. This appeared to demote humanity by locating it on a planet which was no longer at the centre of the universe and and whose privileged location was now occupied by the Sun. Subsequently astronomy in the twentieth century accentuated this demotion by relegating the whole solar system to a corner of one among myriads of galaxies. Human life seemed to have only an insignificant role in relation to the vastness of the universe. However in the last two decades we have witnessed amongst scientists an increasingly acute awareness of how finely tuned the parameters and characteristics of the observed universe are for us as observers to be present at all. Few would now dispute a recent formulation, in its weak form, of what has come to be known as the 'anthropic principle':

> The observed values of all physical and cosmological quantities are not equally probable but they take on values restricted by the require- ment that there exist sites where carbon-based life can evolve and by the requirement that the Universe be old enough for it to have already done so . . . It [this principle] expresses only the fact that those proper- ties of the Universe we are able to discern are self-selected by the fact that they must be consistent with our evolution and present existence.'[8]

It appears that this principle places extremely stringent constraints on the values of many fundamental constants if life is to have anything like the form we know (hence the 'carbon-based' in Barrow and Tipler's formulation) and is to evolve at all in any conceivable universe. These constants include the actual strengths of all the forces that operate in the universe (gravitational, strong and weak nuclear, electromagnetic), the electronic charge, the velocity of light, Planck's constant and various particle masses – and even then the list is not complete. It is this universe that is cognizable, which can generate in itself life and so, eventually, that form of life, ourselves, that can observe it. Far from our presence in the universe being an inexplicable 'surd', our presence is tightly locked into the universe actually having the properties we now observe it to pos- sess. There are, it can now be confidently affirmed, the closest possible links between many quantitative features of the universe being precisely what they are and the possibility of life, and so of us, being here at all.

The anthropic principle in its most widely agreed, 'weak' form, refers to the links between 'carbon-based life' and many universal parameters having particular values. We have already seen that, once life started, there would be an inbuilt tendency for it to increase in complexity of organization in its various manifestations. It is also becoming clear that the acquisition of cognitive skills confers a very great advantage in natural selection. Such skills are dependent on having an increasingly sensitive apparatus for receiv- ing signals from the environment and a highly efficient apparatus for both processing that information and transmitting appropriate sig- nals to the motor system of the organism. More precisely, the four parts of the perceptual apparatus that are needed are input analysers, motivational and behavioural controllers and an energy regulator.[9] All these have to develop together in a process of mutual reinforcement and stimulation and the very process of relating perception, analysis and action is of the essence of cognitive activity, so that the 'mind' becomes the 'cognitive organ of the body'.[10] The systems that have survived this evolutionary process, which is facilitated by social cooperation and the development of language, must *prima facie* be presumed to be giving sufficiently reliable knowledge of the environment to make that survival possible. Hence the evolutionary scientist's approach to a theory of 'knowledge' is one of 'hypothetical realism', affirmed by Konrad Lorenz in the following terms:

> The scientist sees man as a creature who owes his qualities and functions, including his highly developed powers of cognition, to evolution, that age-long process of genesis in the course of which all organisms have come to terms with external reality and, as we say, 'adapt' to it. This process is one of knowledge, for any adaptation to a particular circumstance of external reality presupposes that a measure of information about that circumstance has already been absorbed.'[11]

The advances in cognitive powers must have compensated in natural selection for the increase in vulnerability that must inevitably accompany an increasingly sensitive apparatus for monitoring and sensing the world external to the organism. Indeed, human beings have manifestly only survived their weakness, slowness and general vulnerability by the exercise of cognitive powers which in them reach a unique peak of development. The combination of vulnerability and increased sensitivity to signals from the environment has, as its concomitant, a heightened ability to suffer pain and it is not at all easy to conceive how one could have the former without the latter. Moreover, pain is a necessary danger signal which warns off the organism from courses of action, or feeding habits, or actions in relation to predators, and so on, which would otherwise threaten its survival. We cannot avoid concluding that the pain and suffering consequent upon vulnerability are the inherently necessary price that has to be paid for consciousness to emerge with its associated cognitive powers.

The self-awareness of human individuals is so closely linked to their linguistic and conceptual powers that it is difficult to attribute any distinctive causal advantage it might have had in the processes of natural selection. These same powers clearly facilitated analysis of the environment, of predators and of food resources and the execution through foresight of planned, cooperative action so that the physically relatively weak *homo sapiens* began to establish itself in every conceivable habitat. The subsequent emergence of culture, based on those resources for transmitting knowledge across the generations that we have already referred to, have now led to the domination of the earth by humanity. This domination is undoubtedly the consequence, if only indirectly, of human self-awareness and self-consciousness, as expressed through its cultural systems held together by communication through language and symbol. But this very self-awareness and self-consciousness is the stage on which is enacted the human drama of pain, suffering and the sense of finitude and anticipation of death and all that flows from them – the whole tragedy of the human condition. So that our inner awareness and sense of selfhood both enhance our ability to survive as individuals and as a species and, at one and the same time, snatch from us the fruits of a happiness that is available to a merely animal consciousness. Individuality, and awareness of it, reach a new peak on *homo sapiens* comcomitantly with an increased reliance on socialization for the survival of the species.

CHAPTER 5

What Does It All Mean?

It seems that the human being is alone among living organisms in asking questions about the content and meaning of the world in which it has evolved. Over the course particularly of recent centuries it has acquired a vast new body of information about that world and how human beings have come to exist in it. To that world so understood it reacts in a variety of ways, not all mutually consistent. How does the world appear to human beings in the light of their new knowledge? How does it seem to be? What are the human reactions to the features of the world we have been relating?

To the scientist it is a continuous wonder that the world turns out to be so intelligible and so amenable to rational inquiry based on observation. As Fred Hoyle once said, 'When by patient enquiry we learn the answer to any problem, we always find, both as a whole and in detail, that the answer thus revealed is finer in concept and design than anything we could ever have arrived at by a random guess.'[1] Mathematics, a free construction of the human mind – pure deductions from postulated axioms – turns out to be the necessary means for understanding the fundamental structure and relational networks of the physical world and, increasingly, of being able to articulate the basis of biological complexity.[2] In Einstein's words: 'The eternal mystery of the world is its comprehensibility.... The fact that it is comprehensible is a miracle.'[3] Our earlier consideration of 'evolutionary epistemology', that is, of the evolutionary role of cognitive processes, may serve to diminish our wonder a little – but not overmuch, for penetration of the secrets of the nature of, say, the sub-atomic world and of quantum field theory can hardly be postulated as necessary for biological survival. The powers of human ratiocination and conceptual imagination far exceed the demands for survival. Their extraordinary ability to represent aspects of the world inaccessible to the ordinary senses and incapable of depiction by any extrapolations from ordinary experience is still a striking feature of our relation to the world and of our reactions to that relation.

Because of the witness of the sciences we see the world as an unbroken, even if tangled, web of causal order in which multiple, but discernible, chains of causality interlock and intersect, constituting patterns of intelligible relationships. Sometimes the track of causality becomes too ill-defined to trace and intelligibility is obscured, but it has been the continuously validated experience of three centuries of natural science that gradually the network of relations and interactions becomes clearer and light is cast over a wider swath. So, in this sense, our understanding of the world becomes more and more complete, for the gaps in our ignorance and in our comprehension continue to narrow and often disappear.

Yet, oddly enough, there is always a certain baffling incompleteness to our understanding as evidenced by the limitations on predictability already mentioned in chapter 3. For, although we find the emergence of new properties and behaviours of entities in the natural world intelligible after the event, we would often be incapable of predicting them in advance and, indeed, find them entirely surprising on reflection after the event. As our knowledge of the natural world stretches out in both directions – to the basic constituents of physical reality on the one hand, and to the higher levels of biological complexity on the other – we cannot but be more and more impressed by the way the operation of a few simple principles on a finite number of basic entities produces the vast richness and fecundity of this planet and of the universe of which it forms such a small part. Only the dullest could fail to react with awe at the immense inbuilt and inventive creativity of the world in which we have evolved. The elusive and unpicturable basic sub-atomic entities out of which all else is made, including ourselves, have potentialities unknown and undescribable in terms of the physics that discovers and the mathematics that symbolizes them. Hence at both of the extremities of our comprehension – the sub-atomic and the personal – we face baffling depths in the actual nature of reality that make many scientific writers refer to the sense of 'mystery' that is stirred in them as they contemplate the universe through the lenses of the natural sciences.

This sense of mystery engendered through science has been particularly stressed by Harold Schilling.[4] He traces it firstly to the sense of wonder at the infinity and unfathomability of the unknown, quoting Victor Weisskopf: 'Our knowledge is an island in the infinite ocean of the unknown'[5], – and the larger this island grows, the more extended are its boundaries toward the unknown. Secondly, he encounters it among scientists as they reflect on the infinity and unfathomability of the known, the mysteries at the two extremities of the sub-atomic and biological that we have referred to already. Every apparent answer confronts us with even more numerous unanswered questions.

So there is an ambiguity in our knowledge of the natural world – increasingly rich and exciting to the intelligence, but increasingly eliciting intellectual vertigo as, viewing from the dizzy heights of the new perspectives, we try to plumb challengingly new conceptual depths. But there is another, more ancient, ambiguity that human beings experience in re,⁀rd to the natural order. This is the awareness that the natural order is essential to our existence and nurtures us through its resources but that it can, nevertheless, also be tragically destructive of human existence and aspirations. The root of this is to be found in our inherent ambiguity as parts of nature that, in our self-consciousness, also transcend it as subjects. Again, our distinctively human characteristics emerge as the source of the possibility of enhanced fulfilment concomitant with a sensibility readily offended and pained.

For, finally, as we contemplate the future of our planet in the solar system in its galaxy, we have to reckon with its certain disappearance. The energy of our Sun which sustains life on Earth is finite: the Sun is about half-way through its life and the time left for the existence of the Earth is about the same as the length of time it has already existed. So the demise of all life, including human, on earth is quite certain. Since it is entirely problematic whether human beings will be able to 'colonize' any other planets, we have to ask: Is the whole experiment of life, which has such significance for us in interpreting the universe, after all going to prove futile and abortive? What is the *meaning* of this universe and of our presence in it? Thus we come to ultimate questions and find them not answerable through the resources of science itself.

PART II

Divine Being and Becoming

CHAPTER 6

Asking 'Why?': The Search for Intelligibility and Meaning

At the end of Part I, we recognized that there was a somewhat mixed response on the part of human beings to the hard-won scientific perspective on the being and becoming to be discerned in the natural world. The scientists, we noted, respond with a mixture of wonder, even awe, and intellectual excitement tinged with a sense of mystery concerning the ultimate nature of the world and awareness at the essential incompleteness of our real understanding and comprehension of it all. Such ambiguity in our response to this new perspective on the world is compounded when we reflect on humanity's place and destiny in it, as we contemplate and experience the pain, suffering and evil that it evidences – and finally as we face the enigma of death both of the individual and of the whole human species when the Earth eventually ceases to exist, as surely it will. Are all our thoughts and strivings doomed to ultimate futility? We find we cannot escape the question of the meaning of it all and this inevitably takes us beyond the end of the tether of the natural sciences.

The scientific and theological enterprises are, like many other human endeavours, characterized by their search for intelligibility, for what makes the most coherent sense of the experimental and experiential data with which each are concerned. We cannot help pressing 'why?' questions to their intelligible limits. Science directs such questions to the nexus of events in the natural world: it seeks to provide answers to the question 'why?' by depicting the realities of the natural world in metaphorical language.[1] But there are other broader 'why?' questions than those directed to what is in and going on in the natural world. 'Why is there a universe at all?' 'Why should it be of this particular kind?' 'Why is it open to rational inquiry?' 'Why is it beautiful?' 'Why does it generate a creature that can discern values?'

The religious quest, or rather, its intellectual aspect in the form of the theological enterprise, presses such 'why?' questions to their attainable limits – until to press them further 'becomes plain silly'.[2] The problem is that there is no agreement concerning the point at which this limit is reached, for the point at which one stops is controlled by one's willingness to allow the quest to enter that area of discernment which has a wider, essentially religious, import. This has certainly been the case with respect to what is often regarded as the paradigm of religious questions, namely the mystery-of-existence question 'Why does the world exist?'. Fewer philosophers today than a decade or so ago are willing to dismiss such questions as meaningless by, for instance, asserting that to argue for them is already to assume the existence of (a) necessary being. For example, we find Munitz in 1965 arguing minimally that questions in the form 'Is-there-a-reason-for-the-existence-of-the-world?' are meaningful – even if possibly unanswerable.[3] The philosophical suspicion of such questions is not unfounded if the answer to them is sought as an 'explanation' conceived of as operating in the same way as explanations of events do within the natural causal nexus. There is a genuine difficulty in postulating one ultimate explanation *of* the universe in the same way as we 'explain' individual events *within* the universe. But 'explanation' does not have to be restricted only to causal explanations and the acceptance of this and other developments in philosophy, principally the demise of the Verification Principle in its strong form, has rendered theism as an attempt to respond to such questions a much more lively option than would have been thought philosophically respectable even a decade ago – as was brought out very clearly in the radio interviews with leading philosophers conducted by Keith Ward in 1986.[4] As Ward himself has written elsewhere, 'explanation' might, more usefully, be equated with 'that which renders intelligible' and, in this sense: 'For the Christian, God, as the power making for intelligibility, beauty and righteousness, may be said to explain the universe in that he gives it meaning and intelligibility, provides purpose and significance, and so sets all things within an overall context'.[5] But this is to rush our fences, for at this stage of our inquiry we simply wish to identify some of what we might call these 'limit-questions', recognizing that it is not intellectually and philosophically disreputable to ask them.

I suggested earlier[6] that there are two kinds of search in which we are engaged in relation to the world in which we live. One – primarily intellectual, though not without existential urgency – is the search for intelligibility, inference to the best explanation, where 'explanation' is now to be construed in the qualified sense of the preceding paragraph. This search, involving as it does the mystery-of-existence question in its various forms, adds impetus to that other search – the search for personal meaning in human existence, in general, and our own, in particular. The twentieth-century scientific perspective of a developing cosmos which generated persons now ties together in a stronger bond than ever before these two quests. For it now appears that the universe is such that it is characterized by values of the fundamental constants that are precisely those necessary for our existence (the 'anthropic principle'[7]) and that we are generated within it out of its own constituents by its own natural processes; then, having arrived, we seek intelligibility and meaning in that universe and in those processes. Indeed we cannot avoid, in the light of the scientific perspective, merging these two searches into one by urging our questions about the cosmos in forms that include ourselves: 'What is the intelligible meaning of a cosmos in which the primeval assembly of fundamental particles has eventually manifested the potentiality of becoming organized in forms that are conscious and self-conscious, human and personal, namely ourselves, and whose thinking transcends that out of which they have emerged?'; or, 'If we continue to press for 'explanation' and to search for 'meaning', does not the very continuity of the universe, with its gradual elaboration of its potentialities, imply that any categories of 'explanation' and 'meaning' must at least include the personal?'; or, 'What is the 'explanation' and 'meaning' of a cosmos that generates from within itself entities, *homo sapiens*, who, in knowing and knowing that they know, creatively seek truth; respond to, and themselves create, beauty; strive after goodness, have moral purposes, and create community – and can also ambiguously counter and confound these values?'; or, more darkly, ' What is the 'explanation' and 'meaning' of a cosmos in which pain, suffering and death of sentient creatures is inbuilt as a transformative principle whereby new forms of increasingly conscious life become possible?'; or, darker still, 'Why does the universe generate from within itself by its own inherent, inbuilt processes a creature, *homo sapiens*, which is such a misfit with its environment that, at best, a general sense of incompleteness and lack of fulfilment pervades and colours their consciousness, and, at worst, they are overwhelmed by *angst*, suffering and tragedy?'; or, perhaps not surprisingly in view of all these questions, 'Why do these human beings, the product of the cosmos and its forces, experience a sense often of *sacred* mystery hidden within and veiled by their experience of that same cosmos, both in its particular and general features?'

If we pursue the quest of science to its limits we cannot avoid coming to questions such as these which, while they go beyond the remit and power of the natural sciences to answer, nevertheless demand a response. Difficult though such a response may be, it would be intellectually irresponsible, indeed a twentieth-century *trahison des clercs*, not to ask and seek to answer these questions. To decline to do so is to be less than human and to leave ourselves with no map, however sketchy, by which to steer our lives from birth to and through death.

It is in responding to challenging questions like these, referred to the cosmologies of their own day, that from time immemorial men and women have postulated the existence of an ultimate Reality that is the source of all being as both the meaning and explanation of all that is – that Reality which, in English, we call 'God'. But the postulate of 'God' is inseparable from the question of 'What sort of God?'. Both the postulate and the associated question have been the perennial concern of philosophers and to some of their more recent reflections we must now turn.

CHAPTER 7

'God' as Response to the Search for Intelligibility and Meaning

1 'GOD' IN THE PHILOSOPHY OF RELIGION

Since the demise of positivism, traditional metaphysical questions have increasingly during the last two decades come to be recognized as again worthy of the attention of philosophers. Paramount in such traditional metaphysical questions evoking renewed philosophical consideration is, of course, the question of 'God', both with respect to the epistemological questions concerning what sort of arguments should properly be deployed and the arguments as such. Indeed, Keith Ward affirms that 'Theism . . . has gone onto the attack; and we can see very clearly how it joins hands with science in proposing the possibility of making God the best explanation of how the world actually is.'[1] I have already advocated[2] that theology, like any other human inquiry into the nature of reality, must use the same general criteria of reasonableness as, say, science itself. So that inference to the best explanation is assessed[3] by its fit with the data ('existential relevance'[4]), internal coherence, comprehensiveness and general cogency ('adequacy'[5]), simplicity ('economy'[6]) and fruitfulness in producing new ideas and, in the case of theology, in giving meaning for personal existence. As suggested in the comment of Keith Ward, applying these criteria and coming to the conclusion that the existence of 'God' in the Judeo-Christian sense is probable, has become more frequent in recent years.[7] Needless to say, this conclusion has not gone uncontested.[8] There can be no doubt that the 'question of God' is no longer regarded as simply meaningless, as in the earlier days of 'logical positivism'.

What we can usefully mean by 'God' and how we might depict God's relation to the world and to humanity will only gradually unfold later. For the moment, we would do well in seeking to obtain an insight into the philosophical debate to turn to Richard Swinburne's significant book on *The Existence of God* and the reply he made to J. L. Mackie's criticism of it.[9] There, Swinburne claims that

> most of the well-known *a posteriori* arguments for the existence of God could be construed as inductive arguments in which the observable phenomena cited in the premises (the existence of the universe, its orderliness, the existence of consciousness, various opportunities available for men, reports of miracles, and religious experiences) provided evidence for (in the sense of raising the probability of) the existence of God and that overall they rendered the existence of God more probable than not.[10]

By 'God exists' (= 'There is a God'), Swinburne means that 'there exists a person without a body (i.e. a spirit) who is eternal, is perfectly free, omnipotent, omniscient, perfectly good, and the creator of all things.'[11] He uses 'God' as the name of the person picked out by this description. These descriptions he elaborates thus:[12]

> *person*, used 'in the modern sense', more specifically, not in the sense of *persona* or *hypostasis* of Christian trinitarian doctrine;[13]
> *eternal*, God 'always has existed and always will exist' (not in the sense of 'timeless' or 'outside time');
> *perfectly free*, 'no object or event or state (including past states of himself) in any way causally influences God to do the actions which he does – his own choice at the moment of action alone determines what he does';
> *omnipotent*, God 'is able to do whatever it is logically possible (i.e. coherent to suppose) that he can do';
> *omniscient*, God 'knows whatever it is logically possible that he know';
> *perfectly good*, God 'does no morally bad actions', and does any morally obligatory action;
> *creator of all things*, 'everything which exists at each moment of time (apart from himself) exists because, at that moment of time, he makes it exist, or permits it to exist'.

Swinburne argues that the theist holds that God possesses these properties necessarily in the sense that 'having those properties is essential to being the kind of being which God is ... He could not lose any of the properties analysed [as set out above] without ceasing to be God.'[14] But is 'God exists' necessary too? This is a subtle question to which Swinburne's response is 'that God's essence is an eternal essence; that there is a being who is essentially a personal ground of being (which includes being eternal) is the inexplicable brute fact, a terminus of explanation, how things are.'[15] He terms this a 'factually necessary existence', as distinct from a 'logically necessary existence'.

The contested issues between Mackie and Swinburne concerned *inter alia* Swinburne's claim that 'God is the simplest kind of person there can be because a person is a being with power (to do intentional actions), knowledge, and freedom (to choose, uncaused, which actions to do).'[16] Linked with this claim is Swinburne's insistence that to postulate God as agent in bringing about all-that-is is a *personal* explanation, whereby the occurrence of a phenomenon is explained as brought about by a rational agent doing some action intentionally.[17] Mackie disputed the simplicity of personal explanation, since human personal agents act through a complex causal chain to implement their intentions. His undermining of this claimed simplicity, Mackie argued, reduces the support Swinburne says it gives to the *a priori* improbability of the evidence for regularity in the world of our observations. Swinburne rejects these criticisms as inadequate, finally affirming

> It is very unlikely indeed *a priori* that there should be a Universe made of matter behaving in totally regular ways, giving rise to conscious beings capable of changing themselves and others, making themselves fit for the Heaven of which they have a glimpse in religious experience. Hence the reason which we use about science and history demands that we postulate a simple explanation of these phenomena in terms of a creator and sustainer God.[18]

I have dwelt on Swinburne's account and arguments for theism not because I wish to support their every nuance but because they seem to me broadly to represent the position of many Christian theists and because his has been one of the most ably expounded and philosophically defended expositions of theism of recent years. Many others, of course, have contributed to the revival of the philosophy of religion in the last twenty years, as demonstrated in the representative collection compiled by Thomas Morris on *The Concept of God*.[19] While recognizing that this effort has yielded a better understanding of the arguments for the existence of God, the problem of evil and the nature of claims based on religious experience, he is concerned, in his introduction to this volume, to point out the considerable attention that has been devoted to examining the *concept* of God. He claims that

Beneath the many deep differences that divide philosophers on the nature of God, a single unifying consideration seems to have been operative ... most recent contributors to the literature on divine attributes have worked in the broad tradition of perfect being theology. That is to say, their overall conception of God has been that of a maximally perfect or greatest possible being.[20]

He urges that such a 'perfect being' theology is rationally the method most suited to governing our thinking about God. God as such a 'perfect being' will then be conceived as having some unsurpassable array of properties that make for greatness and which can be possessed together without contradiction. Relying, as this does, on our intuitions concerning what properties make for greatness, this clearly goes beyond the constructing of a concept of God as the result of inference to the best explanation of the existence of the world and of its actual features and characteristics in the style of Swinburne, for example. Such empirically based constructions of the concept of God are more likely to be pertinent to our purpose, in this book, of discerning the extent to which the scientific perspective of the world might or should affect Christian concepts of God. Naturally, we have to recognize that, in the end, no sharp, classificatory lines can be drawn between the concepts of God that the different approaches yield, for there is much overlap and common ground. However, before we can undertake that study of the impact of science on the concept of God, which is the principle theme of Part II of this book, we must examine more closely what the addition of the adjective 'Christian' to 'theism' purports and implies.

2 'GOD' IN CHRISTIAN BELIEF

The foregoing sketch of some philosophical analyses of the concept of God may well have left the reader feeling that what philosophy can deliver is only an arid and desiccated version of the rich depths of the God whom individual Christians trust and worship and whom the Christian church affirms and proclaims. The faith of the Christian church rests on its experience, the principal resource and source for which are those archetypal and seminal experiences and encounters with God enshrined in its scriptures. Such belief is a shared possession which cannot be acquired simply by an individual effort divorced from the entry of the individual into the well-winnowed common inheritance of a community continuous through many generations.[21] Hence in pressing our inquiries into the possible impact of the scientific perspective on the Christian understanding of God, we need first to try to expound the content of this understanding as it has been shared by Christians down the ages, even into our own pluralistic societies. To ascertain this content of Christian belief in God is a subtle and complex task, but we are fortunate in having available a recent concerted effort by leading thinkers in the Church of England, which, in this respect (as in others), stands in the centre of both catholic and reformed belief concerning God – for fortunately the unhappy divisions between the churches have not been in this basic area. I refer to the 1987 report of the Doctrine Commission of the Church of England, *We Believe in God*, [22] the main ideas of which I will attempt to summarize in the following paragraphs (giving page numbers as references in the text and using its general phrasing), for it represents the most recent attempt by any of the mainline churches to expound the content of belief in God in the Christian community. It is the more valuable for our purpose in that it does not attempt to argue for the 'God of the philosophers', surmising, quite rightly, that the God who is believed in and trusted by Christians is thought of in more personal and less abstract terms than are properly appropriate to philosophical discourse.

The Christian Bible, that marriage of the already sacred writings of the people of Israel with focal written sources of the early Christians, is *par excellence* the product not simply of individual authors but also of communities. In the communities that generated and possessed this literature, God was spoken about by means of narrative, so that, to this extent at least, God is personal. The biblical stories express a faith which tried to see a coherent divine purpose in events (pp. 54–6). The God of the Bible who features in these narratives is described in many, often apparently inconsistent, ways – both as severe judge and as loving father, with both what we would regard as 'masculine' and 'feminine' images (in spite of the blinkers with which subsequent believers have seen the texts), as characterized by both 'wrath' and mercy. The relation of the biblical narratives to history is subtle, varied and complex, and the fact that it is impossible to define exactly where sacred history ends and secular history begins is in itself a significant pointer to the nature of God himself – namely that God's action in history is both real and elusive of definitive de-limitation (pp. 58–61). This is notoriously true of attempts to determine what is the 'end' of its principal narratives, most notably that about Jesus himself (pp. 61–3). This fluidity of interpretation should not surprise us for, as the Report puts it,

> Like the hypotheses used by scientists to describe the physical universe, the models used in the Bible to describe God are valid up to a certain point of experience and understanding, but (in theory, at least) they are corrigible in the light of new challenges to faith and further moments of revelation. (p. 64)

This process is to be seen at work within the Bible, or more strictly, the biblical experience, itself – most significantly, as we shall see in a moment, in the way Jesus himself revised and amplified the tradition of the 'Old Testament' he received. In doing this he was, in one sense, being true to those very traditions, for the story of Israel can be seen both as a voyage of discovery of God on the part of the people of Israel and as a story of the activity of God (p. 70). God was discovered and revealed himself as a personal being who is intimately involved both in human life, as provider, healer and friend, and in the natural world as the source of the world's stability and life (pp. 72–4).

Nevertheless, the God of the Old Testament is not just a human person writ large; there is a mysterious otherness about him. He is the Holy One, demanding awe in worship with a holiness inseparable from his righteousness and love. In Israel's religious consciousness the concept of the holiness is bound up with ethical qualities, with sheer goodness. Holiness and love are inseparably linked. God is supremely one in the unity of his love and justice and his attributes are not split between a multiplicity of minor deities, though God's power within persons is often objectified, as 'Spirit' or, later, 'Wisdom', so as not to compromise God's essential otherness from humanity (pp. 75–6). God's goodness could be fully displayed only in the salvation of his people, a salvation which a few prophetic souls saw, because of God's oneness as Creator of all, must be extended to all humanity in God's good time (pp. 76–7).

For Christians, Jesus the Christ constituted a radical revision, *the* most radical revision, of human ideas about God, that is of the understandings of God of the people of Israel, in Jesus's historical setting. He does not invalidate this tradition, nor even that of other religions –

> But by his suffering, death and resurrection he significantly enlarges the range of human experience which can be 'read' as a testimony to

the love and power of God; and in his teaching he offers new 'models' of understanding which go far beyond what was available before. (p. 66)

This authority to reveal the nature of God stems, historically, from a uniquely intimate relation between himself and God that involved an exceptional degree of personal knowledge (p. 67). Jesus addressed God as 'Abba', the family word for 'father' and the title used by disciples for a rabbi: it suggests attitudes both of dependence, security and confidence, on the one hand, and of humility, obedience and reverence, on the other. A new richness of content came to the fore in Jesus' teaching about the activity of God in the world and especially in human life. 'God is one who loves, cares, gives, listens, welcomes, seeks, accepts, forgives, provides' (p. 81). The character and attributes predicated of God that generate such features in his action are focused by affirming a divine fatherhood. This is worked out in parable and prayer (the Lord's Prayer and that in Gethsemane) in terms of both authority and caring, with hardly a hint of 'wrath'.

Jesus was uncompromising in his prophetic message of the immanent confrontation of his contemporaries with God in 'all his holiness, purity, goodness, mercy and love' (p. 84). A response was called for that was, in the end, evoked by his making his death a sacrifice, thereby affirming his teaching about the God whose power extends beyond the grave and whose good will for mankind cannot in the end be thwarted. Because of Jesus' life, suffering, death and resurrection he became for them, as they assimilated this experience, the 'Christ', 'Son of God', the 'Word and Wisdom of God'. What is important to us at this stage of our inquiry is that the God who was made known in his self-disclosure through Jesus was supremely and essentially total self-giving love. God is revealed in Jesus the Christ as the 'Father of a crucified Son' (p. 97) who is 'deeply involved in the total act of redemptive suffering' (p. 98), that is in the life, suffering and death of the historical Jesus. Indeed, the unity between Jesus and God the Father, the Creator (all that Jesus affirmed he was), was so profound that in St John's Gospel the death of Jesus, in spite of all its bitterness and exemplification of the sordid corruption of humanity, could be called Jesus's 'glorification'. Here the evangelist is pointing to a new kind of relation which all might have with God on account of these events.

In the experience of the disciples and the early Church this new kind of relation was sustained in the human community by what they came to call 'God the Holy Spirit', the counterpart of 'the spirit of Yahweh' of the Old Testament. This experience and its interpretation constituted a significant development of the understanding of God, for it denoted a recognition of the personal presence of God the Spirit as 'abiding in the life of the Christian community and of the individual believer, inspiring both, and transforming them into the likeness of Christ' (p. 101). So it moved beyond the Old Testament view of the Spirit as the transcendent God intervening from time to time in his creation. It is the foundation for a specifically Christian and strong emphasis on the immanence of God in his world as a personal presence, awareness of whom is particularly and powerfully vouchsafed to the believing community. This presence of God, strong as was the awareness of it in the Church and in individuals in particular seminal historical experiences, could not, in the end, be confined to the Christian, or even the human, community alone.

The Christian doctrine of God is not a philosophical and metaphysical theory; it is, rather, an attempt to understand and to come to terms with a profound religious experience centred on the life, death, resurrection and teaching of Jesus. This had 'brought a new realization of God's accessibility, a recognition of his entrance into human suffering and of his relationship to his people, and at the same time a new estimate of the persons of Christ and of the Spirit in relation to God himself' (p. 101). But, because it was the love *of God himself* that had been demonstrated in Jesus and which had become accessible through him, this could never lead to the conclusion that Jesus was a 'second god'.

Already we see here the beginnings of the understanding of the one God as triune in his character, as personally transcendent, personally incarnate and personally immanent – 'Father, Son and Holy Spirit', in the classical formularies. 'God, the God of Israel, is also known as the Father of his crucified and redeeming Son, and in the distinguishable person of his sanctifying Spirit. But precisely because these are, theologically speaking, also functions or attributes of the one God, the unity of God is not impaired' (p. 102).

CHAPTER 8

The Concept of God: Implications of Scientific Perspectives

We come now to the crucial stage of this enterprise, to inquire into the extent to which these concepts, models and images of God that have been winnowed and refined in religious experience, in particular the Christian, and have been supported by philosophical reflection, might need to be modified and enriched by the impressive perspectives on the world that the natural sciences now give us. Of course, the philosophical concepts of God have already attempted to take into account many of the broad features of the world that the natural sciences have unveiled. I refer *inter alia* not only to the existence of the world but also to it being an intelligible nexus of relations exhibiting regularities without which personal existence would be impossible. Inference to God as the best explanation – what I take to be the perennial task of 'natural theology' – has always looked closely at what the sciences have been saying about the world, sometimes too closely in the sense that God's finger has been too readily discerned in details of the world's phenomena. However, the undoubted fact that the philosophers of religion have often been concerned to take account of their contemporary scientific world view serves only to encourage us in the task. For their efforts to do so have tended to be only partial and intermittent.

The panorama of the sciences has so widened in the present century that philosophers of religion and theologians have scarcely been able to adjust to the sweeping conceptual changes that they entail. The study of the philosophy of religion and of theology have become such demanding disciplines that these remarks are not intended as criticism but, rather, as a recognition of the magnitude of the task facing all thinkers about God in this century. That is why before setting out on our more particularly theological task it has been necessary to try to set out as coherently and succinctly as possible the perspective on the world that the sciences today actually give, and not that of the mechanistic accounts which have dominated theological exposition for well over three centuries.

It was found necessary in Part I to express our scientific knowledge of the world in terms both of its being – what is there – and of its becoming – what is going on. That account had, moreover, to take seriously the advent of the personal in and through the natural and the loose ends, and indeed mysteries, that this introduced into an otherwise coherent perspective. So we must expect that scientific perspective on the world to affect our understanding of both the 'being' of God and of God's 'becoming', and for it to raise questions about the significance of the personal in relation to God.

The philosophers of religion and the religious believer have now to reckon with their one God's relation to a continuously developing world – and this implies at least a continuously changing relation of God to the world, including persons, and so the further possibility that God is not unchanging in certain respects. So the question of the nature and attributes of God cannot in the end be separated neatly and clearly from the vital question of how God's interaction with a world described by the natural sciences is to be conceived. Traditionally, at least in Eastern Orthodox theology, there has been a distinction made between God's 'essence', what he is in himself, his 'being', on the one hand; and God's 'energies', what he does, his 'becoming', on the other.[1] This can be a useful distinction, provided we recognize that it can never be absolute, for what we are prepared to affirm about God's 'essence' nearly always depends on what we discern of his 'energies', what we believe or infer to be his activity in the world. So in the following our account of the implications of various aspects of the world view of the sciences for our understanding of God will inevitably move between these two poles of our questioning, between asking who or what God is, or is like, and asking how this God interacts with the world.

This latter will be the more explicit concern of chapter 9, but our concern now is certainly with *both* divine being and becoming – with both static and dynamic metaphors. For convenience of exposition in this chapter we attempt to separate them, but it has to be admitted that these two aspects of divinity are inextricably and mutually interwoven. In pursuing this inquiry we shall inevitably partly traversing again ground already covered in many of the classical philosophical treatments of the nature and attributes of God. However, the same territory of the world of nature has a way of being perceived very differently in the context of the wider landscape of late twentieth-century science. A shift of context can alter our judgement of the nature of, the weight to be given to, and the consequences of arguments that have already been well aired in the long tradition of philosophical theology.

1 DIVINE BEING

a Ground of Being

As we saw in chapter 6, the postulate of the existence of *God as the Ground of Being* has become a respectable, though disputed, response to the mystery-of-existence question, 'Why is there anything at all?'. Substantiation of this response has been the aim of the philosophical work already referred to above.[2] The scientific perspective outlined in Part I does not substantially alter the nature of the philosophical debate or the status of the theistic claim, it seems to me, but it does highlight with greater intensity some of the issues at stake. Thus, what one might call the sheer apparent 'givenness' of the world, with its cosmological, biological and social history – its contingency – is not abated by our newfound awareness of the regular lawfulness of its interconnectedness through space and time. We have good reason for thinking that this goes back to the first fluctuations in the quantum 'vacuum', or whatever it was that led to the setting off of the expansion of the universe. Let us suppose for the moment that these speculations do refer to what 'actually happened'. Even so, such a quantum field that undergoes these fluctuations (the quantum 'vacuum') is not, strictly speaking, simply 'nothing at all'. *Its* existence still calls for explanation of some kind – in the sense that it is contingent and need not have existed at all with its particular properties, namely those represented by quantum theory. There is a need too to explain the existence of the mathematical laws by which the properties and transformations of this quantum field can be elucidated and made intelligible and coherent. – There is also a need to explain the existence of the entities, structures and processes that stem from those primordial events and of the laws and relationships that govern their unfolding and evolution. So the mystery-of-existence question becomes even more pressing in the light of the cosmic panorama disclosed by the natural sciences.

But those same sciences now lead us to recognize that the 'mystery' is not confined simply to the fact of experience as such.

For the deepest scientific studies of the very nature of *what* exists run out, in particle physics and cosmology, towards boundaries where the ontological status of the entities, structures and processes propounded have a character that raises profound questions about what it is that science *can* actually affirm about 'reality' at these levels.[3] This has engendered, as we saw in chapter 5, a new sense of mystery about the nature of physical existence and has raised important epistemological questions concerning the deductions made from the results of the interactions of our measuring instruments with this deepest level of the physical world. Furthermore, a sense of genuine mystery is also generated by the other extreme of biological complexity with its experienced properties of consciousness, self-consciousness and personhood. All of which is a good antidote for that peculiarly scientific *hubris* which has too often characterized the accounts of the world in much so-called 'popular science' – the 'scientism' that believes that natural science alone gives clear, direct knowledge of all that is in the world. For if we can run up against such barriers to scientific comprehension in relation to both the physical and personal worlds, then the traditional reticence of theists concerning the nature of God as the Ground of all Being thereby becomes the more acceptable. This recognition of an ultimate ineffability in the nature of the divine parallels that of our ultimate inability to say what even things and persons *are* in themselves.

b One

We saw in our consideration of the scientific perspective that the world exhibits beneath its remarkable diversity, fecundity and complexity an underlying unity.[4] This unity is manifest in both the multiple, intricate interconnectedness[5] of the natural world at many levels and also in the ultimate and beautiful, though abstract, unity of at least some of the fundamental forces and principles that govern the properties of matter and the forms into which it evolves. The natural sciences have demonstrated a remarkable unity underlying the often overwhelming diversity we encounter in the world. This unity refers both to origins and to the principles that govern its development. The 'best explanation' of such a world's existence and character, if any is to be found at all, cannot but be grounded in *one* unifying source of creativity, multiple though its outreach may be. Thus it is that the scientific perspective on the world continues to reinforce the long-held intuition and inference of theists that *God is One* and is the underlying ground not only of the being of all-that-is but also of its deep unity, interconnectedness and wholeness – whatever differentiations within this unity may eventually be required from other, theological considerations (for example, any revelation by this one God of a threefoldness within this unity).

c Of Unfathomable Richness

We saw indeed that this underlying unity was capable of giving rise to immense diversity in the natural world, culminating in the enormously varied richness of human experience and societies. The world is characterized both in its development and in its present state by a hierarchy, or rather hierarchies, of complexity wherein entirely new kinds of properties and modes of existence emerge at new levels that are only understandable in terms of new non-reducible concepts.[6] As the creative source of all that is, *God must be a Being of unfathomable richness* to be able to bring into existence a cosmos with such fecund potentialities.

d Supremely Rational

It has been a perennial feature of their experience over the last three centuries that scientists have been impressed by the intelligibility and comprehensibility of the natural world. This has often generated a sense of wonder and even awe in twentieth-century scientists of many kinds of theistic belief or non-belief, as witnessed by the remarks of Einstein and Hoyle quoted earlier.[7] Often this awareness of a profounder rationality in the nature of things than had previously been imagined enters the general consciousness of the scientific community through encountering an impasse in their inquiries (as it often does in the case of scientific discovery by individuals). One could instance the profounder rationality of quantum field theory which made intelligible, though no longer picturable, the apparently contradictory behaviour, as particles and waves according to the experimental context, of electrons and other sub-atomic particles. Or one could cite the now intelligible way in which the interplay between chance-governed, random events and the lawlike framework constraining them are productive of irreducibly unpredictable new regimes of structures and processes in complex dynamical systems, including those that are living.[8] This has only relatively recently been recognized and resolves a number of puzzles generated by what had been thought of as anomalous or idiosyncratic observations. So twentieth-century science reinforces this experience of the inherent, yet always challenging, intelligibility and putative comprehensibility of the world's entities, structures and processes. This cannot but render more probable than ever before inference to the existence of a supra-rational Being as Creator as the 'best explanation' of such a world's existence and character. In other words, the affirmation of the existence of *God as the supremely rational Creator* is strengthened and its truth rendered more, rather than less, probable by the increasing success of science in discovering the inherent, but in content ever-surprising, rationality of the cosmos.

e Sustainer and Faithful Preserver

Relativity theory in its special form, as we saw earlier[9] does not vitiate the concept of causality, the idea of sequences of causes and effects succeeding each other in time. It modifies the concept only to the extent that it is now realized that causal effects cannot be transmitted at speeds greater than that of light. However, scientific knowledge of the entities, structures and processes of the world, especially of complex living organisms, has shifted the focus of interest of much of the sciences away from the search for 'causes', as such, to seeking to understand networks of intelligible relationships both static, in structures and entities, and dynamic, in processes. So the classical argument of the 'Second Way' of St Thomas Aquinas,[10] which, finding intolerable an infinite chain of alternating causes and effects, goes on to infer the existence of a First Cause (to which everyone gives the name 'God') loses its cogency through this diminished interest in cause-and-effect sequences – even though the whole idea of an infinite series is itself more acceptable now that it is so commonplace in quite elementary mathematics. In any case the concept of God as 'First Cause' is not satisfactory theologically, for it makes God an element, admittedly a limiting boundary one, within the sequence of natural events and so not ultimately different in kind, however much greater in magnitude, from the natural world, thereby lacking the transcendence which is demanded by the primary experience of the divine.

Although for these reasons the concept of God as 'First Cause' terminating a *temporal* sequence has lost its cogency today, the natural sciences have nevertheless led to such a revision of our concept of the nature of time that the relation of God to time needs itself to be reconsidered. This is one of the concerns of the following section, on 'Divine Becoming', but for the moment let us note just two aspects of this relation. First, we cannot now but be aware that time is an aspect of the natural order, being closely integrated with space, matter and energy,[11] and so, for theists, must be regarded, in some sense, as created. Second, the realization that time has a direction,[12] in which there emerge new entities, structures and processes reinforces the idea that God is, as Creator, both its *Sustainer and faithful Preserver* through time. If 'God' is still to be the 'best explanation' of all-that-is, then as Creator he[13] must be regarded as holding all in existence and maintaining the validity of all laws and relations throughout time. It should be noted that there is implied, if God is personal, a moral quality in the divine sustaining and preserving – that of faithfulness or 'steadfast love', as the Old Testament calls it. However, this classical concept of sustaining and preserving as a characteristic of the divine Creator, valid as it is as far as it goes, appears to be singularly static in its impact, words such as 'sustaining' evoking pictures of a somewhat Atlas-like figure holding up the world.

f Continuous Creator

What the scientific perspective of the world inexorably impresses upon us is a dynamic picture of the world of entities and structures involved in continuous and incessant change and in process without ceasing. As we have seen,[14] new modes of existence come into being, and old ones often pass away. In the world new entities, structures and processes appear in the course of time, so that God's action as Creator is both past and present: it is continuous. Any notion of God as Creator must now take into account, more than ever before in the history of theology, that *God is continuously creating*, that God is *semper Creator*. In this respect, God has to be regarded as related to created time as the continuously creating Creator. Thus it is that the scientific perspective obliges us to take more seriously and concretely than hitherto in theology the notion of the immanence of God as Creator – that *God is the Immanent Creator creating in and through the processes of the natural order*. The implications of this will need working out further in our consideration of the divine becoming.[15]

g Personal – Creator of An Anthropic Universe

We have seen[16] that philosophical inferences to the best explanation of all-that-is lead to the conclusion that the postulate of a creator and sustainer God as the agent bringing about all-that-is is a *personal* explanation, whereby the occurrence of a phenomenon is explained as brought about by a rational agent doing some action intentionally. There are, as we shall shortly argues, grounds for believing that God might be 'personal', or 'at least personal', or even, if one is more robust, 'a person'.[17] This belief, indeed experience, is basic and fundamental to the Judeo-Christian religious tradition – one could hardly worship and pray to the 'Ground of Being', and even less to the 'Best Explanation of all-that-is'. We saw, too, that the distinctive contribution of Jesus's teaching to our understanding of God was to heighten and stress this personal relation of God to his people by his referring to God as 'Father' in a particularly intimate way and in the verbs with which he described the actions of this God his Father.[18] So the understanding and experience of God as personal is deeply embedded in the philosophical, theological and religious traditions. What bearing does the scientific perspective have on this conviction?

In our account[19] of the conditions required for the emergence of human persons – our discussion of the so-called 'anthropic principle' – we came to the conclusion that the world does seem to be finely tuned with respect to many physical features in a way conducive to the emergence of living organisms and so of human beings. We also gave reasons why living organisms might develop, through a basically intelligible natural processes, cognitive powers and consciousness as they increased in complexity and flexibility – and how the development of self-consciousness would involve awareness of pain, suffering and death. None of this, we have argued, need imply a reductive account of the content of human consciousness or diminish our awareness of the deep mystery of human personhood. It does indeed seem to be the case that the universe is of such a unique kind that it can generate through its own inherent properties living organisms, including *homo sapiens*. Our presence in the universe is closely interlocked with the universe being of the kind it actually is, down to some very precise physical details. The presence of humanity in this universe, far from being an unintelligible surd, represents an inherent inbuilt potentiality of that physical universe in the sense that intelligent, self-conscious life was bound eventually to

appear although its form was not prescribed by those same fundamental parameters and relationships that made it all possible.

This now well-established 'anthropic' feature of our universe has
been interpreted in various and mutually inconsistent ways. Thus
for some[20] it renders any talk of a creator God more than ever
unnecessary since we would not be likely, would we, to be able to
observe a universe that did *not* have the right conditions for producing us? D. J. Bartholomew, himself a theist, has argued[21] that the
'weak' anthropic principle ('what we can expect to observe is
constrained by the conditions which are necessary for our existence
as observers') is irrelevant to any argument for the initial state of the
universe being divinely determined. For the probability of the initial
conditions and laws of physics being as we now know them to be
(which is the probability relevant to whether or not the initial state
was divinely determined) hardly affects the value of what that
probability would be *given that we exist*. This latter is certainly
close to one in the light of the (non-controversial) 'weak' anthropic
principle. Others[22] have seen in it a new and more defensible
'argument for design', or, rather, an 'argument from design' for the
existence of a creator God. The whole debate is philosophically a
very subtle and puzzling one,[23] depending as it clearly does on the
presuppositions and interpretative framework that one brings to
bear on any assessment of the *a priori* probability of all the
constants, etc. – all the 'fine tuning' – coming out just to have the
values that could lead to life and so to us.

Much of the current argumentation in favour of a theistic
interpretation[24] has been concerned to base itself on a demonstra-
tion that this is indeed the only universe with which we have to deal.
It is certainly the only one of which we have any knowledge and the
one in which we seek meaning and intelligibility. Those arguing in
favour of a theistic conclusion from anthropic considerations frequently reject any notion of the existence of (to us) unobservable,
multiple universes. These have been postulated as existing simultaneously with us now as a result of a multiple splitting occurring at
the beginning of this universe; or existing successively, as a result of
a cycle of expansions and contractions ('hot big bangs' alternating
with 'hot big crunches'); or as forming at every instant of time
through a quantum splitting effect (the not-widely-held 'many
worlds hypothesis' of some theoretical physicists). Those in favour
of a theistic inference from anthropic relationships take this line, it
would seem, because they believe that only if the 'fine tuning' to

which the anthropic principle draws attention is operative in *one* universe can a theistic argument get off the ground. 'Look at these extraordinary coincidences that have made us possible in this one-off universe' is what we seem to be invited to do. So provoked, we are then asked to conclude that the remarkable emergence of persons (and it *is* remarkable, as we shall later have cause to stress) in this one universe is evidence for its origin in a creative personal God.

I myself do not want to dissent from the broad conclusions of this argument, but I urge that it does not depend on our universe being the *only* existing one and in there being no other universes, in any of the three possible senses already mentioned. Some years ago I made a theological appraisal[25] of the anthropic principle in the light of an acceptance of the mutual interplay of chance and law as the basis of the evolving forms in this universe (in the context particularly of biological evolution). I saw, as we shall again discuss below, this interplay as entirely consistent with how a creator God would act. If this is so, and we take seriously the possibility of there being an 'ensemble' of universes, in one of the three senses stated above, then, as I wrote:

> ... if we are [also] to look upon the role of 'chance' as the means whereby all the potentialities of the universe are explored, then we have to extend the time-scale and the ontological range over which 'chance' is thought to operate. Chance must now be regarded as, not only operating ... to elicit the potentialities of matter-energy-space-time over the spatial and temporal scale of our present universe, but also over the ensemble of possible universes, in most of which matter-energy-space-time might be replaced by new entities consistent with other values of the physical constants and possibly acting, presumably, according to quite different physical laws than those we can ascertain in principle in this universe. Even so, the point is that over the extension of space-time (or whatever replaces it) the potentialities of the ensemble of universes, as well as of this particular universe, are being or have been run through, or 'explored' ... For however long it may have taken on the time-scale of our universe, or however many universes may have preceded (and might follow) it [or might exist along with it], the fact is that matter-energy-space-time, in *this* universe, acquired the ability to adopt self-replicating structures which have acquired self-consciousness and the ability to know that they exist and have even now found ways of discovering how they have come to be.

So it is that we come to stress the particularity of our universe. For in this universe there are certain basic given features ... which limit what can eventually be realized through its dynamic, evolutionary processes.... Man's existence is non-necessary, that is, is contingent, in the sense of his not being present in all possible actual worlds, whose existence he can infer [on the 'ensemble of universes' assumption], and the same could also be affirmed of any other self-conscious being composed of particles of the kind that make up this universe.[26]

Whatever the constraints and framework of meta-laws and supervening relations that operate in bringing about the range constituting any postulated ensemble of universes, they must be of such a kind as to enable in one of the universes (*this* one) the combination of parameters, fundamental constants, etc., to be such that living organisms, including ourselves, could come into existence in some corner of it. So, on this argument, it is as significant that the ensemble of universes should be of such a kind that persons have emerged as it would be if ours were the only universe. Whether our purview is that of the present cosmos (broad enough on any account) or of the whole range of a hypothetical ensemble of universes, it is still a striking fact that the conditions were such on this planet Earth, in this galaxy, in this universe, for living organisms and self-conscious persons to come into existence. The fact is that it has happened at least once, here, and was thus among the range of potentialities of the whole natural order, whether this extends over many universes or only this one. Hence any argument for theism based on 'anthropic' considerations may be conducted independently of the question of whether or not this is the only universe.

Thus we return, after this digression, to the tricky question of how one should interpret these recent discoveries that the universe we observe is so 'finely tuned' to the existence of living organisms, including ourselves, whose presence therefore makes this a cognizable universe. The universe appears to be such that it has generated through its own processes, following their own inherent principles of unfolding new forms, a part of the universe (us) that knows that it exists in such a universe and moreover, knows that it knows. We have stressed that the emergence of cognizing living organisms, *homo sapiens*, is intelligible, with hindsight, through our increasing understanding of the evolutionary processes and of human biology, coupled with the anthropological sciences. However, this should not lead us to underplay just how unexpected our arrival on the scene is from the point of view of the natural sciences. Because of their inevitably reductionist methodology, which constitutes no criticism of them, the sciences are acutely limited in their explanatory power of precisely what new kinds of organized modes of being can emerge at levels of complexity above that at which the science in question operates. *Post hoc*, such developments can seem intelligible while not being strictly predictable. Most of all is this the case with the emergence of humanity and the experience of being persons.

We have earlier[27] given some account of the singularity and distinctiveness of personhood, even within a purely biological context. But now is the point at which the truly astonishing character of this emergence of personhood can be properly emphasized. For, we may well ask, why did the world, before the emergence of living organisms, and *a fortiori* of humanity, not just go on being an insentient, uncomprehending mechanism – 'merely the hurrying of material, endlessly, meaninglessly'.[28] The fact is, it didn't; and it is indeed significant, as John Durant has remarked,[29] that, with all its impressive knowledge of the physical and biological worlds and of our human physical nature, science can tell us nothing about why we have the experience of subjectivity. It is this that generates all the language of personal experience and personal interaction that constitutes for most people the bulk of their waking lives, and is reflected in our literature, art and music, indeed in our general culture. Although biology helps us to understand how our cognitive processes help survival and the neuro-sciences are beginning to help us see how our brains might be effective cognitively, this is light-years away from describing the actual experience of cognition, let alone the myriad other facets of subjectively experienced human personhood. We do not seem to be much nearer bridging this gap than the early pioneers of the scientific method 300 years ago.

We are certainly nearer, as outlined in Part I, to explaining how matter can become self-reproducing, and so living, and thereafter to become more and more complex with acquisition of cognitive powers conducive to survival, but this in no way describes how we think, feel, etc., in ourselves the way we do – that is, what our lives are actually like to ourselves. If we only had the sciences to go on, we would have no reason to predict or expect the arrival of personhood on the scene in *homo sapiens*, to suppose that the world could have persons in it at all. The subjectivity of our self-conscious personhood is quite unpredictable from even our present state of sophisticated science. With hindsight we see it emerging little by little, but once persons have arrived something qualitatively new has appeared. A real boundary is encountered by the natural sciences at the threshold of personality. In saying this I am not intending to introduce any note of mystification into the discussion, but I do mean that we should recognize frankly our actual incomprehension of the nature of the 'person'. There is a huge gap between what mechanism, and even organicism, can predict and any plausible explanation of the presence of persons in the universe eludes science as such. To use our earlier terms, the concept, and so actual instantiation, of personhood is the most intrinsically irreducible of all emerging entities that we know.

It seems, therefore, that the universe has through its own inherent processes – and there is no need to depart from this well-warranted assumption – generated a part of itself which, as persons, introduces a distinctively new kind of causality into itself, namely that of personal agency. The 'anthropic principle', the fine-tuning that allows the emergence of life and humanity, emphasizes the deep connection between the presence of life and of ourselves, on the one hand, and the intrinsic properties of the physical universe, on the other. Yet this very connectedness itself poses a problem because of those unique features of personhood already emphasized[30] which not only render the nature of persons irreducible to other scientific levels (a common feature of the relation between different levels[31] but also introduces the possibility of a new kind of explanation, namely *personal* explanation.

So we cannot help asking what kind of universe is it, if it can generate such entities as persons? As I have put it elsewhere,[32] if the stuff of the world, the primeval concourse of protons, neutrinos, photons, etc. has, as a matter of fact and not conjecture, become persons – human beings who possess 'inner' self-conscious lives in relation to other human beings – then how are we properly to interpret the cosmological development (or the development of the ensemble of universes) if, after aeons of time, these fundamental particles and energy have evidenced that quality of existence we call 'personal', with its distinctive self-awareness and new kind of agency in the world? Does not the very intimacy of our relation to the fundamental features of the physical world, the 'anthropic' features, together with the distinctiveness of personhood, point us in the direction of looking for a 'best explanation' of all-that-is (both non-personal and personal) in terms of some kind of causality that could *include* the personal in its consequences? That is to say, the single 'best explanation' of all-that-is, this 'X', would have to be of a quite different essence, over and beyond the order of created beings. In other words 'X' must transcend the personal in such a way that 'X' could be the ground of that distinctive mode of actual being we call personal, as well as of the non-personal being we have already considered. Since the personal is, for the reasons given above, the highest category of entity we can name in the order of created beings, and since 'God' is the name we give to this 'X', we therefore have good reason for saying that *God is (at least) 'personal'*, or 'supra-personal' and for predicating personal qualities of God as less misleading and more appropriate than impersonal ones – even while recognizing, as always, that such predications must remain ultimately inadequate to that to which they refer, namely, God.

h Purposive

It is of the nature of human persons to have purposes particularly in their seeking to embody their values in individual and social life. Of our innate 'values' – those goal-seeking patterns of behaviour that are built in by evolution and cannot be altered by human beings – some, what G. E. Pugh[33] has called the 'selfish' ones, we share with the higher primates, but others, the 'social' ones, only partly so; and yet others, the 'intellectual' ones, are distinctively human. For, as persons, we are also characterized by continually endeavouring to do what we 'ought' do, to respond in action to more than what simply 'is'. These distinctively human values cannot, it seems to me, be reduced to the purely biological, as the programme of some sociobiologists claims, and are distinctive of the emergence of personhood in human beings.[34] If that is so, then human beings have arrived on the scene as potential carriers of values, so the creator God who gives them such personal existence cannot but in his own inherent self be an ultimate source of values, since by their very nature values transcend the physical and biological and partake of the nature of the personally purposive. Any relationship of such a creator God to created persons would *ipso facto* be personal in character and it becomes eminently reasonable to affirm that such a personal, creator *God has purposes* that are manifest in the existence and destiny of persons embodying values.

It is at this point that the inadequacy of our talk only of the 'being' of God, of God as the one Ground of Being, becomes increasingly apparent. For it is of the nature of the personal not only to be capable of bearing static predicates, referring to stabler settled characteristics, but also of predicates of a dynamic kind, since the flow of experience is quintessential to being a person. So the 'static' predicates, such as 'supremely rational', 'omniscient', 'omnipotent', 'sustaining', 'preserving', 'faithful', and so on, with which we have hitherto been largely concerned to talk of God, must be enriched by other and more 'dynamic' predicates appropriate to the personal – as we saw was also implied by our earlier inference that God must be an immanent, continuously creating Creator. To put it another way, for our models of God to be personal they must be dynamic as well as static. So it is more appropriate to develop our consideration of the creative actions and activity of a personal God under the heading of 'Divine Becoming'.

2 DIVINE BECOMING

It is distinctive of free persons that they possess intentions and purposes and act so as to implement them. If, then, we accept the clue to the nature of the Creator afforded by the existence of such free-willing purposive persons in the universe it becomes proper to ask: can we infer from what is going on in the natural world[35] anything about what might properly be called the 'purposes' of God as personal Creator acting in the created world? That is, can we discern the purposes of this personal God in any ways that are consistent with what we now know of the universe through the sciences? The monotheistic religious traditions, especially Christianity, make strong claims to know aspects of God's purposes. We do not want to derogate from these claimed revelations but does the scientific perspective on the natural world, including humanity, enhance and add to or diminish and subtract from our notions of the purposes of God in creation that the Judeo-Christian tradition in particular has affirmed? More broadly, is our understanding of God the personal Creator as the 'best explanation' of all-that-is enriched by what science shows us concerning the being and becoming of the natural world, including humanity?

a *Joy and Delight in Creation*

We have seen[36] that the natural world is immensely variegated in its hierarchies of levels of entities, structures and processes, in its 'being'; and abundantly diversifies with a cornucopian fecundity in its 'becoming' in time. From the unity in this diversity and the richness of the diversity itself, we earlier adduced,[37] respectively, both the essential oneness of its source of being, namely the one God the Creator, and the unfathomable richness of the unitive Being of that creator God. But now we must reckon more directly with the diversity itself. The forms even of non-living matter throughout the cosmos as it appears to us is even more diverse than what we can observe immediately on the Earth. Furthermore the multiply branching tree of terrestrial biological evolution appears to be primarily opportunist in the direction it follows and, in so doing, produces the enormous variety of biological life on this planet. As Charles Darwin himself put it in a famous passage,

> It is interesting to contemplate a tangled bank, clothed with many plants of many kinds, with birds singing on the bushes, with various insects flitting about, and with worms crawling through the damp earth, and to reflect that these elaborately constructed forms, so different from each other, and dependent upon each other in so complex a manner, have all been produced by laws acting around us ... There is grandeur in this view of life, with its several powers, having been originally breathed by the Creator into a few forms or into one; and that, whilst this planet has gone cycling on according to the fixed law of gravity, from so simple a beginning endless forms most beautiful and most wonderful have been, and are being evolved.[38]

We can only conclude that, if there is a personal Creator, then that Creator intended this rich multiformity of entities, structures, and processes in the natural world and, if so, that such a Creator God takes what, in the personal world of human experience, could only be called 'delight' in this multiformity of what he has created – and not only in what Darwin, in that same passage, called 'the most exalted object which we are capable of conceiving, namely the production of the higher animals'. The existence of the *whole* tapestry of the created order, in its warp and woof, and in the very heterogeneity and multiplicity of its forms, must be taken to be the Creator's intention. We can only make sense of that, utilizing our resources of personal language, if we say that *God has joy and delight in creation*. We have a hint of this in the satisfaction attributed to God as Creator in the first chapter of *Genesis*: 'And God saw everything he had made, and behold, it was very good.'[39] This naturally leads to the idea of the 'play' of God in creation on which I have expanded elsewhere,[40] in relation to Hindu thought as well as to that of Judaism and Christianity. That this 'play' of God in creation is, in certain respects, akin to a game of chance is something that has become increasingly apparent from a number of developments in the sciences and it is to this aspect of the sciences and our perception of the world that we must now turn.

b Ground and Source of Law ('Necessity') and 'Chance'

Our games obey given rules but, because of the involvement of an element of chance, there is a certain unpredictability and open-endedness in their outcome which, indeed, constitutes their attraction and fascination. Interestingly, these same features are also aspects of the natural world that the sciences have now discerned.[41] We saw in Part I[42] that there are various kinds of system in the natural world which may be differentiated with respect to their predictability or otherwise. In particular, we noted that there are non-linear complex dynamical systems that can undergo transitions at the observable macro-level that are unpredictable, even though all of their subsidiary processes are governed by deterministic laws. Their existence has only gradually and recently become increasingly clear to scientists in a number of diverse fields. In the form of 'dissipative systems'[43] they are particularly relevant to our understanding of biological systems. For, as we saw,[44] they gave us a clue as to how the interplay of random, chance-like events at the micro-level could lead to a form of self-organization that is also self-reproducing and so living – that is, the transition from non-living to living matter was rendered intelligible by its consistency with the properties of these kinds of physico-chemical system. Such transitions in such systems would be unpredictable before the event but intelligible afterwards as being within the range of possibilities available to the system as a whole, for they are the results of the lawlike amplification of the effects of a single or of a few micro-events. This creative interplay of 'chance' and law is even more obviously apparent in the evolution of living matter by natural selection, but what we mean by 'chance' in this context first needs closer examination.

Micro-events are unpredictable by us in two ways:

1 They can be unpredictable because we can never possess the necessary detailed knowledge with the requisite accuracy at this micro-level of description. In such cases talk of the role of 'chance' can mean either (a) we cannot determine accurately

the micro-parameters of the initial conditions determining the macro-events (e.g., the forces on a tossed coin), while often knowing the overall constraints that must operate on the system as a whole (e.g., the symmetry constraints making for equal probabilities of heads and tails); or (b) the observed events are the outcome of the crossing of two independent causal chains, accurate knowledge of which is unattainable both with respect to the chains themselves and to their point of intersection.

2 Micro-events can also be unpredictable because of the operation of the Heisenberg Uncertainty Principle[45] at the sub-atomic level and this unpredictability is inherent and ineradicable.

Both of these two categories of micro-events unpredictable as they are, produce effects at the macroscopic level which operate in a lawlike framework that constrains their possible consequences. These 'lawlike' constraints may be viewed as delimiting the scope of the consequent events or as providing them with new and unexpected outcomes. Both ways of viewing the matter are pertinent to one of the most significant arenas in which there is an interplay of 'chance' events in a lawlike framework, that of biological evolution.

We saw earlier[46] that biological evolution depends on a process in which changes occur in the genetic information carrying material (DNA) that are random with respect to the biological needs of the organisms possessing the DNA; and in particular, are random with respect to its need to produce progeny for the species to survive. What we call 'chance' is involved both at the level of the mutational event in the DNA itself (1(a) and/or 2, above), and in the intersecting of two causally unrelated chains of events (1(b), above) – those that give rise to the change in the DNA and the consequences of such changes for those features of the organism that affect its survival in its particular biological and ecological niche.

The original mutational events are random with respect to the future of the biological organism, even its future survival, but these changes have their consequences in a milieu that has regular and lawlike features. For the biological niche in which the organism exists then filters out, by the processes of natural selection, those changes in the DNA that enable the organisms possessing them to produce more progeny. The details of how such 'selection' operates in any given case are, of course, individual to that species but the statistics of the process are amenable to mathematical description in an entirely lawlike fashion. This interplay between 'chance', at the molecular level of the DNA, and 'law' or 'necessity' at the statistical level of the population of organisms tempted Jacques Monod, in his influential book *Chance and Necessity*,[47] to elevate 'chance' to the level almost of a metaphysical principle whereby the universe might be interpreted. As is well known, he concluded that the 'stupendous edifice of evolution' is, in this sense, rooted in 'pure chance' and that *therefore* all inferences of direction or purpose in the development of the biological world, in particular, and of the universe, in general, must be false. In so arguing, he thereby mounted, in the name of science, one of the strongest and most influential attacks of the century on theism. For, as Monod saw it, it was the purest accident that any particular creature came into being, in particular *homo sapiens*, and no direction or purpose or meaning could ever be expected to be discerned in biological evolution. Even if there were a creator God, for all practical purposes he might just as well not exist, since everything in evolution went on in an entirely uncontrolled and fortuitous manner.

The responses to this thesis and attack on theism – mainly, it is interesting to note, from theologically informed scientists, and some philosophers, rather than from theologians – have been well surveyed by D. J. Bartholomew[48] and their relative strengths and weaknesses analyzed. I shall here follow what I consider to be the most fruitful line of theological reflection on the processes that Monod so effectively brought to the attention of the twentieth century – a direction that I began[49] to pursue in response to Monod and which has been further developed by the statistically informed treatment of Bartholomew.

There is no reason why the randomness of molecular event in relation to biological consequence has to be given the significant metaphysical status that Monod attributed to it. The involvement of what we call 'chance' at the level of mutation in the DNA does not, of itself, preclude these events from displaying regular trends and manifesting inbuilt propensities at the higher levels of organisms, populations and ecosystems. To call the mutation of the DNA a 'chance' event serves simply to stress its randomness with respect to biological consequence. As I have put it elsewhere:

Instead of being daunted by the role of chance in genetic mutations as being the manifestation of irrationality in the universe, it would be more consistent with the observations to assert that the full gamut of the potentialities of living matter could be explored only through the agency of the rapid and frequent randomization which is possible at the molecular level of the DNA.[50]

This role of 'chance', or rather randomness (or 'free experiment') at the micro-level is what one would expect if the universe were so constituted that all the potential forms of organizations of matter (both living and non-living) which it contains might be thoroughly explored. Indeed, since Monod first published his book in French in 1970, there have been those developments in theoretical and molecular biology and physical biochemistry that cast new light on the interrelation of what we call chance and law (or necessity, to use Monod's term) in the origin and development of life – namely the investigations of the Brussels school led by Ilya Prigogine[51] and of the Göttingen school led by Manfred Eigen.[52] They demonstrated that it is the interplay of chance and law which is in fact creative within time, for it is the combination of the two which allows new forms to emerge and evolve; so that natural selection appears to be opportunistic.

This has been superbly illustrated by Richard Dawkins[53] with his computer programme for what he calls 'biomorphs', two-dimensional patterns of branching lines generated by random changes in a defined number of features combined with a reproduction and selection procedure. It was striking how subtle, varied and complex were the 'biomorph' patterns after surprisingly few 'generations', that is, reiterations of the procedure. Such computer simulations go a long way towards making it clear how it is that the complexity and diversity of biological organisms could arise through the operation of the apparently simple principles of natural selection. For these involve only the interplay and consequences of random processes (in relation to biological outcome) in the lawlike framework of the rules governing change in biological populations in complex environments. These rules are what they are because of the 'givenness' of the properties of the physical environment and of the already evolved other living organisms with which the organism in question interacts. All these constraints themselves arise from the inherent properties of the world in which the organism is developing and so go back to that basic contingency of the universe itself having the particular laws, relationships, entities, structures and processes it in fact has.

This givenness, for a theist, can only be regarded as an aspect of the God-endowed features of the world. The way in which what we call 'chance' operates within this 'given' framework to produce new structures, entities and processes can then properly be seen as an eliciting of the potentialities that the physical cosmos possessed *ab initio*. Such potentialities a theist must regard as written into creation by the Creator's intention and purpose and must conceive as gradually being actualized by the operation of 'chance' stimulating their coming into existence. One might say that the potential of the 'being' of the world is made manifest in the 'becoming' that the operation of chance makes actual. *God is the ultimate ground and source of both law ('necessity') and 'chance'.*

I have elsewhere[54] attempted to express this characteristic of the Creator's mode of action – a characteristic of which we have only in this century really become aware – by means of a musical analogy, a model of God as composer, and to this we shall revert in chapter 9. To a theist, it is now clear that God acts to create in the world *through* what we call 'chance' operating within the created order, each stage of which constitutes the launching pad for the next. The Creator, it now seems, is unfolding the potentialities of the universe, which he himself has given it, in and through a process in which these creative possibilities and propensities, inherent by his own intention within the fundamental entities of that universe and their inter-relations, become actualized within a created temporal development shaped and determined by those selfsame God-given potentialities.

However, the actual course of this unfolding of the hidden potentialities of the world is not a predetermined path, for there are the irreducible unpredictabilities in the actual systems and processes of the world to which we have already referred (micro-events at the Heisenberg level and non-linear dynamical complex systems). So there is an open-endedness in the course of the world's 'natural' history. In other words, we now have to conceive of God as involved in explorations of the many kinds of unfulfilled potentialities of the universe he has created – and we must recognize that the transition from 'causal' to anthropomorphic-narrative language cannot be avoided at this juncture. It thus transpires that the creative action of God is to be seen as genuinely innovative and adaptive, but not inchoate and without purpose. For there are, as we saw, inbuilt propensities – a theist would say 'built in by God' – in the natural, creating processes which, as it were, 'load the dice' in favour of life and, once living organisms have appeared, also of increased complexity, awareness, consciousness and sensitivity, with all their consequences. New though such a conception may be for theists, especially Judeo-Christian believers in God with their sense of creation as the expression of divine will and purpose (perhaps less so for Hindus with their sense of the play, *lila*, of God in creation[55]), nevertheless this proposal, far from being inherently inimical to belief in God actually enriches our understanding of divine creation. For the original quantum vacuum, or whatever current theory postulates as the origin of our universe, must have had the potentiality of being able to develop so as to display those qualities of complexity, awareness, consciousness and sensitivity that characterize the higher forms of life. It is this which is significant about the emergence of life in the universe and the role of chance is simply what is required if all the potentialities of the universe, especially for life, are going to be elicited effectively. As I have expressed it elsewhere:

> if we propose that the world owes its being to a Creator God then I see no reason why God should not allow the potentialities of his universe to be developed in all their ramifications through the operation of random ['chance'] events; indeed, in principle, this is the only way in which all potentialities might eventually, given enough time and space, be actualized. Or, to change the metaphor, it is as if chance is the search radar of God, sweeping through all the possible targets available to its probing.[56]

D. J. Bartholomew has urged that God and chance are not only logically compatible, as the foregoing has argued, but that there are 'positive reasons for supposing that an element of pure chance would play a constructive role in creating a richer environment than would otherwise be possible'.[57] He argues that 'chance offers the potential Creator many advantages which it is difficult to envisage being obtained in any other way.'[58] Since in many natural processes, often utilized by human beings, chance processes can in fact lead to determinate ends, for many of the laws of nature are statistical, 'there is every reason to suppose that a Creator wishing to achieve certain ends might choose to reach them by introducing random processes whose macro-behaviour would have the desired character.'[59] Thus the determinate ends to which chance processes could lead might well be 'to produce intelligent beings capable of interaction with their Creator'.[60] For this it would be necessary, Bartholomew suggests, to have an environment in which chance provides the stimulus and testing to promote intellectual and spiritual evolution. Indeed, he goes further and asserts that

> a world of chance is not merely consistent with a theistic view of nature but, almost, required by it ... It is more congenial to both faith

and reason to suppose that God generates the requisite degree of randomness much as we do, by deterministic means. We emphasize again that this does not imply or require fore-knowledge of the consequences at the micro-level on God's part. He is concerned with macro-effects.[61]

Such a 'strong' view on the part of Bartholomew of the role of chance in the divine purposes has repercussions for how we might conceive of God's interaction with the world. What is clear at this juncture is that, in a world in which chance plays the role both Bartholomew and I have depicted, God is taking risks in his creation and, as we shall see, most of all with created humanity.

It seems that we now have to take account of: (1) this new perspective of God the Creator as acting through chance operating within the constraints of law, that is, of the God-given properties and propensities of the natural world; (2) a renewed emphasis[62] on the immanence of God in the processes of the creative and creating world; and (3) our earlier recognition of the irreducible unpredictability of much of what goes on in the world.[63] These considerations steer us towards new models of God's creative action that stress that the rationality that is evidenced in the creation is one that is exploratory of new possibilities, generating them through the conjunction of chance and law. They lead us to see that *God the Creator explores in creation*.

c Self-limited Omnipotence and Omniscience

Considerations such as these on the role of 'chance' in creation impel us also to recognize more emphatically than ever before the constraints which we must regard God as imposing upon himself in creation and to suggest that *God has a 'self-limited' omnipotence and omniscience*. For, in order to achieve his purposes, he has allowed his inherent omnipotence and omniscience to be modified, restricted and curtailed by the very open-endedness that he has bestowed upon creation. This open-endedness and unpredictability of the world's processes increases with the complexity of organization of the entities and structures undergoing them, particularly when these are living and most notably in the human experience of that freedom possessed by the human-brain-in-the-human-body.

The attribution of 'self-limitation' to God with respect to his omnipotence is meant to indicate that God has so made the world that there are certain areas over which he has chosen not to have power (for example, human free will, as generally recognized by theologians). Similarly, the attribution of 'self-limitation' to God in regard to his omniscience is meant to denote that God may also have so made the world that, at any given time, there are certain systems whose future states cannot be known even to him since they are in principle not knowable (for example, those in the 'Heisenberg' range and certain non-linear systems at the macroscopic level). If there is no particular point in time of which it could truly be said of those systems 'this will be its future state', then it could not be known at any instant, by God or by us, what the future state of such systems will be. It seems that God has made the world so that, in these systems, he himself does not know their future states of affairs, since they cannot be known.

As we saw in chapter 7,[64] God's 'omniscience' has to be construed as God knowing at any time whatever it is *possible* that he know at that time. This excludes such incoherences as God possibly knowing that $2+3=6$ etc., and also knowing in advance what human beings would freely actually choose, since it would be logically incoherent if God did know this *and* human beings were genuinely free. The unpredictability for us of events in the sub-atomic ('Heisenberg') range and in non-linear, dynamic macroscopic systems is not 'logical' in this sense but, I would suggest, they are also unpredictable for God. For in these situations it transpires that the unpredictability is inherent in the nature of the systems themselves: there are no 'hidden variables' in the 'Heisenberg' case; and, in the non-linear case, there may not only be no closed solutions, but the same Heisenberg Uncertainty Principle also sets a limit to the accuracy with which the determining initial conditions *can* be known. This is, then, a limitation on God's omniscience. But in these cases not a purely logical one (as in the arithmetical example above): it is a *self*-limitation, because God as Creator 'chose' (that is what is implied by God being Creator) to create a world in which these subatomic constituents and non-linear systems had such an unpredictable character. Their unpredictability, their inherent indeterminacy, is not logically necessary but contingent – the contingency of the way God made these particular kinds of systems with these properties. If this expansion of what is 'impossible' is allowed, then God is still omniscient in the sense of Swinburne's definition but, in respect of these particular kinds of events and systems, only contingently so – a contingency of God's own choosing by creating them thus. It is this aspect of God's knowledge of the world he has created to which I refer as the 'self-limitation' of God's omniscience.

These considerations do not, of course, preclude God from knowing the probabilities of the sequence of events in such systems and so of knowing, and – we shall later suggest – of influencing, the general direction of the history of these natural events, in particular, and of nature, in general.

d Vulnerable, Self-emptying and Self-giving Love

Thus it is that we come to a recognition that in creating the world continuously God has allowed himself not to have overriding power over all that happens in it nor complete knowledge of the direction events will take. This self-limitation is the precondition for the coming into existence of free self-conscious human beings, that is, of human experience as such. This act of self-limitation on behalf of the good and well-being, indeed the existence, of another being can properly be designated as being consistent with, and so exemplifying the ultimate character of *God as 'Love'*. For in human life – and it can only be a human analogy – love is supremely manifest in self-limiting, costly action on behalf of the good and existence of another. The designation of God *as* 'Love' is, of course, a specifically Christian insight and I am not suggesting that without the revelation of God in Jesus the Christ we could have known this explicitly simply by reflecting on the world. But such reflections leading to the notion of God's self-limitation of his omnipotence and omniscience at least render it meaningful to speak of the *vulnerability of God*, indeed of the *self-emptying* (kenosis) *and self-giving of God* in creation. This is an insight that has been recovered for the church in recent years especially by the writings of Jürgen Moltmann and in W. H. Vanstone's *Love's Endeavour, Love's Expense*.[65]

It appears that not only does God remain faithful and reliable in his giving being to the world but he has also concomitantly made himself vulnerable to its costly becoming. He has put his ultimate purposes at risk by incorporating open-endedness, and so eventually human freedom, into the created world. Yet this expresses a transcendent rationality of a subtle kind for, as Bartholomew argues, it seems to be the only way of bringing into existence intelligent, self-conscious, sensitive, free beings who can relate personally to God who 'chose to make a world of chance because it would have the properties necessary for producing beings fit for fellowship with himself'.[66] There were many branching lines in biological evolution but, in fact, one did lead to human beings who are distinctive in knowing the world (including, now, their own evolutionary origins), who know that they know, can relate as persons and can act freely with intention and purpose. We are beginning to recognize, as was pointed out earlier in this chapter,[67] in what respects the arrival of human persons on the biological scene is intelligible in the light of their precursors and in what respects the leap that constituted the transition to humanity is conceptually baffling. Any theistic account of the existence of *this* kind of natural order and process must therefore incorporate into its understanding of God the Creator the notion that God had a purpose in creating such distinctive beings capable of inferring his existence and seeking to come into relation to him through prayer and worship, as has always characterized humanity from its first glimmerings of self-consciousness.

As we have just seen, the conditions for the emergence of open-endedness in natural systems – and so, in due course, the experience of freedom of the human-brain-in-the-human-body – involve a subtle interweaving of chance and law, with consequences that are often not readily predictable in principle (and, indeed, are often inimical to too narrowly-conceived human interests). If God willed the existence of self-conscious, intelligent, freely-willing creatures as an end, he must, to be self-consistent, logically be presumed to have willed the means to achieving that end. This divine purpose must be taken to have been an overriding one, for it involves as a corollary an element of risk to his purposes whereby he renders himself vulnerable in a way that is only now becoming perceivable by us. This idea that *God took a risk in creation* is not new – as evidenced by the traditional theology implicit in the 'narratives' of creation in the Old Testament – but is now, I am suggesting, reinforced and given a wider context by these biological considerations.

To instantiate truth, beauty and goodness, that is value, in the created order, the possibility of generating a *free* being had to be incorporated as a potential outcome of the cosmic processes. The cost to God, if we may dare so to speak, was in that act of self-limitation, of *kenosis*, which constitutes God's creative action – a self-inflicted vulnerability to the very processes God had himself created in order to achieve an overriding purpose, the emergence of free persons.

e Natural Evil

God's act of creation is not, as we saw, something done once for all – creation still proceeds and God is immanently present in and to the whole process. These processes that the natural sciences now unveil for us include the operation of chance in a law-like framework as the origin of life; the emergence of new forms of life only through the costly processes of natural selection with death of the old forms; and the emergence of sensitive, free, intelligent persons through a development that inevitably involves increasing sensitivity to pain and the concomitant experience of suffering *pari passu* with a growing consciousness and self-consciousness. Death, pain and suffering constitute the sting of what has often been called 'natural evil', those events, involving apparently pointless suffering and tragedy, which are inimical to human health, welfare and happiness, and indeed life. 'Natural evil' refers to those events that stem from the non-human, natural world – including *inter alia* earthquakes, floods, 'accidents' (the crossing of two independent causal chains), as well as the breakdown of the biological organization of the human physical/mental organism.[68] Pre-eminently it is such disruption of human bodily and mental organization, whether arising spontaneously (as in the malformation of a growing human embryo or in cancer) or as the result of the invasion of other organisms (disease), that are for us at the same time the most tragic of human experiences and the most directly experienced manifestation of how delicately and subtly balanced – and so vulnerable – is the intricate, dynamically balanced, network of the human living organism.

We have seen how it is that 'chance', or randomness, together with 'law' (the regularities resulting from the lawlike framework within which 'chance' operates) through their mutual interplay are necessary in any universe that is to be the matrix for the emergence of free-willing, responsible, conscious and self-conscious persons. So that in willing this end, instantiated in *homo sapiens*, God inevitably wills also the means – and these cannot but involve those random effects of 'chance' that are inimical to humanity and other living organisms and constitute the 'natural evil' to which all life is heir. It is this incidence of random processes within the regularities of a biological system, this combination of 'chance' and 'law', that, while it can be the root of individual tragedies, is also the fundamental basis for there being any life at all and any particular form of biological life, especially free-willing, self-conscious life such as our own. The chance disorganization of the growing human embryo that leads to the birth of a defective human being and the chance loss of control of cellular multiplication that appears as a cancerous tumour are individual and particular results of that same interplay of 'chance' and 'law' that enabled and enables life to exist at all. Hence such interpretations based on the understanding that the sciences have afforded us now mitigate and diminish greatly the problem of the existence of 'natural evil' and its widely assumed undermining of theistic belief.

Nothing, however, can diminish our sense of loss and tragedy as we experience or witness particular natural evils, especially in individuals known to us. But, at least, we can now better understand how it is that God wills into existence the kinds of living creatures that depend on the operation of the same factors that produce those particular 'natural' evils. The interplay of 'chance' and 'law' is the necessary condition for the existence of certain good eventualities and the 'natural evil' consequences need not be regarded as either avoidable or as intended in themselves by God. Even God cannot have one without the other.

God has created a universe in which, it transpires, certain situations have unpredictable outcomes and in which it is the existence of such situations that enables propensities towards complexity, consciousness and freedom to become actualized in the universe on the surface of the Earth, at least. God, we suggested, has thereby, and for those ends, in his acts of creation implicitly limited himself from knowing the particular outcomes of certain processes and also, as a consequence, his power over them. So we come to regard God's omniscience and omnipotence as 'self-limited' in these senses in order that the universe should be of a certain kind – namely, capable through its open-endedness and flexibility of generating complexity, consciousness and freedom. Again, in this wider context, the new perspectives of the sciences help to draw the sting of the problem of 'natural evil' and so contribute to a more defensible theodicy.

f A Suffering God

If God is immanently present in and to natural processes, in particular those that generate conscious and self-conscious life, then we cannot but infer that *God suffers in, with and under the creative processes of the world* with their costly, open-ended unfolding in time.[69]

Rejection of the notion of the impassibility of God has, in fact, been a feature of the theology of recent decades. There has been an increasing assent to the idea that it is possible 'to speak consistently of *a God who suffers eminently and yet is still God, and a God who suffers universally and yet is still present uniquely and decisively in the sufferings of Christ.*'[70] As Paul Fiddes points out in his survey and analysis of this change in theological perspective, the factors that have promoted the view that God suffers are new assessments of 'the meaning of love [especially, the love of God], the implications of the cross of Jesus, the problem of [human] suffering, and the structure of the world'.[71] It is this last-mentioned – the 'structure of the world' – on which the new perspectives of the sciences bear by revealing the world processes to be of such a character, described above, that involvement in them by the immanent Creator has to be regarded as involving suffering on the Creator's part. God, we find ourselves having to affirm, suffers the 'natural' evils of the world along with ourselves because – we can but tentatively suggest at this stage – he purposes to bring about a greater good thereby, the domain of free-willing, loving persons in communion with himself and with each other.[72]

The magnitude and scope of the divine loving vulnerability that puts itself at risk in creation only becomes fully apparent with the arrival on the scene of *homo sapiens*. For human beings can not only constitute the highest fulfilment of the Creator's purposes but, through the essential gift of freedom, they are also that part of the created order most capable of frustrating the divine will and purpose and of sinking to depths of degradation and denial of values in ways not open to, or actualized in, any other creature. They are also capable of experiencing to a unique degree pain, suffering and the loss which is death. With the arrival of human beings on the earth the free creation of value – of truth, beauty and goodness, to use for brevity the classical trio – first became possible, along with their deliberate and wilful rejection. This paradox of the creation of a humanity capable of alienating itself from the source of its own being merits deeper inquiry but, at this point, I wish to draw attention principally to the support for the notion of divine passibility which comes from the scientific perception of the role and inherent inevitability of pain, suffering and death in a universe capable of evolving free, intelligent persons.

g God and Time

The revived insight that God suffers in the processes of creation and, supremely, with suffering humanity, raises again[73] the question of God's relation to time. For if God 'suffers' with creation in some sense analogous to that of human suffering, God must be conceived as being changed through this interaction with the world. Indeed, this is precisely how the narratives of the biblical tradition depict God – the story of God's dealings with his people and God's reactions to their response, or lack of it. They depict God as somehow 'in time' in unashamedly anthropomorphic language, while acknowledging the impossibility of doing justice to what God is in himself.

Analyses of the relation of the question of the relation of God to time show that a number of important traditional attributes of God (for example, his personhood, his ability to act in the world,[74] his ability to know the world as temporal and changing[75]) lose coherence and meaning if God is regarded as 'timeless' in the sense of being 'outside' time altogether in a way which means time cannot be said to enter into his nature at all, so that he possesses no succession in his experience – that is, nothing akin to temporality. To affirm, as we have done, that God is, in some sense, 'personal' can only have any meaning if God experiences something like the succession of conscious states that being a person involves in ourselves. To be a person with consciousness *is* to be aware of a succession of states of mind (and in our case, though not God's, of body too).

Yet, we have urged[76] that God is also the Creator *of* the physical time which is so closely integrated with space, and so with energy, and so with matter, in the understanding that twentieth-century physics has given us – while recognizing that temporal relations (that is, in physical time) nevertheless have distinct differences from spatial ones.[77] If God *creates* time, does he not 'transcend' it in the sense of viewing the whole course of 'our' time from the mountain top, as it were, of another dimension – 'above' or 'outside' time so that our 'before', 'now' and 'after' are all spread out for him to see? In which case, does not God see ahead in time so that all is 'actually' predetermined – and our talk of unpredictability has to be taken to refer only to human and not divine foreknowledge? But we had to recognize that events at the sub-atomic ('Heisenberg'), quantum micro-level, and often also the development of non-linear dynamical systems, are unpredictable. At best only the *range* of possible outcomes of certain events (e.g., of a quantum measurement, or in a complex, non-linear dynamical system) is predictable and the actual event itself is not predictable. The future of the quantum or complex system is genuinely open and genuinely new states of the system occur. On these grounds we argued also that the outcome of such events must also be inherently unpredictable to God, if God is to be self-consistent and faithful to his own laws and constrained by the laws of logic and mathematics, as he must be for the concept of God to have any coherence at all. *A fortiori*, if human free will is to be genuine and not illusory, even if more constrained than we think as we experience it, then God cannot so 'transcend' the time in which we act that he can know precisely and definitively what our future free actions will be. As Keith Ward puts it:

> If genuinely free creatures are admitted, there is an overwhelmingly strong argument against Divine immutability and for Divine temporality. For the free acts of creatures will partially determine the initial conditions of the next temporal segment of the world. Before he creates that next segment, God must therefore know what choices have been made. The creation is consequent upon God's knowledge, which depends in turn upon free creaturely acts; so God must be conceived as responding to free acts moment by moment, as they are decided.... The combination of non-temporal knowledge, non-temporal creation and free creaturely action is contradictory.[78]

However, as was pointed out in relation to 'Heisenberg' microevents and non-linear dynamical systems that are irreducibly unpredictable, this does not mean that God cannot have the most complete knowledge that is possible of the probabilities of the outcomes of the operations of our free will – rather as a parent might in relation to a child's decisions, or a wife in relation to her husband's. That is, God will have full knowledge of all possible outcomes of our decisions and because of this comprehensive knowledge of us and of all the circumstances, he will know their relative probability of occurrence – but he cannot know certainly what *will* happen if our wills are to be genuinely free.

How then are we, in the light of these various considerations, best to conceive of God's relation to time? These and related questions have, for centuries, been central to the philosophical and theological discussions of major issues such as free will, predestination, the purported changelessness and impassibility of God and the relation of time to eternity, to name but a few. We are primarily concerned here with the impact of the perspectives of twentieth-century science on traditional debates, the percipience of which must-still command respect.

Special relativity raises a particular difficulty in all talk of God's relation to 'time'. For that theory replaces the one, universal flowing time assumed by Newton and by common sense, by many different 'times' specific to different observers, each with their own positions and velocities, that is, their own frames of reference. To which of these 'times' does God relate? Could he relate to all of them? However, as John Polkinghorne points out:

> We can picture each observer's 'instant' as being a three-dimensional slice through four-dimensional spacetime... An *omnipresent* observer, whose direct contact with the way things are is not located at a point within the slice but spread out all over it, would in due course experience everywhere and everywhen. That would be true whatever his choice of time axis... The omnipresent God has no need to use signalling to tell him what is happening and so he has instant access to every event as and when it occurs.[79]

Moreover since the succession of any particular created, causal sequences is independent of the reference frame of any and all observers, there is no incoherence in conceiving of God as having experience of, and so relating to, them all successively in his own self-awareness.

There is no reason why succession in God should not relate to each and every such framework, just as God relates to many other multiple aspects of the created order. This is indeed one sense in which God might be said to 'transcend' all created times. As John Polkinghorne also points out,[80] there is a natural frame of reference that cosmologists use when speaking of the age of the universe; 'cosmic time' provided by certain changing features of the whole universe. Hence there is no incoherence stemming from relativity in our continuing to speak of God's experience of 'time' in the created order rather than of 'times', meaning by the use of the singular this 'cosmic time'.

Also of general significance is the renewed support that the theory of general relativity now gives to the idea, already noted, in accord with St Augustine's famous assertion,[81] of physical ('clock') time being an aspect of the created order, for in that theory time is closely interlocked conceptually with space, matter and energy. Our own sense of psychological time, the sense of succession of our conscious states, with which our own sense of personhood is so bound up, is closely related to this physical time. For we move freely from one sense of time to the other even though they seem, often, to proceed at different rates while sharing many interactions and running in parallel. This relationship can perhaps at least make intelligible to us how God's own inherent self-awareness of successive states (which must be attributed to God if God is to be 'personal' in any meaningful sense) might be closely linked to physical, created time, while yet remaining distinct from it. On such a model, God would not be 'timeless' and could be thought of as the Creator of every instant of physical time. Creation by God would be regarded as that activity whereby God gives existence to each instant of physical time, the 'now' of the hand of the clock, and each instant has no existence prior to its being so created with all the entities, structures and processes that fill it. Keith Ward's suggestion that 'One might say that God timelessly generates, by the necessity of his own nature the infinite series of temporal states in which he freely acts'[82] is in accord with this, though couched in language derived more from theological than scientific discourse. This idea of God eternally giving existence to each successive moment of time, expressed in either of these two ways, illuminates the concept of God the Creator as sustaining and preserving the world.

On this interpretation, then, the future does not yet exist in any sense, not even for God; God creates each instant of physical time with its open, as yet undetermined, outcomes, fecund with possibilities not yet actualized. If the future does not yet exist for God, any more than it does for us, there is no question of God seeing ahead what the future is going to be, even though he can still have purposes to implement in that forthcoming future. That does not preclude God in his omniscience (qualified in the ways we have already suggested[83]) from knowing comprehensively, in a way not open to us, not only what these possibilities might be but also their relative probabilities of occurrence. This created time is, in Schilling's striking phrase, 'the carrier or locus of innovative change',[84] and it has a direction in which new systems emerge through the cosmic, inorganic, chemical and biological evolutionary processes. According to this proposal, God is conceived as holding in being in physical time all-that-is at each instant and relating his own succession of divine states (the divine 'temporality') to the succession of created instants without himself being subject to created physical time. Moreover, God transcends *past* time in the traditional sense of having total knowledge of it all stored in the perfect, permanent memory of God. But even God cannot know the future with absolute certainty when he has not yet given existence both to the time in which it will be located and to the location in this of the systems and persons that are irreducibly unpredictable with respect to their temporal histories.

Our own psychological time, of course, does not transcend physical time, indeed it is the captive of it, but our experience of our own succession of conscious states is sufficiently distinct from physical ('clock') time to make it at least intelligible and conceivable how temporality within God, God's own awareness of succession within the divine life, could be relatable to created physical time. God transcends created time as its Creator (we shall have to affirm, in accord with some later considerations, that created time is 'in God'), but is himself immanent in created time, being present to every moment of it as he creates it. There is no created time to which God is not present as he gives it existence, just as he is present to all space.[85]

To summarize, we can affirm that: *God is not 'timeless'; God is temporal in the sense that the Divine life is successive in its relation to us – God is temporally related to us; God creates and is present to each instant of the (physical and, derivatively, psychological) time of the created world; God transcends past and present created time: God is eternal*, in the sense[86] that there is no time at which he did not exist nor will there be a future time at which he does not exist.[87]

A consequence of this understanding of God as transcendent yet personal, and so possessing succession – that is, some kind of temporality – in conjunction with the acceptance that God is passible, is that God can no longer be thought of as immutable in the strong, classical sense of not changing at all. But the relation of the passible God to time is entirely consistent with a weaker, though more intelligible and relevant, sense of immutability, namely that God cannot change in character (and so in purpose, intent and disposition).[88] This is, indeed, precisely the sense in which we attribute 'consistency, faithfulness and reliability' to persons.[89] As the Report *We Believe in God* puts it:

> we meet in the Old Testament an insistence that 'the Living God' is to be recognized by his capacity to react and respond and adapt his actions to changing circumstances, and to find a way round each new frustration. Such a God, by virtue of creating in Space and Time a

universe with some degree of inbuilt freedom, exposes himself to
being acted upon and, in that sense, being compelled to change.[90]

h God and 'Imaginary' Time

The foregoing exposition has spoken of time as if it were meaningful
to think of time as extrapolatable backwards at least as far as the
'point' in time, the singularity, from which the expansion of our
known universe began (the 'hot, big bang'). This is indeed the
presumption of the most generally held picture of the cosmic
development, whether or not the phase of expansion we now
observe was preceded by an 'inflationary' stage – which has also
been conceived of as occurring on the same time scale. However,
we must also consider now that speculative proposal in which, as
we saw earlier,[91] Hartle and Hawking in their attempt to combine
quantum with gravitational theory were led to the idea that the
further one goes back along the ordinary 'real' timescale the more it
has to be replaced by a new parameter which includes also a
mathematically 'imaginary' component (i.e., one involving i, the
square root of -1). According to Hawking,[92] using this 'time', involving an imaginary component, leads to the disappearance of the
distinction between time and space. Furthermore, space-'time' (this
imaginary time) proved to be finite in extent and yet 'have no
singularities that formed a boundary or edge'.[93] This conceptualiza-
tion, it must be remembered, is still highly controversial, is not
widely accepted by physicists and still does not have a basis in a
properly formulated quantum theory of gravity. According to this
speculation:

> There would be no singularities at which the laws of science broke
> down and no edge of space-time at which one would have to appeal to
> God or some new law to set the boundary conditions for space-time.
> One could say: 'The boundary condition of the universe is that it has no
> boundary'. The universe would be completely self-contained and not
> affected by anything outside itself. It would neither be created or
> destroyed. It would just BE.[94]

By the point at which biological organisms appeared on the Earth,
the postulated imaginary component in Hartle and Hawking's physical time would have diminished to insignificance in their theory. So,
with this cosmology, we are still free to employ the concept of the
personal to interpret God's relation to the universe, which goes on

being created by God. Moreover, the mystery-of-existence question still has to be pressed for, as Hawking himself has put it,

> The usual approach of science of constructing a mathematical model cannot answer the questions of why there should be a universe for the model to describe. Why does the universe go to all the bother of existing? Is the unified theory so compelling that it brings about its own existence? Or does it need a creator, and, if so, does he have any other effect on the universe? And who created him?[95]

To Hawking's question 'Does it [the universe] need a creator?', we have been urging the answer 'yes' on the grounds that, from the existence of the kind of universe we actually have, considered in the light of the natural sciences, we do infer the existence of a creator God as the best explanation of all-that-is. We have, so far, been attempting to discern more accurately the character and attributes of this creator God. But his further question 'Does he [a creator God] have any other effect [other than creating it] on the universe?' calls for more deliberation. For it is to the inability of twentieth-century, scientifically educated, human beings even to conceive of how such a creator God could plausibly interact with, act in or through, the regular lawlike world, which they believe the sciences to have established as fact, that disbelief in even the existence of a creator God is widely attributed. So we turn, in the next chapter, to the question of God's interaction with the world.

CHAPTER 9

God's Interaction with the World

1 THE CONTEMPORARY DISCUSSION

a 'The God Who Acts'

Various modes of interaction of God with the world have engaged the faith and attention of believers in God down the ages and some of these have already been part of our concerns. They may, following M. J. Langford,[1] conveniently be classified into:

1 The creative activity of God.
2 The sustaining activity of God.
3 God's action as final cause.
4 'General providence'.
5 'Special providence'.
6 Miracles.

Langford illustrates the distinctions involved in this classification by instancing three ways in which a leader and guide of a climbing party can control events. There is, he suggests, the initial planning of the expedition, corresponding to 1 and 2. Then there is the actual leading of the party up the rock face, the control that involves the smooth and predictable running of the climb, corresponding to 3 and 4. Finally, there is the exercise of leadership in the *ad hoc* actions and decisions in emergencies which, though perhaps predictable in general, are not so in detail, corresponding to 5 and 6.

Insofar as God may be conceived of in personal terms and may be regarded as having purposes which he is working out in the world, category 3 can be subsumed into the others, for they all imply purposive action on the part of God. Reasons for affirming the creative and sustaining activities (1 and 2) of God in the natural, evolving world have already been given in chapter 8, and there are those who regard these as an adequate representation of all of God's activity in the world and doubt the need for the other categories at all. Thus John Macquarrie affirms that the doctrine of general providence (4) in the form that 'asserts that the same God who gave the world being continues to govern its affairs' is 'just another way of asserting his constant creating and sustaining energy', for creation is not to be thought of as a past event with God as 'a kind of absentee landlord who set things going long ago and now leaves the world to its own devices'.[2] This latter has also been the contention of chapter 8 above, with its emphasis on God's immanent creative presence in the natural world; but, we have to ask, does it follow that assertion of the reality of God's creative and sustaining energy exonerates us from any further decision about or analysis of God's interaction with world?

Christoph Schwöbel has urged that 'talk about divine providence does not add anything to our understanding of divine agency as the work of God, Father, Son and Holy Spirit' – that is, apart from, as he argues, God's 'creative and sustaining activity, apart from God's agency in Christ and apart from God's agency in the inspiration of the Holy Spirit'.[3] In this context by divine providence Schwöbel means, along the same lines as Macquarrie,

(1) Apart from what can be said about creation, redemption and salvation, there is a divine ordering of events in the ordination of all things to an end and this applies generally to the way things go in the world, as well as specifically to the way things go in my own life. (2) This divine ordering can (at least to some extent) be discerned in the course of worldly events ... what we mean by 'providence' concerns the correlation of our understanding of divine agency with our experience of the way things go in the world.[4]

Such a belief in divine providence is founded existentially on Christian experience, indeed on religious experience in general, and forms the presupposition of prayer, worship and the daily lives of believers in God. It is not therefore to be summarily dismissed and subsumed under the more abstract categories of the creative and sustaining activity of God. In any case the problems it raises concerning *how* God can actually interact with a world that is increasingly describable in scientific, psychological, sociological and historical terms also underlie any notion of God's immanent creative and sustaining activity in the world, as well as his activity in those more individual and personal contexts.

But the discernment ((2) in the above quotation from Schwöbel) of both the 'divine ordering of events in the ordination of all things to an end' (1) in 'the way things go in the world' and of 'the way things go in my own life' (1) are notoriously obscure and incapable of clear verification, in this life, at least. God's act of *creatio ex nihilo*, of giving being to all-that-is, must in principle remain ultimately ineffable and mysterious, so that tendering possible models of and analogies for this act, as we shall, is all that is possible. However, this prescinding of God's ultimate act of creation from the requirement to explain *how* God creates does not apply so obviously to the other postulated kinds of divine action. Now the affirmations that God is continuously acting creatively in the world through its natural processes, that he acts to redeem and save in history and that he shapes the course of individual lives are all central to Christian belief. Their very plausibility and intelligibility is widely questioned today in the light of, it is often claimed, that scientific perspective which we have been elaborating. The examination of this issue is more central to our concerns here than whether or not the traditional term 'providence' has any continuing usefulness. Only if we think it plausible that events in nature, society, history and individuals might be intelligibly and plausibly regarded as in any sense the results of *God's* interaction with them would it become worthwhile to speak of 'providence' in the general course of events (4 above) or in special, particular clusters of events (5 and possibly 6 above). Even then we would still have to admit our difficulty in unambiguously discerning what God was doing.

There can be little doubt of the centrality of this question for the plausibility of belief in the God of the Judeo-Christian tradition. For the worship of both Jews and Christians affords a prominent place for the reading of their scriptures, much of which consists of narrative interpreted as the actions of God in history to which the worshipper is invited to attend as exemplifying the nature and character of the God active in those events and still active today. Vernon White has, somewhat uncompromisingly, described as the 'demands of revelation regarding the nature, scope and efficacy of God's activity in the world' that we do not ignore the biblical account of God as one who 'acts personally, universally, with priority and sovereign efficacy; he acts in relation to particular events in which he finds ends as well as means.'[5] In a somewhat more detached vein, Langford summarizes the Old Testament as giving 'continual testimony to belief in an intensely active and personal God, one who both provides for and governs the world',[6] and he concludes also that the New Testament presents a portrait of an intensely personal and active God, which is the foundation of the Christian doctrine of special providence... the actual words and actions of Jesus are the most important examples. Apart from the allegedly miraculous episodes, these are manifestly 'natural', in the sense that they illustrate the use of nature rather than its suspension, but on a Christian interpretation they are all particular manifestations of the love of God himself.[7]

The biblical themes have constituted one of the principal formative strands in Christian theology – though, it must be stressed, not the only ones. Nevertheless their continued influence is obvious even in a post-Christian country such as modern Britain, when a lightning strike on an ancient cathedral is seriously interpreted by certain Christian ministers as an act of God in which he is showing his disapproval of the beliefs of a theologian recently consecrated therein as a bishop! More seriously, with both greater sophistication and immensely more scholarship, for a decade or so after the end of the Second World War, there was dominant in Western Protestant Christianity a 'biblical theology' which, while certainly not fundamentalist, held to 'a doctrine of unique historical revelation through God's self-declaring actions.... God is known through the particular acts in which he shapes the history of Israel and redeems all of humankind.'[8] Their emphasis is apparent even in the titles of the books of major exponents of this biblical theology, such as *God Who Acts: Biblical Theology as Recital* (G. Ernest Wright, 1952) and *The Book of the Acts of God* (Reginald H. Fuller, 1957). However, as Thomas Tracy has put it, 'Biblical theology has crumbled under a number of pressures.'[9] For, when pressed to say what God has actually done in the supposed 'mighty acts' that biblical theologians find in the Scriptures, the answers turn out to be accounts of what the ancient Hebrews, or the early Christians, *believed* God to have done. The biblical theologians accepted that nothing outside the usual laws of nature or the processes of history would have been recorded from the viewpoint of one without faith – they would have been, as Langdon Gilkey put it in a key article deflating the claims of biblical theology, 'epistemologically indistinguishable from other events for those without faith'. But, as he continues,

for those of faith it must be objectively or ontologically different from other events. Otherwise, there is no mighty act, but only our belief in it... Only an ontology of events specifying what God's relation to ordinary events is like, and thus what his relation to special events might be, could fill the now empty analogy of mighty acts, *void since the denial of the miraculous.*[10]

The italicized phrase reminds us that the biblical theologians adopted that scepticism concerning the occurrence of 'miracles', in the sense of events 'breaking the laws of nature', which is characteristic of our scientific age. The point now is not whether or not they were right to do this, but that the whole exercise of 'biblical theology' as an exposition of God's acts in history was based on theological and philosophical presuppositions which had not been adequately examined. As Gilkey puts it,

> When we use the analogies 'mighty act', 'unique revelatory event', or 'God speaks to his people', therefore, we must understand what we might mean in systematic theology by the general activity of God. Unless we have some conception of how God acts in ordinary events, we can hardly know what our analogical words mean when we say: 'He acts uniquely in this event' or 'this event is a special divine deed.'[11]

So the question now is: 'What kind of conception of how God acts in or, more generally, interacts with, the world can we possibly have in the light of scientific perspectives on that world – the presuppositions of which also underlie our scientific, psychological, sociological and historical explanations of events in human experience?' We are concerned with human experience as well as events in the natural, non-human world, for if God is presumed to interact with human beings, then these interactions eventually have to take the form of changes in ourselves (including our brains) as we initiate actions that would have been otherwise but for God's influence. To some recent attempts to answer this question and to a re-examination of the implications of scientific perspectives we must now turn.

b Presuppositions

Consideration of how God might plausibly be conceived of as interacting with the world has for over three centuries been largely coloured by two presuppositions which were taken to be either as validated by the world-view of the natural sciences or, at least, as being implications of it. It would not be too strong to aver that these were two ghosts that still haunt some theological thinking even of recent decades. I refer to (1) the understanding of the natural world basically as a mechanism, controlled by inviolable 'laws of nature', deterministic and therefore, 'in principle' at least, predictable; and (2) the dualist assumption that human beings consist of two entities – mind and body – and that these represent two different orders of reality, sometimes denoted respectively as 'matter' and 'spirit', whose relationship, admittedly problematical, mysterious even, is regarded as exemplified in the human experience of being an agent.

With presupposition (1), it is not possible to conceive of God's interaction with the world, other than his general and perpetual sustaining of it in existence, except in terms of God 'intervening' in the natural course of events. That is, God is regarded as bringing about results which would have been otherwise in the absence of such 'interventions' by God, namely exemplifications of the law-determined processes which the sciences reveal. I have inserted the single inverted commas here, and occasionally later around the verb to 'intervene' and its derivatives when applied to God's action in the world, because I believe there is some ambiguity about its meaning. For example, David Brown[12] is very concerned to defend theism against a 'deism' characterized as 'belief in a non-interventionist God', for he believes that 'for certain types of religious experience such a ['interventionist'] framework is essential' and argues, for example, that 'the argument [for belief in God] from religious experience is only effective when appeal is made to the type of experiences for which such a framework is essential'. However, I have considerable reservations about the use of 'intervention' on the part of God as that which distinguishes deism from theism, as if 'theism', on the contrary, necessarily involves God 'intervening' in his created world as a kind of *deus ex machina* interrupting other-wise orderly created processes.

It seems to me that what Brown wishes to argue for (*inter alia* the validity of religious experience as above, and later on in his extensive work, the doctrines of the Incarnation and the Trinity) depends on God being conceived of as in continuous *interaction* with and a continual influence on the created order, in general, and human experience, in particular – rather than on God 'intervening' in any way disruptive of the natural and human processes he has created. As I hope will become clear, it is possible to think of this continual, and effective, interaction of God with the world in ways that are not crudely 'interventionist' in the manner I have just depicted, yet can still serve to underpin the doctrines Brown is rightly, in my view, concerned to defend.

This is also the view of William P. Alston who, in a very clarifying article,[13] reflects that:

> Many people think, and I myself at one time thought, that the belief that God enters into active interaction with his creatures, a belief crucial to the Judeo-Christian tradition, requires us to suppose that God directly intervenes in the world, acting outside the course of nature ... Just by virtue of creating and sustaining the natural order God is in as active contact with his creatures as one would wish ... If God speaks to me, or guides me, or enlightens me by the use of natural causes, he is as surely in active contact with me as if he had produced the relevant effects by direct fiat ... After all, when one human being directly interacts with another ... the agent is making use of aspects of the natural order ... And surely this does not imply that we are not in active contact with each other in such transactions. However necessary direct intervention may be for the authentication of messengers, it is not required for genuine divine-human interaction.[14]

For Alston (it is interesting to note in relation to our subsequent discussion), 'when we speak of 'special' acts of God, the specialness attaches to our talking rather than to the action itself ... Our account is rather in terms of how the subject is thinking about the matter, what the subject believes about it ... it is only the demarcation of 'special' acts of God that is made to rest on human reactions. Members of this class share with innumerable other happenings the objective feature of being acts of God, a feature that attaches to them however we think, feel, or experience!'[15]

Those who share 'interventionist' views seem to be assuming that if God is 'omnipotent', then he has the power to achieve particular purposes, to 'set aside' his own laws operative in the world he has created. So, what can be said to constitute God's knowledge and power is pertinent to this issue.

c Objections to Divine 'Intervention'

There have been weighty objections to such a picture of God as *deus ex machina*; some of the relevant considerations[16] are as follows.

1 The idea of an 'intervening' God appears to presuppose that God is in some sense 'outside' the created world and has in some way, not specified, to come back into it to achieve his purposes. Yet we

have already found good reason why the presence and immanence of God within the created order needs to be re-emphasized. A mechanistic view of the world inevitably engenders, as it did in the eighteenth century, a deistic view of God and of his relation to it.

2 The very notion of God as the faithful source of rationality and regularity in the created order appears to be undermined if one simultaneously wishes to depict his action as *both* sustaining the 'laws of nature' that express his divine will for creation *and* at the same time intervening to act in ways abrogating these very laws – almost as if he had second thoughts about whether he can achieve his purposes in what he has created. Even if one conceives of these 'interventions' as rare, as made only for significant purposes such as, say, the education of humanity in God's ways or for the revelation of his purposes, one still faces the question of whether it is a coherent way to think of God's action in the world in the light of other insights into the nature of God of the kind we were formulating in the last chapter.

This theological unease about the concept of an intervening God has been very well expressed by David Jenkins in his Hensley Henson Lectures:

> it ... becomes clear that the God who is held to be in some decisive sense the author of the whole [human] story, in some real sense the basic presence in and animateur of the whole story, and in some truly imposing sense the purpose and possibility of the entire story, when and if it reaches its end – that this God cannot and ought not to be thought of ... as if he were the supreme *controller* of the universe who *manages* its affairs by a series of direct interventions for which he alone is responsible and to which response is inevitable in a cause-and-effect way.[17]

3 Furthermore, one has to recognize, with Hume, that adequate historical evidence for such a contravention of the originally divinely established laws of nature could never, in practice, be forthcoming. *Ex hypothesi* the 'laws' are themselves statements of both regularities in sequences of events (as Hume saw them) and also expressions of underlying fundamental relationships and realities (as modern science more frequently sees them). So one would need vastly *more* evidence for the occurrence of any event supposed to have contravened such 'laws of nature' than for one not thought to be doing so – and it is of the nature of our fragmentary historical (even contemporary) evidence that this cannot be forthcoming. Any

favourable assessment that the historical evidence could indeed be interpreted as evidence for a divine 'intervention' would clearly be sensitively dependent on the degree to which the assessor believed *a priori* in the possibility of such 'intervention' ever occurring. Scientists who are theists still find it difficult to conceive of such 'interventions' except as very rare occurrences indeed – and, even then, often prefer to regard such supposed interventions of God in the world's processes and events as manifesting the existence of 'higher laws' or a 'profounder rationality' than have yet become clear to us.

4 There are, of course, also well-known moral objections to simplistic ideas concerning God's intervening in events, both in the natural world and in human affairs, that have to be regarded in retrospect as inimical to human life and welfare. If God *can* intervene consistently with his own being and purposes, why did he not do so to avert disasters in the world of nature or human history, floods in Bangladesh or concentration camps in Auschwitz? Some, like David Jenkins, feel very strongly about this:

> A God who uses the openness of his created universe, the openness and freedom of men and women created in his image and the mystery of his own risky and creative love to insert additional causal events from time to time into that universe to produce particular events or trends by that eventuality alone would be a meddling demigod, a moral monster and a contradiction of himself.... God is not an arbitrary meddler nor an occasional fixer. This is morally intolerable, and no appeal to the mysteriousness of particularity or its scandal can overcome this... However he [God] interacts or transacts he cannot intervene as an additional and inserted and occasional historical cause.[18]

Not all (many did not) agree with such a forthright position, but Jenkins' remarks do serve to highlight the difficulty which many theists feel and which also leads many, if not to atheism, to wistful agnosticism.

To what extent are considerations such as those listed above dependent on presupposition 1 concerning a mechanistic, predictable lawlike universe as the world-view authenticated by the sciences, and indeed also by the commonsense interpretation of events in human affairs? It will emerge that this is not the world-view licensed by the sciences, at least, and to this extent the whole debate takes on a new slant.

d *The Analogy to Personal Agency and Dualism*

Meanwhile we need also to look briefly at presupposition 2 in the 'intervening' model for God's action in the world, that of a dualistic interpretation of human nature and, specifically, of mental experience. That God is not to be conceived of as a 'God of the gaps' in our knowledge of the natural, including the human, world is widely agreed – for such a 'god' has the habit of shrinking to nothingness as our knowledge increases. A parallel set of considerations has deterred many theologians from thinking of God as First Cause if 'cause' in this attribution means a cause within the natural nexus of linked events. It has been generally thought that, insofar as God may be said to be causally related to all-that-is, it is in the way that a personal agent may be regarded as causing things to happen by realizing intentions in action. So it is that the affirmation of the notion that God can and does act in the world has been modelled on the relation of human intentionality, will and purposes to human action in our bodies and through them to the world at large, the world of entities and processes described by the sciences. A dualistic view of human nature qualifies neatly, it has seemed traditionally, as a suitable model for the relation of God to the world. The ultimate ineffability, mysteriousness and transcendence of God appears to be properly analogous to that parallel mystery concerning the nature of human consciousness, a property of that purported distinct entity, the 'mind'.

Two of the distinguished attempts in recent years – those of Schubert Ogden[19] and Gordon Kaufman[20] – to resolve the problem of how God acts in the world have relied on this analogy of divine to personal agency. However, both are vulnerable to the criticism[21] of resting too heavily on an implicitly dualist, Cartesian even, account of human nature and so of human agency. As Thomas Tracy puts it,

> The disconcerting thrust of such criticism is that the person concepts at work in these proposals are philosophically problematic at just those points where they appear to be most useful theologically.... Both Ogden and Kaufman seem to trade on a strong distinction (though not necessarily the same distinction) between the agent and his body as the basis for talk of a God who can be distinguished from the world but who acts upon or through it.[22]

Whether or not these criticisms of these particular authors are justified to the extent these remarks of Tracy suggest is less important for us at this stage than that we recognize the critical sensitivity of talk about God's action in the world to the wider philosophical discussion concerning the nature of human action[23] and the mind/body problem.[24] But those wider discussions have been strongly influenced by scientific developments which thereby alter greatly not only the context of theological discussion but the very plausibility even of some of these relatively recent offerings.

e How?

A major problem created for belief in God is generated by this scientific milieu which, quite properly, presses on the theist the question 'How can one conceive of God acting in the world?' The contemporary sceptic expects, again quite reasonably, that any analogies the theist may wish to make between God's action(s) in the world and human agency should, for them to be intelligible and plausible, be consistent with our best knowledge of that agency. As we shall see later in this chapter, there are grounds for thinking that presuppositions 1 and 2 are no longer warranted by science, so that the whole question of God's action in the world is ripe for reassessment – not least because we now have to ask how God might act in a lawful universe in which 'much of the order arises from the aggregate properties of random events.'[25]

But to ask 'How does God act in the world?' is a more complex question than first appears. Owen Thomas[26] has usefully distinguished the following senses of 'how?' relevant to this question:

A By what means?
B In what way or manner?
C To what effect?
D With what meaning or for what reason or purpose?
E To what extent or degree?
F On analogy with what?

The different positions adopted with respect to how God acts in the world address different combinations, or only one, of these various senses of 'How?'. They also differ, as Thomas points out,[27] in the extent to which they are analogies or theories (metaphysical analyses of the relation of divine activity to processes and events in the created order), or combinations of both – or neither, for example the 'two perspectives and languages' approach.[28]

Thomas further provides[29] a succinct and helpful analysis of the various approaches to this question which have been offered classically and in recent theological studies.[30] The reader is referred to his analysis, for it is not our aim here to provide a an overview of the whole discussion but to highlight any repercussions upon it of the twentieth-century scientific perspective. Nevertheless it will be helpful, for clarity, to set the scene by reproducing his classification and some of his comments (quotations are from his chapter 14, see n. 10).

f Views on Divine Action

Apart from the two-languages approach, the following distinct positions need to be considered.

Personal action (addressing 'how?', F above)   'based on the analogy of human personal action in the world as elaborated in the philosophy of action', already discussed in relation to the views of Ogden and Kaufman.[31] This approach is not really offering any explanation, or theory, of God's action. It is indeed an analogy employed in all of the other approaches (including that of 'biblical theology'), though in ways that differ with regard to the aspect of human action that is stressed. The possibility of particular divine actions occurring is given credibility by this analogy, but it can help in addressing the 'how?' questions A to E only if it spells out far more than most authors have attempted *how* human intentions and purposes, as described in mentalistic language, can take effect in the physical system of the human brain and body, and thereby in the world at large. In other words, the analogy can reduce to mere assertion of the claimed similarity between human and divine action unless there is further clarification of the position assumed on such matters as the nature of the human person, the mind-body problem and the philosophy of human action.

Primary cause (addressing 'how?', A and E above)   'God as primary cause acts in and through all other secondary causes in nature and history. . . . In its traditional form this view is a complex theory with the occasional use of the artisan-instrument analogy [of human action]. In its liberal form [e.g., Kaufman[32]] it is neither a theory nor an analogy but simply an affirmation'. Particular divine actions do occur, according to this view.

Process theology (addressing 'how?', A, B, E and F above)[33] 'holds that God acts in all events by influence or persuasion. By being prehended or experienced God offers an initial aim to each emerging event, which aim may be accepted in varying degrees... The analogies offered are those of self-body, mind-brain, and self-constitution.' Particular divine actions do occur, according to this view.

Uniform action (certainly addressing 'how?', E and, less clearly, B above)   'God's action in the world is understood as uniform and universal, and [in the form proposed by M. Wiles[34]] the appearance of particular divine activity is given by the variety of human response.' No *particular* divine actions can be said to occur on this view. This approach merits fuller discussion for it has been specifically propounded to meet the considerations of section c (1 to 4) which tell so heavily against any model of God's action in the world whereby God is said to 'intervene' in some explicit sense in the course of ordinary events. It is supported as a currently defensible view in the light of these considerations which otherwise would seem fatal to traditional views, and certainly to those of 'biblical theology' (which, it must be admitted, is the assumption of most expository sermons!).

The authors who propose various nuanced versions of this 'uniform action' approach seem to hold the presuppositions to which we earlier referred – namely those of a law-governed, determinist world (1) and an implicitly dualist account of human nature (2).[35] This is an assumption which they share with the proponents of other views such as the postulate of a primary cause and process theology. Consequently, with intervention by God in the events of the deterministic world of presupposition 1 becoming implausible, the analogy for God's action provided by the dualistic human model of presupposition 2 involves such a sharp dichotomy between God and the world that no *continuing* interaction of God with, or action of God in, the world becomes at all intelligible. So it is not surprising that authors sharing these presuppositions tend to gravitate in their conclusions towards affirming, as the *only* action of God, his 'one' act of creation and sustaining of all-that-is, his giving of being and keeping in being of the universe.

Thus for Kaufman the 'whole complicated and intricate teleological movement of all nature and history should be regarded as a single all-encompassing act of God.'[36] Maurice Wiles in his Bampton Lectures for 1986[37] affirms, in agreement with these authors, that the idea of divine action should be in relation to the world as a whole rather than particular occurrences in it . . .

For the theist, who is necessarily committed to a unitary view of the world, the whole process of the bringing into being of the world, which is still going on, needs to be seen as one action of God . . .

. . . we can make best sense of this whole complex of experience and of ideas if we think of the whole continuing creation of the world as God's one act, an act in which he allows radical freedom to his human creation. The nature of such a creation . . . is incompatible with the assertion of further particular divinely initiated acts within the developing history of the world.

g An 'Ontological Gap' at the 'Causal Joint'?

The trouble with this conclusion of these authors, explicitly and frankly spelt above out by Wiles, is not only the bleak prospect it holds out for the life of the individual in his or her relation to God in their lives, but its close dependence on presuppositions 1 and 2 which are themselves questionable and, as I shall argue, have no support in the natural sciences. It is indeed difficult to imagine *how* God might be an agent in a world conceived of as ruled by deterministic laws at all levels when the only analogy for such agency has itself been formulated in dualistic terms that involve a gap dividing action in the 'body', and so in the natural world, from intentions and other acts of the 'mind'. This is an *ontological* gap between two kinds of entities across which it is difficult to see how in principle a bridge could be constructed. Use of the analogy of human action does not exonerate the theologian from entering into the very fraught issue of how mental acts might be conceived of as issuing in, indeed even *being*, processes in the human body and thereby in the natural world. This is a somewhat daunting task, it must be admitted. But it does seem to be the case that, just at this crucial point, theologians expounding apparently very different understandings of how God acts in the world, or of whether he does so or does not do so, tend to resort to just assertion that there *is* such a link in the case of human action and that the link in God's action is analogically similar. They make such assertions usually without saying anything about human action itself, which illuminates *how* God might be conceived of exercising his influence on events in the world.

This omission is not confined to those holding the 'uniform action' position. For example, Austin Farrer's treatment[38] of the notion of God as agent – his use of the concept of 'double agency' – has been regarded[39] as one of the best attempts to say what talk of God's action might be understood to mean. The notion of double agency asserts that events in the world (natural events and human actions) can be regarded as both acts of God and those of finite agencies:

> two agencies of different level taking effect in the same finite action, the finite agency which lives in it, the infinite agency which founds it ... On the theistic hypothesis everything that is done in this world by intelligent creatures is done with two meanings: the meaning of the creature in acting, the meaning of the Creator in founding or support-ing that action ... Where the creature concerned is non-intelligent there are not two meanings, for only the Creator has a meaning or intention. But there are still two doings; it is the act of the Creator that the creature should either act or be there to act.[40]

However, advocacy of this paradox[41] comes perilously close to that mere assertion of its truth already criticized, since Farrer on his own admission can give no account of the 'causal joint' between the agency of the Creator and even human action:

> The causal joint (could there be said to be one) between God's action and ours is of no concern in the activity of religion. ... Both the divine and the human actions remain real and therefore free in the union between them; not knowing the modality of the divine action we cannot pose the problem of their mutual relation.[42]

The problem is, as Wiles stresses, that 'We do not understand the modality of the divine action in a way which enables us to define its relation to our finite human acting.'[43] But if this is the case for the interaction of the divine with the human, which is at least intuitively intelligible by analogy with personal interaction, it is *a fortiori* harder to conceive of the 'causal joint' between the divine and natural non-human events. The hiatus in his exposition frankly admitted by Farrer in the above quotation is also to be found in other recent authors.

For example, Michael Langford[44] works with the idea of God, in his 'general providence', intelligently planning and governing events in a continuing way. The divine 'steering' of nature to fulfil God's purposes he sees as also applying to 'specific events rather than to general movements'. This 'special providence shares with general providence the idea of intelligent control'.[45] But Langford chooses to be 'agnostic about the methods by which God acts, assuming that he does so'.[46] He is properly 'wary of the request for an account of the "mechanism" of his [God's] action, since this may suggest that whatever the manner may be, it must be akin to the way in which one part of a machine works on another part'.[47] He then employs the 'fruitful image'[48] of God as creative artist.[49] However, although he considers that this analogy does 'bring out some of the meaning of the idea of [God as] 'steering' nature',[50] yet it still does not, and is not meant to, 'indicate how God initiates change'.[51]

This is also the position of Vernon White, who asserts that 'if we can and must accept in human experience the hidden causal efficacy of human intention in physical action, without knowing its precise causal modality, then we can surely affirm by analogy the hidden causal efficacy of divine intention on creaturely activity without knowing its modality.'[52] This is true as far as it goes, the analogy does help us to conceive *that* God might act in the world, but does not render the notion at all plausible without more spelling out of the analogy. This requires supplementary conceptual resources that explicate human action to make the idea of God's acting in the physical world at all clear. For without some plausible (certainly not mechanistic) account of *how* God might interact with the causal nexus of individual events in the world, including human-brains-in-human-bodies, we cannot with integrity assert that God does, or might, do so.[53]

This absence of explication of the causal joint is also the weak point of Vincent Brummer's otherwise admirable treatment of *What Are We Doing When We Pray?*[54] In the course of an analysis of divine agency and natural law, Brummer has to resort to a rhetorical question at the crucial point:

> By our actions we cause contingent events by bringing about con-
> ditions necessary for them which would otherwise be subject to
> chance. But if human persons can intervene in the course of nature in
> this way, why cannot God do so as well? Divine action in the world
> need therefore not take the form of miraculous intervention in viola-
> tion of the natural order, any more than human action need do so.[55]

The analogy referred to in the question in this quotation has, as we have seen, often been used as the basis for arguing that God, supposedly like us, on presuppositions 1 and 2, *does* 'intervene' in the world. The mere assertion of the analogy to human action without any further explication of it, and so also analogically of divine action, leaves us still sceptical of the mere possibility of the latter. For we experience our intentions becoming actions in the physical world as a basic feature of our existence, but in the case of all events in the world other than those we initiate we observe only the events themselves and not God as such intending or acting in them. So we cannot use *our* experience as such for saying that God does actually act in these other, vastly more numerous, non-human natural events – whatever other good grounds there might be for supposing that there is such a continuously creating Reality which we name as God. We need further grounds for the plausibility of such an assertion.

For all these authors the notion of God as personal agent remains central to the whole concept of God, as we have also seen already in chapters 7 and 8, and to the widespread human experience of relationship to God being *personal*. These concepts and convictions therefore remain vulnerable to the criticism that the analogy from human agency to divine action cannot do the work it is intended to do – namely render the idea of God acting in the world intelligible – in the absence of any spelling out of the 'causal joint' in *both* human *and* divine action in the world. It is to the absence of this explication of the 'causal joint' that we must attribute the fact that so many contemporary theologians have to resort simply to the assertion that God *does* act in the world with no further attempt to make the idea intelligible other that drawing the analogy to human agency.

It is therefore important to examine if new scientific perspectives throw any light on the deterministic and dualist presuppositions 1 and 2 relevant to the question of the 'causal joint'.

2 How God Might Interact with the World in the Perspectives of Science

In chapter 8 we recognized a number of significant ways in which our scientific understanding of what is in the world and of what has been and is going on in it has modified, indeed enriched, our reasons for believing in God as Creator of that world, and what we are to mean by 'God' – that is, our understanding of various aspects of such a God's relation to the created world and what that relation implies about the nature of God. We saw *inter alia* that the intelligibility of the natural world pointed to the basic rationality of God as Creator; the regularity of its processes to the divine faithfulness to the created order; and the continuity of these processes and their emergent character to the continuing immanence of the divine creative activity. We saw also how the omnipotence and om-niscience of God had to be understood with important qualifications of the way they have been interpreted both by many philosophers of religion and by traditional piety. The way of regarding these essential attributes of God that most commended itself was seeing God as having a self-appointed vulnerability towards the events and processes of the world in the creation of which there had been a self-emptying (*kenosis*) by God's own self. If, as we argued, the source of the being of the world is other than itself, then we inferred that the 'best explanation' of that world is a creator God who must be at least personal and who possesses a mode of rationality creative of and exploratory in new possibilities in the world. But now we have to inquire if scientific perspectives on the world can make any contribution to our conceiving of how God so described might interact with that world.

a Unpredictability, Open-endedness, Flexibility and Propensities

Although the natural sciences have traditionally concerned themselves with the regular, predictable, law-governed phenomena of the natural world, they have had to recognize in the twentieth century that there are systems, at every level of complexity, whose future development is unpredictable. These were:[56] subatomic systems, at the ('Heisenberg') micro-level; many-bodied Newtonian systems at the micro-level of description; and non-linear dynamical systems at the macroscopic level.[57] Awareness of the existence of this last-mentioned category is relatively recent in spite of the wide range of situations that are unpredictable in this way – for example, turbulent liquids, some networks of chemical reactions or of neurones and the weather. It must be stressed that the non-linear, macroscopic, open systems in question are as deterministic at the micro-level as any 'classical' system. Their unpredictability at the macro-level results from the nature of the solutions to the mathematical equations that govern the behaviour of these systems as a whole, and from their sensitivity to initial conditions.

Thus the world looks less and less like the deterministic mechanism that has been the presupposition (1 on p. 147 above) of much theological reflection on God's action in the world since Newton. It is now seen to possess a degree of openness and flexibility within a lawlike framework so that certain developments are irreducibly unpredictable and we have good reasons for saying, from the relevant science and mathematics, that this unpredictability will remain.

We also saw that the historical course of natural development manifested a kind of rising curve of such unpredictability at the macroscopic level, especially in the open-endedness of the biological evolutionary development and ultimately in the increasing freedom of conscious organisms. The most immediate and notable instance of the latter is, of course, the experience of human freedom which one is strongly inclined to associate with the non-linear far-from-equilibrium dynamical complexity of the neuronal network constituting the human brain.

The history of the relation between the natural sciences and the Christian religion affords many instances of the gap in human ability to give causal explanations, that is, instances of unpredictability, being exploited by theists as evidence of the presence and activity of God who thereby filled the explanatory gap. But the advance of the natural sciences showed just how vulnerable was such a 'God of the gaps', as science gradually filled these supposed opportunities in which such a 'god' could flex his 'omnipotent' muscles. But we now have to reckon with a new irreducible kind of unpredictability in systems such as those mentioned above and so with a new flexibility in the events occurring in such systems – *rigid* determinism no more universally rules at the macroscopic level than it does, as recognized since the 1920s, at the subatomic level.

We therefore have to take account of, as it were, permanent gaps in our ability to predict events in the natural world. Should we propose a 'God of the *unpredictable* gaps'? There would then be no fear of such a God being squeezed out by increases in scientific knowledge. But this raises two further theological questions: (1) 'Does *God* know the outcome of these situations that are unpredictable to us?', and (2) 'Does God act within the flexibility of these situations to effect his will?' As regards question 1, his omniscience might be such that he would know and be able to track the minutiae of the fluctuations, unpredictable and unobservable by us, whose amplification leads at the macroscopic level to one outcome rather that another, also unpredictable by us. Only if we answered question 1 affirmatively (i.e., if we thought of God, even if not we ourselves, as being able to predict the outcome of any initial conditions) could we then go on to postulate that God could act to change the initiating, subsequently amplified, fluctuation event so as to bring about a macroscopic consequence conforming to his will and purposes – that is, also to answer question 2 affirmatively. God would then be conceived of as acting, as it were, 'within' the flexibility of these unpredictable situations in a way that, in principle, could never be detectable by us. Such a mode of divine action would always be consistent with our scientific knowledge of the situation, which itself includes our recognition of only a limited ability to predict on our part, and sometimes of a total inability to do so. If this were the case, God would be conceived of as actually manipulating quanta, atoms and molecules in these initiating fluctuations in the natural world in order to produce the results that he wills. This seems to be the argument of John Polkinghorne in *Science and Providence*, where he, rightly in my view, stresses that 'the concept of divine immanence helps us to understand something of the scope of God's activity'.[58] But, although he has just quoted approvingly the statement of John V. Taylor in *The Go-between God*, to the effect that 'the hand of God ... must be found not in isolated intrusions, not in any gaps, but in the process itself',[59] Polkinghorne nevertheless thinks that the 'notion of flexible process helps us to see where there might be room for divine manoeuvre, within the limits of divine faithfulness'.[60] His subsequent contention that God's immanent action will always lie hidden in those complexes whose precarious balance makes them unsusceptible to prediction'[61] seems to me to be vulnerable to the criticism that this is simply God putting what could only be called an 'intervening' finger into those, to us, unclosable gaps in the predictability of the natural world manifest particularly in the form of (often complex) non-linear systems. On this understanding, God would himself both have to be able to predict the outcome of his actions within the 'flexible process' and also actually to make some micro-event, subsequently amplified, to be other than it would have been if left to itself to follow its own natural course, without the involvement of divine action. This is the dilemma if God is conceived of as acting in some way *within* the processes at their micro-level, that is by the 'isolated intrusions' that John Taylor precludes.[62]

Such a conception of God's action in these, to us, unpredictable situations would then be no different in principle from the idea of God intervening in a deterministic, rigidly law-controlled, mechanistic order of nature of the kind thought to be the consequence of Newtonian dynamics. The only difference, on this view, would seem to be that, given our irreducible incapacity to predict the histories of many natural systems, God's intervention (for that is what it would properly have to be called) would always be hidden from us, whereas previously, God's intervention in a mechanistic, rigidly law-controlled, world could always have been regarded as open to verification by us provided we could ascertain the natural laws usually operative. For then we would know what regularities were not being conformed to, what laws were, so to speak, being set aside.

Thus, although at first sight this introduction of an unpredictability, open-endedness and flexibility into our picture of the natural world seems to help us to suggest in new terminology how God might act in the world in its unclosable 'gaps', the above considerations indicate that such divine action would be just as much 'intervention' as it was when postulated in relation to a mechanistic world view. This analysis has, it must be stressed, been grounded on the assumption that God *does* know the outcome of natural situations that are unpredictable by us (i.e., on an affirmative answer to question 1). It assumes total divine omniscience and prescience about all natural events.

However, we have already[63] given reasons for regarding God's omniscience, at least in some respects, as 'self-limited'. This means that God does *not* know which of a million radium atoms will be the next to disintegrate in, say, the next 10^{-3} seconds and only (like ourselves) what the average number will be that will break up in a given time interval. The proposal of self-limiting omniscience means that God has so made the natural order that it is, in principle, impossible, for him and for us, to predict the outcomes of certain classes of events – which is what I take 'in principle' to mean in this context.[64] In other words if, in the above example, it is genuinely indeterminate which particular radium atom will break up in a particular given time interval, there would then be no question of God's being able to intervene in the micro-events at this level to influence the natural order. Not only these events at the subatomic level but a wide range of macroscopic events are also unpredictable in principle and therefore indeterminate.[65] It must be concluded that the outcomes of these kinds of macroscopic event cannot be known to God and their manipulation by God would then be impossible (in this universe with its actual created characteristics). There just does not exist any future, predictable state of such systems *for* God to know.

For such reasons, we earlier[66] propounded that God's omniscience and omnipotence must be regarded , in some respects, as 'self-limited'. This, we hinted, is the origin of the natural order possessing that genuine degree of open-endedness and unpredictability required for the interplay of chance and law in its creative processes and, eventually, for real human freedom to emerge. On this view God bestows a certain autonomy not only on human beings, as Christian theology has long recognized, but also on the natural order as such to develop in ways that God chooses not to control in detail. That natural order he allows a degree of open-endedness and flexibility which becomes the natural, structural basis for the flexibility of conscious organisms and, in due course, of the freedom of the human-brain-in-the-human-body, that is, of persons.

We concluded above that this new awareness of the unpredictability, open-endedness and flexibility inherent in many natural processes and systems does not, of itself, help directly to illuminate the 'causal joint' of how God acts in the world. But it does help us to perceive the natural world as a matrix within which openness and flexibility and, in humanity, freedom might naturally emerge. It also provides as apt context within which free persons can fruitfully act – namely one where there is regularity enough on which to base decisions and action but also one which provides unexpected challenges to conscious organisms and which is not so rigid that the exercise of creativity and spontaneity is impossible.

We saw in Part I[67] that the processes of the natural world displayed certain tendencies, some of them strong enough to be called *propensities* in the sense that Karl Popper has again recently brought to our notice.[68] These include propensities for an increase in complexity which is the basis for an increase in organization in living organisms, itself the basis for the emergence of consciousness and so of self-consciousness. These propensities must be regarded on any theistic interpretation of the universe as built-in and intended by God their Creator. So that, although we have had to infer that God cannot predict in detail the outcome of in-principle unpredictable situations, this does not derogate from his having purposes which are being implemented through the inbuilt propensities that load, as it were, the dice the throws of which shape the course of natural events. The world has, it seems, been so constituted, a theist would say 'created', that there is a kind of ratchet effect such that once a certain level of complexity, and then organization, and then consciousness and then self-consciousness has been attained, these form the 'launching pad', as it were, for the next exploration of new possibilities. And this movement continues even though retrogressions are still possible and, from time to time, actually occur. As D. J. Bartholomew puts it, 'God chose to make a world of chance

because it would have the properties necessary for producing beings fit for fellowship with himself.'[69]

In summary, it would seem that the new scientific awareness of
unpredictability, open-endedness and flexibility and of the inbuilt
propensities of natural processes to have particular kinds of outcomes show that the world we have is the kind that could be the
matrix in which free agents could develop; and that in itself it has
such a degree of open-endedness and flexibility that we are
justified[70] in attributing an exploratory character to God's continuing creative action. However, we also found that these features
of the world did not, in the end, help us very much in unravelling the
problem of how best to conceive of and articulate God's action in
the world, the question of the 'causal joint', much as they altered our
interpretation of the meaning of what is actually going on in that
world. Defining the problem as that of the 'causal joint' between God
and the world is inappropriate, for it does not do justice to the
many-levels in which causality operates in a world of complex
systems multiply interlocking at many levels and in many modes. It
is to this major feature of the world as perceived by the sciences
that we must now turn.

b Top-down Causation

We saw in Part I[71] that, in a number of natural situations, causality in
complex systems constituted of complex subsystems at various
levels of interlocking organization could best be understood as a
two-way process. Not only did events at the 'lower' levels in the
hierarchy of complexity in the long run (however slightly) influence
how the total inclusive system-as-a-whole behaved, but also the
state of the system-as-a-whole could itself properly be regarded as a
causal factor influencing events in the 'lower' subsystems, constraining them to follow one course rather than another. Now the events
at each particular level, or in each particular subsystem (whichever
way of speaking is appropriate to the particular situation, and sometimes it could be both) are explicated and described in language that
makes use, on the critical-realist view adopted here, of the concepts
which refer to the realities operative at those levels. This is true also
of the system-as-a-whole, so that real features of the total system-
as-a-whole may well be properly regarded as causative factors in,
constraints upon, events happening within the subsystems at lower
levels – events, which, it must be stressed, in themselves are describ-

able in terms of the sciences pertinent to that lower level. Thus we drew attention to the examples[72] of the seemingly coordinated movement, or chemical transformation, of individual molecules in, respectively, the hexagonal flowing 'cells' of Bénard convection in a liquid and the spatial organization of a previously homogeneous reaction system. In biological systems, especially, we noted[73] how such 'top-down' causation happens in evolution so that selective evolutionary processes may properly be regarded as the cause of changes that are established in the DNA of living organisms. We noted particularly[74] that such considerations were providing significant clues to how conscious brain states could be 'top-down' causes at the 'lower' level of neurones – and so conceivably of human actions stemming from brain states. This constitutes a new insight into the nature of human agency very pertinent to our central problem.

In the light of these features of the natural world, might we not properly regard the world-as-a-whole as a total system so that its general state can be a 'top-down' causative factor in, or constraint upon, what goes on at the myriad levels that comprise it? I suggest that these new perceptions of the way in which causality actually operates in our hierarchically complex world provides a new resource for thinking about how God could interact with that world. For it points to a way in which we could think of divine action making a difference in the world, yet not in any way contrary to those regularities and laws operative within the observed universe which are explicated by the sciences applicable to the level of complexity and organization in question. It also provides an appropriate and helpful model of how natural events, including the unpredictable ones and the outcome of freely-willed human decisions, could work their way up through the hierarchy of systems and contribute to the state of the whole. It therefore helps us to model more convincingly that interaction, dialogue even, between human decisions and actions, on the one hand, and divine intentions and purposes, on the other. It is in such a context that the significance of prayer, worship and the sacraments are rooted.

Attempts to hold together the notions of God's transcendence over the world, his ultimate otherness, with that of his immanent Presence in, with and under the world often find it helpful to deploy models of the world as being, in some sense, 'in God', but of God as being 'more than' the world, and so as the circumambient Reality in which the world persists and exists ('pan-en-theism').[75] He is the

God in whom 'we live, and move, and have our being.'[76] This is the model that St Augustine has depicted so memorably and in such graphic terms, addressing God thus:

> I set before the sight of my spirit the whole creation, whatsoever we can see therein (as sea, earth, air, stars, trees, mortal creatures); yea and whatever in it we do not see ... and I made one great mass of Thy creation ... And this mass I made huge, not as it was (which I could not know), but as I thought convenient, yet every way finite. But Thee, O Lord, I imagined on every part environing and penetrating it, though every way infinite: as if there were a sea, everywhere and on every side, through unmeasured space, one only boundless sea, and it contained within it some sponge, huge, but bounded; that sponge must needs, in all its parts, be filled with that unmeasurable sea: so conceived I Thy creation, itself finite, full of Thee, the Infinite; and I said, Behold God, and behold what God hath created; and God is good, yea, most mightily and incomparably better than all these ...'[77]

On this model of God's relation to the world-as-a-whole, the total world system is seen as 'in God' who (uniquely) is present to it *as a whole*, as well as to its individual component entities. If God interacts with the 'world' at this supervenient level of totality, then he could be causatively effective in a 'top-down' manner without abrogating the laws and regularities (and the unpredictabilities we have noted) that operate at the myriad sub-levels of existence that constitute that 'world'. Particular events could occur in the world and be what they are because God intends them to be so, without at any point any contravention of the laws of physics, biology, psychology, sociology, or whatever is the pertinent science for the level of description in question. Furthermore, we should expect the irreducible unpredictability, open-endedness and flexibility that characterize lesser complex dynamical systems within the world also to be a feature of the world-as-a-whole, rather in the same way that the succession of human brain states has an unpredictability (from outside) that may be related to human freedom. Might not this be the correlate of divine freedom in relation to the world?

In thus speaking of God, it has not been possible to avoid talk of God 'intending', of God's 'freedom', that is, to avoid using the language of personal agency. For these ideas of 'top-down' causation by God cannot be expounded without relating them to the concept of God as, in some sense, an agent, least misleadingly described as personal. We cannot examine further the usefulness, or otherwise, of this notion of 'top-down' causation by God without looking again at the dualistic assumptions about human nature which, as we saw, have so frequently been presupposed in attempts to use the model of human agency for God's action in the world.

c Personal Agents As Psychosomatic Unities

Over recent decades the pressure from the relevant sciences[78] – studies of the evolution of brains, pharmacology, brain biochemistry, neurophysiology, neuropsychology, psychology, the brain sciences, and the cognitive sciences in general, to name only a selection – has been inexorably towards viewing the processes that occur in the human brain and nervous system, on the one hand, and the content of consciousness, our personal, mental experience, on the other, as two facets or functions of one total unitive process and activity.[79] One could instance the well-known effects of hormone balance, of brain lesions, and of drugs on both personality and the content of mental experience and the research on the unity, or rather disunity, of the experience of patients with 'split' brains. I have argued elsewhere[80] that the mind-body identitist view which most readily accords with such observations is in fact quite acceptable to Christian theology – and is indeed also consistent with Biblical presuppositions concerning human nature – provided it is qualified by being held with the proviso that the language of mental events is not reducible to that of the physical and neurological sciences which are also attempting to describe the one unitive process that is going on when we think. The description of an event in the mind/brain in non-reducible mentalist language is regarded, and this is the force of the qualification, as referring to a *real* feature of the unitive mind/brain event. This is indeed a widely held view amongst philosophers on the mind-body problem, sometimes denoted as 'soft materialism', though what is then to be meant by 'materialism' needs considerable qualification,[81] since matter is thereby recognized as capable of thought when it is in the form of the human brain in the human body.

We have already seen[82] that combining a non-dualist account of the human person and of the mind-body relation with the idea of top-down causation illuminates the way in which states of the brain-as-a-whole (a) could be causally effective at the level of neurones, and so of action; and (b) could actually also be mental states to which non-reducible mentalist, including first person, language could legitimately refer as a real modality of that total unitive event which is the activity of thinking accomplished by the human-brain-in-the-human-body. A total brain state, experienced as 'I intend to do x as I do x', has a causal relation to, is a constraint upon, a series of subsystems (down to muscles and their coordinated actions), which just *is* the intended action and which is fully explicable in terms of the sciences appropriate to those levels (muscle biochemistry, physiology, anatomy, etc.).

My suggestion is that a combination of the notion of top-down causation from the integrated, unitive mind/brain state to human bodily action ((a) above) with the recognition of the unity of the human mind/brain/body event ((b) above) *together* provide a fruitful clue or model for illuminating how we might think of God's interaction with the world. According to this suggestion the state of the totality of the world-as-a-whole (all-that-is) would be known only to the omniscience of God and would be the field of the exercise of his omnipotence at his omnicompetent level of comprehensiveness and comprehension. Just as our human personal subjectivity (the sense if being an 'I') is a unitive, unifying, centred influence on the conscious, willed activity of our bodies, and this is what characterizes personal agency, so God is here conceived as the unifying, unitive source and centred influence on the world's activity. We are exploring here the notion that the succession of the states of the system of the world-as-a-whole is also a succession in the thought of God, who is present to it all; and that this is a model for, is analogous to, the way, it has to be presumed, a succession of brain states constitutes the succession of our thoughts. In this model, God would be regarded as exerting continuously top-down causative influences on the world-as-a-whole in a way analogous to that whereby we in our thinking can exert effects on our bodies in a 'top-down' manner.

Earlier[83] we surmised that 'the causal effectiveness of the whole brain state on the actual states of its component nerves and neurones is probably better conceived of in terms of the transfer of information rather than of energy.' This now affords a further clue to how the continuing action of God with the world-as-a-whole might best be envisaged – namely as analogous to an input of information, rather than of energy. But since God is personal, this flow of 'information' is more appropriately described as a 'communication' by God to the world of his purposes and intentions through those levels of the hierarchy of complexity capable of receiving it. The implications of this will have to be considered later.[84]

This holistic mode of action and influence is God's alone and distinctive of God. God's continuous interaction with the whole and the never-ending constraints he exerts upon it could thereby shape and direct all events at lesser levels so that his purposes were not ultimately frustrated and were attained. Such interaction could occur without ever abrogating at any point any of the natural relationships and inbuilt flexibilities and freedoms operative at all the lower levels, and discerned by the sciences and ordinary human experience – any more than the 'program' of the software used in a computer overrides the laws of solid state physics operating in the processes going on in the hardware.

Only God in his transcendence is present to the totality of all-that-is as well as, in his immanence, also to the individual entities that comprise created existence. Accordingly, the relation of God's experience is of the world-as-a-whole as well as of individual entities and events within it. By analogy with the relation of our private awareness and the corresponding descriptions of our own mental states to scientific accounts of our brain states and our bodily actions, I suggest that only God could be aware of the distinctiveness of any state of that totality and what states might or might not succeed it in time (or whatever is the appropriate dimension for referring to 'succession in God'). So this divine knowledge would always be hidden from and eternally opaque to us, existing as we do at levels at which the conceptual language will never be available for apprehending God's own 'inner' life. The best we can do, as we have already urged, is to stretch the language of personal experience as the least misleading option available to us. According to this approach, we are free to describe any events at our own level of existence in the natural terms available to us (e.g., those of the sciences) and at the same time to regard those same events, whether private and internal to us or public and external to all, as manifesting God's overall intentions, that is, his general providence. For God could have brought it about that they are what they are and not something else by that overall comprehensive constraint which he exerts, in a top-down causative way, upon all lesser events in the totality of existing entities. God is thus to be conceived of as all the time the continuing supra-personal, unifying, unitive Agent of all-that-is. We must go on recognizing – and this is essential to the whole proposal – that, in the light of our earlier discussion, God himself has chosen to allow a degree of unpredictability, open-endedness and flexibility in the world he continues to create.

What does this imply about the 'causal joint' between God and his action on the world? I would emphasize, with Kaufman and Wiles,[85] that God's action is on the world-as-a-whole, but to stress more strongly than they do that this maintaining and supporting interaction is a continuing as well as an initial one; and can be general or particular in its effects. The freedom of God to affect the world is indeed reinforced and protected in this model. The idea of God's continuous interaction with the world as being best conceived of in terms of 'top-down' causation also helps to bridge what some, for example Hugh Montefiore,[86] have viewed as a tendency towards postulating the 'God of the deists' in the kind of immanence that I have urged here and elsewhere.[87] I attempted to meet this criticism by stressing[88] that the creative processes of the natural order, involving chance operating in a lawlike framework, are themselves the immanent creative activity of God – and a musical analogy can, I think, help us to imagine this (see below, chapter 9, section 3b).[89]

The notion of top-down causation has the merit of allowing us to understand how initiating divine action on the state of the world-as-a-whole can itself have a causative effect upon individual events and entities within that world. Any change in God's interaction with the world-as-a-whole can on this top-down causative model thereby influence particular events in the world, within those limitations of unpredictability, open-endedness, and flexibility in nature (including humanity) that God himself has created. Moreover, such divine causative influence would never be observed by us as a divine 'intervention', that is, as an interference with the course of nature and as a setting aside of its observed relationships.

d How?

It might be helpful in clarifying this way of looking at the interaction of God with the world to revert to Owen Thomas's classification[90] of 'how?' in the question, 'How does God act in the world?':

A *By what means?* This question amounts to an earlier one, namely, 'What is the "causal joint" in this postulated holistic interaction?' Any description of the world-as-a-whole pertinent to an answer is available only to God, who alone has that relevant and requisite experience of the world-as-a-whole. This is analogous to our description of our own brain states being privately accessible only to us and then only in mentalistic language. There is therefore still a lacuna in our explication of the God/world 'causal joint', but it has reached an inevitable boundary, namely that between the world-as-a-whole and the inner life of God within which God represents the world to himself in such a way that he can alter its overall state. I have suggested that the influence of God on the world-as-a-whole might be appropriately conceived of in terms of a flow, an 'input', of information rather than of energy. Now, as pointed out elsewhere,[91] at all levels observable by us any input of information requires *some* input of matter/energy, however minimal. So we still have a problem of the 'causal joint', now in the form of: How can God exert his influence on, make an input of information into, the world-as-a-whole without an input of matter/energy? This seems to me to be the ultimate level of the 'causal joint' conundrum, for it involves the very nature of the divine being in relation to that of matter/energy and seems to me to be the right place in which to locate the problem, rather than at some lower levels in the created order at which divine 'intervention' would then have to be postulated with all of its difficulties.

B   *In what way or manner?* – by continuously interacting, as a top-down agency, with the world-as-a-whole but without infringing any of its natural relationships, so that no 'interventions', in the sense of rupturing previously observed regular relationships, occur to our observation.

C   *To what effect?* – primarily on the world-as-a-whole, but thereby on any constituent entity or event in the world that God wishes to influence, within the God-imposed limits of the creation's inbuilt unpredictability, open-endedness and flexibility which include the exercise of human freedom. These effects operate in a top-down manner through the boundary conditions and constraints that the state of the whole exerts upon all subsidiary, constituent entities and processes.

D   *With what meaning or for what reason or purpose?* – the question of theodicy still remains open for discussion, though certain guidelines can already be discerned from the character of those self-imposed limits (see C above).

E   *To what extent or degree?* – on the world-as-a-whole and thereby and selectively, according to God's working out of his purposes, on individual entities and events as he purposes.

F   *On analogy with what?* – on analogy with the personal agency of the psychosomatic unity of the human mind-brain acting in a top-down causative manner on the human body and so affecting events at lower levels, as described by the relevant sciences, and so also effecting action in the world. This process is analogous to an input of 'information' and so to the kind of patterning and redisposition of the material world that our brains-in-our-bodies continuously perform.

This treatment of the God–world interaction is, of course, but a variation on the widely adopted analogy of personal agency for God's action in the world. But I would suggest it renders this analogy more apt and convincing by its taking account both of the psychosomatic unity of the 'personal' and of top-down causality by the human 'agent'. It is offered as an enrichment of what Galilee and Hebblethwaite[92] interpret as the general thrust of Farrer's account, including his agnosticism over the modality of divine action, which is 'not to be confused with agnosticism over the meaning of the basic analogy of action with which Farrer operates or over the necessity of its use'.[93] Their description of Farrer's approach, albeit in terms of 'Spirit' (which, in this context, is a term for God's outreach into the world-as-a-whole) and going further theologically than the stage we are at present at, nevertheless coheres with the kind of understanding of God's interaction with the world developed above:

> In his treatment of divine providence, Farrer invites us to think much more holistically of the web of creaturely interaction as the field of divine action than the analogy of one agent among others might suggest. Although each created energy-system is given the power to 'run itself its own way' neither the natural world nor the human world is a closed system, impervious to the divine Spirit. On the contrary, the divine Spirit 'radiates' upon his creation, superimposing higher levels of organization and drawing the various threads of evolution, history and individual life-stories into the providential patterns we observe. The modality of the divine Spirit's operation may be unknown, the hand of God perfectly hidden, but the effects of divine agency in the emergence of man, in salvation-history, and in the lives of Christ and the saints are not hidden at all.[94]

In conclusion, it would seem that new perspectives afforded by the natural sciences on the processes of the world, including especially those on top-down causation and on the human-brain-in-the human-body, have provided not only a new context for the theological debate about how God might be conceived to interact with the world but have also afforded new conceptual resources for modelling it. There have been a number of ways in which this interaction of God with the world has in fact been modelled by different authors and we now need to consider some of these.

3 MODELS OF GOD'S INTERACTION WITH THE WORLD

These have to be reconsidered in the light of the understanding of divine being and becoming that we developed[95] in response to the new perspectives on the world which the natural sciences have stimulated. The past few decades have witnessed attempts by various authors to meet this challenge by proposing new models, or older models revised, in response to various pressures, including those from the sciences. In doing so they have participated in that rebirth of images of God's relation to the world which is the general and perennial task of theology. Not, of course, that a plethora of models (we shall employ this word, rather then 'images' in accordance with our earlier usage) were at all lacking in the Judeo-Christian tradition to represent this relation.

a Models of the God–world Relation

John Macquarrie[96] has usefully and perceptively classified these models as being broadly either 'monarchical' or 'organic'. The former stress 'God's transcendence over and priority to the world'[97] and the relation between God and the world is asymmetric: the world is dependent on God, but not God on the world; God affects the world but not *vice versa*; and so on. The latter, 'organic', approach 'envisages . . . a much more intimate relation between God and the world than the monarchical model. It does not abolish the ideas of transcendence and priority of God, it qualifies them . . . I should prefer myself to regard it as a variety of theism, differing from classical theism in the stress which it lays on elements of intimacy and reciprocity in the God-world relation.'[98]

The monarchical models include *inter alia* God as Maker, Father (conceived in patriarchal terms[99]), Lord, King and Sovereign of the universe. Even within such models of kingship, two different pictures may be distinguished,[100] namely, those of the 'philosopher-king' and the 'saviour-king'. The former is the model of a king 'by whose wisdom and power everything is so controlled that nothing can be present in the kingdom which is alien to his will'.[101] In the latter model, which predominates in the Bible, what happens in the realm of the 'saviour-king' is often not as he wishes and he is 'constantly meeting, redressing and redeeming that which is alien to his will'.[102]

The organic models with their stress on intimacy and reciprocity between God and the world are less prominent in the Bible, though certainly not absent – for example, the notion of God as closer to human beings than their own breath; Hosea's picture of God as the faithful husband; God as the Shepherd of Israel; the image of creation as the garment worn by God; in the Wisdom literature, the idea of *Sophia* going out from God as the personal agent and expression of God's own being in creation; and, in the New Testament, the doctrine of the incarnation according to which God embodies himself in creation in a created human being.

There have been a number of proposals in contemporary theology to soften the distinction between these two limiting models both of which, it must be noted, are used by biblical authors with no apparent sense of disparity. Thus Sallie McFague,[103] *inter alia,*[104] has urged the model of God as Mother along with that of God as Father, and the Doctrine Commission of the Church of England (not expected to be ultra-radical theologically) has stressed in its 1987 Report that the model of God's relation to the world as that of *parent*-child 'is of great importance in both Judaism and Christianity'.[105] Sallie McFague also goes on to explore the models of God as Lover and God as Friend in a very interesting and fruitful way. In such exercises it is important to remember that, as we indicated in the Introduction,[106] such models utilize metaphors, with the concomitant and simultaneous 'is' and 'is not' character of their affirmations. Hence different models can be employed together without contradiction and with mutual enrichment of our perception.

As we saw earlier in this chapter, personal agency has traditionally been used as an analogy for God's interaction with the world and has recently been subject to much reassessment. Although traditionally the soul/body relation has not been widely used in Christian theology for the God/world relation, except in certain limited ways, in recent years process theologians have extensively used the analogy in the form self:body::God:world. As we saw, holistic conceptions of the human person which have arisen in response to scientific knowledge and which conceive the 'self' and the 'body' as two aspects of one total unity, then serve in combination with this analogy to facilitate a non-interventionist way of thinking of God's agency in the world and a more intimate and internal form for God's knowledge of the world. The metaphor of the world *as* God's body has been explored particularly by Sallie McFague and by Grace Jantzen.[107] The former assesses this model sympathetically, especially for its world-affirming and ecological implications and for its ability to stress God's genuine involvement in the suffering and joys of the world, but she does not lose sight of the metaphorical character of such language.

Grace Jantzen goes further and regards the world as God's body in a much stronger ontological sense – God is no longer 'incorporeal', for God is embodied in the world as the medium of God's life and action. Her exposition of this concept is stimulating for its illuminating qualifications of much that is now inconsistent with our scientific understanding of the world in many more monarchical and near-deistic ways of speaking of God's relation to the world. However, in the end, one cannot but think that her position steers too near to a pantheism in which all-that-is becomes identified so closely with God that God's role as Creator is compromised. Furthermore, the world, all-that-is, is not an integrated organism in anything like the sense that *our* bodies are a single organism – it is, rather, a nexus of intricately interacting living organisms interlocked within various assemblies of inorganic systems, the vast majority of which have no direct interaction with living organisms. Moreover, the problem of the existence of evil becomes particularly intransigent if the world *is* God's body, for then evil becomes a part of God's own being. Yet, in its very indiscretions, if one may, not disrespectfully, so put it, this attempt to depict the world *as* God's body serves to remind[108] us how few have been models adequate to expressing God's intimate contact with and presence to and in the world which God is deemed to have created. The notion of God as Creator is fundamental to the Judeo-Christian concept of God and various ways of conceiving this creative activity of God lie behind these models for God's relation to the world. Indeed, the difficulties hinted at in the idea of the world as God's body and the plethora of alternative models for God's relation to the world suggest that it should be fruitful to examine more closely what we might mean by saying that God 'creates' all-that-is.

b Models of God's Activity as Creator[109]

There are two ways, broadly speaking, in which the activity of divine creation has been modelled in the Judeo-Christian tradition, according to another analysis of John Macquarrie[110] – the models of 'making' and of 'emanation'. The basic analogy in the former is that of a craftsman making something for use – for example, a potter making a pot, something that did not exist before in that form. This model points to the dependence of what is created on the creator for both its form and existence; to the intention and purpose in the mind of the creator that is implemented; and to the relatively independent existence that is accorded to what is created by the act of creation. Such models for divine creation are defective insofar as they imply that the 'matter' on which the act of creation operated was already in existence – that is they do not express the idea of *creatio ex nihilo* which is so essential to the doctrine of God as Creator, as the *one* source of being of all-that-is. Nevertheless they do serve to stress the transcendence of God and that the act of creation entirely stems from the free, divine initiative. However, they also inevitably tend to establish a distinct gap between the Creator and what is created.

The other model – that of emanation – is less biblical but early entered Christian theology and has served historically[111] to supplement, and even correct, the other model. The classical example of 'emanation' is that of the Sun emitting from within itself its rays which permeate the Earth, where they stimulate warmth and life. Thus it is, the model suggests, God from within God's own being goes out to be actively involved in giving and sustaining the being of all-that-is. An 'admirable statement of what may be called the Christian form of creative emanation', as Stephen Hobhouse puts it,[112] is afforded by William Law in regard to the human condition:

> The creation, therefore, of a soul is not the creation of thinking and willing, or the making that to be and to think, which before had nothing of being or thought; but it is the bringing the powers of thinking and willing out of their eternal state in the one God into a beginning state of a self-conscious life, distinct from God.

And earlier in the same work:

> Here, O man, behold the great original and the high state of thy birth.... Thou beginnest as time began, but as time was in eternity before it became days and years, so thou wast in God before thou wast brought into the creation; and as time is neither a part of eternity, nor broken off from it, yet come out of it; so thou art not part of God, nor broken off from him, yet born out of Him.[113]

This model of emanation certainly places a proper stress on the immanence of God in the created order and the continued closeness of God to that which is created. Yet it avoids the danger of identify-

ing God's presence in the created world too much with the world –
the danger of regarding that world almost as an extension of the
divine being and of the same 'substance', or mode of being, as God.
Furthermore it entails a sense in which creation goes on all the time
and is not just a one-off event. However, it can sometimes also
convey the impression that the process of emanation is inevitable in
the sense that God's nature is of such a kind that emanative creating
is constitutive of God's own being in such a way that no deliberate,
free act of will and love on God's part is involved in the process. It is
then being pressed too far, for the notion of creation being a
freely-willed expression and act of God's love must be retained.

Too often attempts to combine the insights of both of these kinds
of traditional model, as Macquarrie advocates,[114] result only in an
uneasy juxtaposition with no sense of a really unified picture emerging. Moreover, the second model of emanation, in particular, does
not, as we had hoped these models would, illuminate very much the
actual notion of 'creating', the act of creation. It is at this point that
the aesthetic activity of artistic creation, in its widest sense, has
recently been much canvassed as a suitable model for creation by
God.[115] For a work of any kind of art is given being by the artist's
own spontaneous activity. Its form is chosen by the artist and, once
decided upon, this form exercises a constraint on the artistic activity. The proposal of artistic creation as a model of divine creation
seems to have been introduced into the modern discussion first by
Dorothy Sayers in *The Mind of the Maker*:

> The components of the material world are fixed; those of the world of
> imagination increase by a continuous and irreversible process, without
> any destruction or rearrangement of what went before. This represents
> the nearest approach we experience to 'creation out of nothing', and
> we conceive of the act of absolute creation as being analogous to that
> of the creative artist . . . This experience of the creative imagination in
> the common man or woman and in the artist is the only thing we have
> to go upon in entertaining and formulating the concept of creation.[116]

This suggestive model takes somewhat different forms according to
the human creative process that is being referred to.

Dorothy Sayers herself, as might be expected for a distinguished
novelist, took as her prime example that of creative writing. She
discerned a threefoldness in the response of a reader's mind to a
written work which 'corresponds to the threefoldness of the work
(Book-as-Thought, Book-as-Written, Book-as-Read), and that again
to the original threefoldness in the mind of the writer (Idea, Energy,

Power)';[117] and this threefoldness she saw as inevitable because of the structure of the creative mind. She had expounded this earlier in the concluding speech of St Michael in her play *The Zeal of Thy House*, which she quotes thus in her later book:

> For every work (or act) of creation is threefold, an earthly trinity to match the heavenly.
>
> First, (not in time, but merely in order of enumeration) there is the Creative Idea, passionless, timeless, beholding the whole work complete at once, the end in the beginning; and this the image of the Father.
>
> Second, there is the Creative Energy (or Activity) begotten of that idea, working in time from the beginning to the end, with sweat and passion, being incarnate in the bonds of matter: and this is the image of the Word.
>
> Third, there is the Creative Power, the meaning of the work and its response in the lively soul: and this is the image of the indwelling Spirit.
>
> And these three are one, each equally in itself the whole work, whereof none can exist without the other: and this is the image of the Trinity.[118]

The explicitly trinitarian interpretation is not our immediate concern; rather it is the percipient analysis she provides of the act of creative imagination, for this passage comes closer to what is being postulated of *divine* creation than any of the other analogies we have looked at hitherto. It possesses the essential feature of bringing into existence that which exists up to this point only as an idea in the mind of the maker. The novelist's freely willed initiative in the process is unambiguous, so his or her 'transcendence' over the novel is quite clear. But, the model also involves the writer's 'immanence' in the created work since 'if . . . he is to perform an act of power in creation, [the writer] must allow his Energy to enter with equal fullness into all his creatures, whatever portions of his personality they emphasize and embody.'[119] The model also has the further advantage that it incorporates a certain freewheeling independence from the creator of that which is created. For, as Dorothy Sayers pointed out, the characters created by the author in a novel begin, in her experience, to take on a certain life of their own which reacts upon their author as a constraint upon his development of the plot. This is certainly a feature of God's relation to a world that God is going on creating but which contains free-willing self-conscious creatures that God has endowed with a degree of autonomy. As Austin Farrer later expressed it:

> The Creator of the world is not to be compared with those bad novelists who make up the plot of their story first, and force the characters to carry it out, all against the grain of their natures. He is like the good novelist who has the wit to get a satisfying story out of the natural behaviour of the characters he conceives.[120]

To that extent, any scheme that the author originally had is perpetually at risk, vulnerable to a natural development of the action consistent with the personal development of the characters as they interact. All of this is analogous to what we wish to affirm about God's relation to human action, but one wonders if the model is really adequate, for human agents possess an autonomy far greater than that of any character in a novel vis-à-vis its author.

It would seem, from Dorothy Sayers's account of her own experience, that the playwright has to be concerned, even more that the novelist, with the internal coherence and consistency of the created characters, for they have to come to life on the stage and be performed by actors and actresses who need to enter into their parts if they are to be convincing. So the writing of a play perhaps provides a better model for divine creating. In order to strengthen this model of the playwright, Maurice Wiles has proposed that we should think rather of an improvised drama 'in which the actors are each given the basic character of the person he or she is to represent and the general setting in which their interaction is to be worked out but in which they are left free to determine experimentally how the drama is to develop'.[121] Then the drama might well develop in principle, though not in detail, in the way the playwright always intended and would be, in a sense, both the playwright's and the actors'. This seems to be as far as one can go in elaborating this particular model without it becoming too cumbersome.

Taking account of this possibility that the interaction between the creator of a work of art and what is being created determine the eventual outcome is also a feature of other artistic models of divine creating: 'In artistic activity a certain struggle or adventure is involved – the endeavour to contain or express spontaneity within form. ... Having freely chosen to create something in a particular 'medium', God may no longer be free to escape the constraints which that medium imposes.'[122] Such constraints, for a sculptor, may be imperfections, such as a sudden change of grain in the stone or a knot in the wood which is being worked, so that to continue with the creative work the artist has now to exploit this impediment so as to fulfil his creative intentions – a crucial test of inventive skill. This model thereby affords a hint of how the divine creating could become also a divine redeeming.

There comes a point at which the work of any author is regarded as 'finished', such is the limitation of our finitude: even the extemporizing play in Wiles's model presumably comes to point when the players and spectators leave. But, as Dorothy Sayers says, we have to consider

> God as a living author, whose span of activity extends infinitely beyond our racial memory in both directions. We never see His great work finished . . . We are thus considering the temporal universe as one of those great serial works of which instalments appear from time to time, all related to a central idea whose completeness is not yet manifest to the reader. Within the framework of its diversity are many minor and partial unities – of plot, of episode, and of character.[123]

But the art form *par excellence* into which time enters as an inherent, essential and constitutive element is music. There is, of course, a long tradition, going back to Pythagoras and Plato, of using the experience of music to model one's understanding of the universe. Many, too, in the Christian tradition have resorted to music for this purpose, notably Kepler:

> Thus the heavenly motions are nothing but a kind of perennial concert, rational rather than audible or vocal . . . Thus there is no marvel greater or more sublime than the rules of singing in harmony together in several parts, unknown to the ancients but at last discovered by man, the ape of his Creator; so that, through the skilful symphony of many voices, he should actually conjure up in a short part of an hour the vision of the world's total perpetuity in time; and that, in the sweetest sense of bliss enjoyed through Music, the echo of God, he should almost reach the contentment which God the Maker has in His Own works.[124]

Karl Popper, from whom this splendid quotation was obtained, himself remarks that 'a great work of music (like a great scientific theory) is a cosmos imposed upon a chaos – in its tensions and harmonies inexhaustible even for its creator',[125] here echoing a common theme both in classical (Greek and Roman) and the biblical literature[126] of creation by God being the formation of order, a 'cosmos', out of 'chaos'.

Music is especially appropriate as a source of models for divine creativity for a number of reasons. In music there is an unfolding in time of the composer's intentions and the significance of any given moment is constituted by both what precedes it and by the way it forms a growth point for what follows. Particular notes, rhythms, harmonies and dissonances – all that constitutes the music – have a different impact on the listener according to what has gone before. And this instantaneously experienced effect itself is the initiating point of and gives a distinctive meaning to its sequel. This is analogous to the way in which any meaning and significance we might wish to attribute to any given stage of the world's history are dependent both on what precedes and follows the point in question. In music new melodies and developments emerge intelligibly, yet inventively, out of earlier themes and fragments; and similarly in the processes of the world new forms develop, often surprisingly, though *post hoc* intelligibly in the light of the sciences, from what precedes them.

We saw earlier[127] that in the ongoing processes of the world new, and increasingly complex, forms of both inorganic and living matter emerge by a combination of what we briefly designated as 'chance' and 'law' and that to their mutual interplay is to be attributed the inherent creativity of the natural processes of the world. The question for any theistic doctrine of creation is then: how is the assertion of God as Creator to be interpreted, indeed rendered intelligible, in the light of this interplay between random chance at various levels and 'necessity'? This necessity arises from the stuff of the world having its particular 'given' properties and lawlike behaviour, which can be regarded as possessing potentialities that are, as it were, written into creation by the Creator's intention and purpose and are gradually actualized by the wide-ranging exploration that the operation of 'chance' makes possible. It is here that musical creativity appears to be especially helpful as a model of God's creative activity. For in music there is an elaboration of simpler units according to, often conventional, rules intermingled with much spontaneity, surprise even. God as Creator we might now see[128] as a composer who, beginning with an arrangement of notes in an apparently simple subject, elaborates and expands it into a fugue by a variety of devices of fragmentation, augmentation and reassociation; by turning it upside down and back to front; by overlapping these and other variations of it in a range of tonalities; by a profusion of patterns of sequences in time, with always the consequent interplay of sound flowing in an orderly way from the chosen initiating ploy.... Thus does a J. S. Bach create a complex and interlocking harmonious fusion of his seminal material, both through time and at any particular instant, which beautiful in its elaboration, only reaches is consummation when all the threads have been drawn into the return to the home key of the last few bars – the key of the initial melody whose potential elaboration was conceived from the moment it was first expounded.

The listener to such a fugue experiences,[129] with the luxuriant and profuse growth that emanates from the original simple structure, whole new worlds of emotional experience which are the result of the interplay between an expectation based on past experience ('law') and an openness to the new ('chance' in the sense that the listener cannot predict or control it). Thus might the Creator be imagined to enable to be unfolded the potentialities of the universe which he himself has given it, nurturing by his redemptive and providential actions those that are to come to fruition in the community of free beings – an Improvisor of unsurpassed ingenuity. He appears to do so by a process in which the creative possibilities, inherent (by his own intention) within the fundamental entities of that universe and their inter-relations, become actualized within a temporal development shaped and determined by those selfsame potentialities.

This model could be further refined if it referred to a composer extemporizing a fugue on a given theme – as on the famous May evening in 1747 at Frederick the Great's court in Potsdam when Johann Sebastian Bach, visiting his son Carl Philipp Emmanuel, was called upon by the king to improvise, playing on one of the king's prized new Silbermann 'piano-fortes', a three-part fugue on a theme supplied by the king himself. Not every subject is fit for such full development, so next day Bach chose a theme of his own and proceeded to improvise on the organ a *six*-part fugue – an extraordinary feat. Or perhaps a more modern model for those of other tastes might be the extemporization of a jazz virtuoso, say, in Preservation Hall in New Orleans. Introduction of improvisation into this model of God as composer incorporates that element of open adaptability which any model of God's relation to a partly non-deterministic world should, however inadequately, represent.

This model of the world process as the unfolding music of the divine Creator-Composer also illuminates his relation to the human listener to that 'music'. Although a given human work of musical composition attains a kind of consummation in its closing cadence, it would be nonsense to suggest that the 'meaning' of a musical work was to be found only there. Each instant, with its concurrent stored memory of the past as the ambience of the present and its ability already to be forming the reaction to the music yet to be heard, has a significance which is *sui generis* and takes its meaning from its relation to the whole that is being gradually unfolded.

The model also helps us to imagine a little better what we might mean by God's immanence in the world.[130] There is no doubt of the 'transcendence' of the composer in relation to the music he creates – he gives it existence and without the composer it would not be at all. So the model properly reflects, as do all those of artistic creativity, that transcendence of God as Creator of all-that-is which we, as 'listeners' to the music of creation, wish to aver. Yet, when we are actually listening to a musical work, say, a Beethoven piano sonata, then there are times when we are so deeply absorbed in it that for a moment we are thinking Beethoven's musical thoughts with him. In such moments we experience

> music heard so deeply
> That it is not heard at all, but you are the music
> While the music lasts.[131]

Yet if anyone were to ask at that moment, '*Where* is Beethoven now?', we could only reply that Beethoven-*qua*-composer was to be found only in the music itself. The music would in some sense be Beethoven's inner musical thought kindled in us and we would genuinely be encountering Beethoven-*qua*-composer. The whole experience is one of profound communication from composer to listener. This very closely models, I am suggesting, God's immanence in creation and God's self-communication in and through what he is creating. The processes revealed by the sciences are in themselves God acting as Creator and God is not to be found as some kind of *additional* factor added on to the processes of the world. God, to use language usually applied in sacramental theology, is 'in, with and under' all-that-is and all-that-goes-on.

The necessity for music to be performed for it actually to communicate to the listener, for it to *become* music, also gives rise to some suggestive analogies to divine creation. For what the composer writes down is only a kind of blueprint, an outline sketch, of his intentions which only come to fruition at the hands of the performers, his interpreters. Humanity is called upon to be a sensitive co-creator with God of the music of creation, for only human beings in the created world are capable both of discerning what God is doing in the natural world through the sciences; and of having an insight into God's intentions, through reflection upon their direct and mediated experiences of God. God's creative intentions are reflected in and also come to fruition in and through human creativity.[132] Now the performance of a musical composition depends very much on the perception of the individual composer's intentions at a later period by musicologists and by the performers they influence. These perceptions change, so that one can, perhaps, draw suggestive parallels between those who insist that the playing of Bach, for example, on period instruments is the only authentic style and those who wish to express their own insights into Bach on modern instruments. I leave it to the reader to elaborate this possible extension of the analogy.[133]

Clearly the model of God-the-Composer creating the music of creation is a rich and fruitful one, for it gives insights both into the relation of God as Creator to the creation and into our human apprehension of and participation in the creative process. Together with the other artistic models of divine creativity, it points to an aspect of the divine interaction with the world that we have not yet sufficiently taken into account and to which we must now turn. This is the notion that, if God is a *personal* Creator who has been acting in and through a created order that has a created inbuilt propensity to develop into self-conscious persons who are characterized by their uniquely developed ability to communicate with each other, then it would be consistent with such ideas to expect that the creator God would, in ways to be examined, seek to communicate with created persons. There would be little point in the divine artist-playwright-composer creating, never to have his/her works appreciated or responded to, their Creator unidentified and undiscerned. It is in the context of this possibility of the self-communication of the divine in the natural order that we can then consider more fully, in the light of the interpretations already given of the divine interaction with the world, both what has conventionally been called 'special' providence and 'miracles'.

4 GOD'S SELF-COMMUNICATION: SPECIAL PROVIDENCE AND MIRACLES[134]

Consideration of how we might today conceive of God's continuing interaction with the world has led, not surprisingly, to the perennial model of God as a personal agent interacting with and acting on the world – a model modified and enriched by recent insights into the unity of the mental and physical in the human-brain-in-the-human-body and into top-down causation. Now the meaning of an action by a human agent is not to be found by scientific analysis of the physiological, chemical, and mechanical processes going on in the agent's body, but by discovering the person's reasons and intentions, that is, the mental events which are involved in the action in question. That meaning is expressed in terms of its own language (of reason, intention, etc.) even if the meaning has to be conveyed through physical signs, on paper, or as sound vibrations, or whatever. The model of personal agency therefore suggests that if God is to be regarded as, in some sense, an agent interacting with and acting on the world, then we should look for the meaning of those events in *God's* reasons and intentions, i.e., God's own purposes. For the affirmation of God as Creator is an answer to the questions we ask about the meaning of the existence of the world and of the processes that occur in it. Such an attribution of meaning is at least rendered intelligible by the analogous attribution of meaning in mental terms which we give to the physical actions of human agents, even if we cannot absolutely prove its applicability. It is therefore appropriate to inquire into the reasons and intentions, that is, the purposes, that God is implementing in the world – or, rather, those that God *aims* to implement, since the world actually contains created autonomous agents who can frustrate his purposes.

The model of personal agency for God's interaction with and action on the world has a further implication. For developmental psychology and studies on the acquisition of language skills make it abundantly clear that the sense of being a self, of being a particular person, arises only in so far as we interact and communicate with *other* persons. Our selfhood seems only to be able to be constituted if we are in personal contact with others – and this is a deep-seated need that continues throughout our lives. Thus any model based on ourselves as agents of our bodies and God as in some sense a personal agent interacting with and acting on the world implicitly involves the notion that God must be a *communicating* selfhood. Now we express our meanings – our intentions, reasons and purposes – through our bodies, especially, though not only, through our speech organs. *Our* meanings are discerned, with varying degrees of accuracy, by other personal agents, but – we may well ask – who discerns *God's* purposes that constitute, as it was suggested in the previous paragraph, the meaning of the world and its processes?

It appears that human beings are *par excellence* those created entities who uniquely seek to discern, even to create, meaning in the structures of their existence – natural, personal and social. We have had to stress that God's meanings are to be found within the very texture of the network of the processes that constitute the world. But within those processes, there have emerged those intricately ramified and interlaced structures we call human brains, the very processes of which so operate that they can discern meanings in the natural world and in their own processes. It is as if the Creator has endowed matter-energy-space-time, the stuff of the universe, with a propensity now actualized in humanity to discern the meaning in the cosmic process which its Creator has written into it. For in humanity, the stuff of the world has acquired a form and functionality that makes it capable of reading those meanings in existence which are the immanence of the transcendent God of the whole cosmic process. The way in which God has made himself heard and understood is by endowing the stuff of the world with the ability in *homo sapiens* to acquire discernment of his meanings and to listen to his self-communication, his word, in creation. 'By the *word* of God were the heavens made.'[135] If indeed the world is created, then that creation is the expression of the purpose and intention of God its Creator, and these purposes have apparently expressed themselves in and through a cosmic evolutionary process which has generated within its own fabric beings (ourselves) who can listen to and discern God's meanings. God as the personal agent of creation has created human beings capable of receiving his self-communication. His meanings, those communications which he addresses to the human beings who emerge with this capacity, cannot but be patterns of meaning within the world of nature. We recall[136] that top-down causation in complex systems (and notably in the brain–body relation) is frequently characterized by an input and consequent flow down to lower levels of 'information'. That is, God can quite properly be conceived of as sending signals to humanity through particular events and through special clusters or patterns of events that God himself has initiated through his general ('top-down') interaction with the world.

John Macquarrie has usefully elaborated what talk of God's 'meaning' indicates in this context.[137] He freely interprets the opening of St John's Gospel, 'In the beginning was the Word...', as 'Fundamental to everything is meaning...', and that 'God is to the world as meaning is to a process or series of events', presumably the interpretation of ' ... and the Word was God' of John 1:1. When he speaks of God as meaning he has in mind

> a unity that gives order to the world-process and confers significance on its constituent parts; and also the idea that the process has direction and moves towards some goal.... The theist claims by contrast [to the atheist] that he discovers and participates in a context of meaning that is prior to himself and has a ground independent of him.[138]

Since God is worshipful, talk of God as a context of meaning, he continues, implies that 'this context [of meaning] is to be discovered on the personal and historical level as well as on the physical'. However, 'there is no simple pantheistic identification of God with the world-process. He is the partly hidden, partly revealed meaning coming to expression in the process.'[139]

As we have seen,[140] the events and entities of the world consist of natural hierarchies of complexity so that the aspects of God's meaning(s) expressable by any one level in these hierarchies cannot but be limited to that for which it has the capacity. Hence the 'meanings' of God so unveiled, the 'revelation' of God so afforded, by the various and distinctive levels of the natural order can only be complementary and individually incomplete without the others. What is expressed in the different orders of creation and in the pattern of events involving these multiform levels of complexity will not all have the same pertinence to human beings in their search for meaning and intelligibility. They would be expected to vary in what they communicate to us of God's meaning(s), in their ability to unveil God's purposes, according to the level at which they operate in the natural hierarchies of complexity, levels of which we have distinctive kinds of knowledge. As Charles Raven put it over thirty years ago, in the creative process 'from atom and molecule to mammal and man each by its appropriate order and function expresses the design inherent in it and contributes, so far as it can by failure or success, to the fulfilment of the common purpose.[141] So we might expect that God, the transcendent Creator, immanent in the created world which is his self-expression, should make his meanings known most fully not only to but in and through those creatures, human persons, that mirror and reflect God's own nature of transcendence-in-immanence by themselves possessing a subjective transcendence over their objective physical embodiment.

Moreover, although God is not more present at one time or place than at others (he is not a substance present at various concentrations) – all is of God at all times – human beings find that in some sequences of events in created nature and human history, God unveils his meaning more than in others. God is equally and totally present to all times and places but human awareness of that Presence is uniform neither in intensity or content. God may well communicate meaning which is neither comprehended nor apprehended. There are meanings of God waiting to be unveiled but not all are read: some events will be more revealing than others. In such a notion of the varied degrees of unveiling of the meaning(s) that God has written in his creation, of different degrees of what we can now properly call 'revelation', we are simply elaborating further the model of human agency for the relation of God and the world. For our bodies are a causal nexus of events and we are the agents of many of its activities – yet some of our actions, gestures and responses are more characteristic and revelatory of our distinctive selves than others. Thus it is not improper to seek in the world for those events and entities, or patterns of them, which reveal God's meaning(s) most overtly, effectively and distinctively. Some events will be more revelatory, more indicative of God's presence and purposes, than others – while they all continue to be intelligible in terms of the accounts given of them by the science(s) appropriate to their level in the hierarchies of natural complexity.[142] Yet, as Grace Jantzen has pointed out,

> there is a disanalogy between God's revelatory presence and the presence of a person revealed through his activities. Part of the reason that some activities of a person are more revelatory of him than others is that persons have only limited freedom . . . Thus one of the grounds for differentiating the degrees of revelatoriness of a person's behaviour is removed in the case of God: we cannot think that any of God's actions are less deliberate or less free than others.[143]

God is free to act without any constraints other that those he imposes on himself to implement his overall purposes, for his omnipotence to do anything logically possible is, we have suggested, self-limited.[144] The restriction on God–human communication comes from our side, our limited ability to discern and listen. So the point about degrees of revelation of God in the events of the world remains and it is in the light of this, and of the whole understanding of God's interaction with the world, that we are now in a position to consider those items in Langford's classification[145] that we have not yet discussed, namely 'special providence and miracles'.

These terms have been used with a variety of nuances and I can but refer the reader to the useful discussions *inter alia* of Langford and of Macquarrie.[146] Our present reflections bear on these discussions as follows. We have argued above that *particular* events or clusters of events, whether natural, individual and personal, or social and historical, (a) can be specially and significantly revelatory of the presence of God and of the nature of his purposes to human beings; and (b) can be intentionally and specifically brought about by the interaction of God with the world in a top-down causative way that does not abrogate the scientifically observed relationships operating at the level of the events in question. The combination of (a) and (b) renders the concept of God's special providential action intelligible and believable within the context of the perspective of the sciences, always with the proviso, as Langford puts it, that 'the presence of special providence is never guaranteed by events; it is an interpretation of events that depends on faith. It may be compatible with reason, but it can never be absolutely demanded by it.'[147]

The situation as regards 'miracle' is more complex. We are free, of course, to use the word 'miracle' in whatever new way suits us in the present intellectual climate and it has, in fact, undergone much redefinition in the course of time. As Langford points out,[148] the English word 'miracle' in a *biblical* concordance translates words standing for 'wonder', 'an act of power' or 'a sign'. Nevertheless, since the general establishment of the non-biblical idea of an 'order' of nature, ordinary usage of the word 'miracle', and not only by Christians, implies 'some contrast with the natural order' and an event 'not fully explicable by naturalistic means',[149] where the 'natural order' here referred to can in our age mean only that established by the sciences. This is a much stronger claim than in the case of 'special providence', for events falling under that description do not demand some necessarily extra, non-natural causal factor at their own level of operation. Whether or not one considers that events have occurred that fulfil these criteria of the miraculous depends ultimately on one's judgement of the historical evidence. This latter will itself be influenced both by one's *a priori* attitudes towards the very possibility of such events occurring in principle; and additionally, for the theist, by whether or not the claimed miracle is generally consistent with one's understanding of the nature of God and of his purposes for the world and for humanity – understandings themselves at least partly dependent on revelation of a kind entirely consistent with one's knowledge of the natural world through the sciences.

Given that ultimately God *is* the Creator of the world and that he is free to set aside the self-chosen limitations (other than those that are logically necessitated) of his own omnipotence that we have been detecting through our consideration of the nature of the created world, we cannot rule out the possibility that God might 'intervene', in the popular sense of that word, to bring about events for which there can never be a naturalistic interpretation. The freedom of God to effect his purposes cannot ultimately be gainsaid. But we have given cogent reasons[150] for questioning whether such direct 'intervention' is normally compatible with and coherent with other well-founded affirmations concerning the nature of God and of God's relation to the world. The historical evidence that such an intervention *has* happened will therefore have to be especially strong and the event in question of a kind that renders it uniquely revelatory in its particular context of God's purposes, *his* 'meaning' in the senses we have discussed above. We may well conclude from the historical record, given the growing ability of the sciences to give intelligible naturalistic explanations of an increasingly wide range of phenomena, that there are in the end very few events that pass through this sieve. If they do do so, they will be of inestimable significance for our understanding of God in his relation to the humanity to whom he has vouchsafed such a revelation by such a means. Consideration of this possibility must certainly be on the agenda. Meanwhile, under pressure from the scientific perspective on the way the world goes, a more holistic and coherent model of God's continuing interaction with and on the world has emerged – one consistent with our new understandings of the natural order and with that experience of the divine that has shaped the religious consciousness of humanity. For because our brains-in-our-bodies are part of the natural order, God's continuing interaction with and action on the world can include human persons – so that the traditional language of the Christian religion which sees the relation of God to humanity in personal terms and to be a real interaction, can be maintained and preserved as intelligible and not at all inconsistent with our scientific perspectives.

POSTSCRIPT

In Part II of this volume I have been trying to express how we might refer both more accurately and more adequately to that ultimate Reality that is God in the light of what we know of natural being and becoming, as expounded in Part I. The notion of 'being' and 'becoming' as applied to the natural world that the sciences depict have distinguishable meanings. For it is intelligible to see the natural world as containing entities and structures undergoing processes, even though quantum physics has to speak more circumspectly with respect to such easily visualizable distinctions. In doing so, these developments in physics reinforce philosophical reflections such as those of John Macquarrie:

> The fact that whatever becomes both is and is not shows that the distinction between being and becoming is of a peculiar kind. In so far as what becomes is, then becoming must be included in being as well as distinct from it. Two consequences seem to follow. The first is that being cannot be identified with a static, changeless, undifferentiated ultimate.... the fundamental contrast between being and nothing would seem to be made possible only in so far as being includes becoming and gets differentiated, otherwise being and nothing would be indistinguishable.... we talk about being and distinguish it from nothing only in so far as it includes becoming ... The second consequence is that becoming is unintelligible apart from some conception of being, in which the becoming is included. A mere flux would be a chaos, and so would a sheer pluralism.[1]

But what of *divine* 'being' and 'becoming'? God, we have suggested, is the ultimate Reality, Being-itself, who 'all the time' (we have to say, meaning *our* time) gives being to[2] all other, dependent realities that constitute the world, all-that-is. In giving being to entities, structures and processes *in* time, God cannot have a *static* relation to that time which is created with them. Hence we have to speak of a dynamic divine 'becoming' as well as of the divine 'being'.[3]

God as ultimate Being gives ordered being to ('lets-be') a world that has sufficient order to be constituted of continuing entities and structures; but God as ultimate Becoming also gives the world an existence of a kind that exhibits an unfolding and opening up, an actualization of created potentialities, that leads to a fruition and a flourishing in and to which God is present. Now the divine Being is not one being, that is one existent, among other existents. God is not *a* 'being' in that sense or even the sum of all beings, for God's being is the source of all the other existents. God is Being itself. God is the one who 'lets-be' and who is totally distinct from, over against, all-that-is: God is 'wholly other'. We encapsulate this in affirming that God is 'transcendent'.

But God creates and dynamically 'lets-be' in created time and so God as the divine Becoming continually interacts with that which becomes in the created order. For God would not be Creator unless the divine Being and the divine Becoming were facets of the same ultimate divine Reality. God so conceived is deeply involved with time and natural becoming. God is present at all times and spaces and to all created entities, structures and processes. We encapsulate this in affirming that God is 'immanent' – and this in no way subsidiary to our affirmation of his transcendence.

God is the Transcendent One who is immanent in the created world; God is the Immanent One who is transcendent over the created world; and only if God is both could God be continuing Creator. The predication of creativity to God is rooted in this conjunction. Thus 'creativity' is a basic attribute[4] of God and is closely linked with other more fundamental aspects of the divine nature, namely God's transcendence and immanence, that God is ultimate Being and Becoming. *Both* transcendence and immanence have, paradoxically, to be affirmed of God. A famous attempt by Gregory of Nyssa to resolve this paradox involved asserting another, believed to be more acceptable: namely, that God is both knowable and unknowable. God, it was suggested, is unknown in his essence (*ousia*) yet makes himself known in his energies (*energeiai*) – in his works, the results of his creative activity. But the usefulness of this idea turns on what knowing God 'in his acts' might mean.[5] It is doubtful[6] whether this distinction of Gregory of Nyssa should indeed be the basis of the later, more metaphysical, one made by St Gregory Palamas, according to which: 'to know God is to know and participate in his "acts", flowing from the three divine persons, but the divine substance remains entirely transcendent and incommunicable, the totally mysterious, indescribable reality shared by the persons.'[7] It turns out not to be helpful simply to equate the transcendent with the unknowable in God and immanence with the knowable: for we need to affirm, as true to religious experience as well as for reasons of coherence, that God is revealed *and* hidden both in his transcendence and in his immanence.

We have made much use of personal predicates of God as being the least misleading available and preferable to saying nothing at all about God. However, we must not be misled by this into so emphasizing the personal that the concept of *a* 'person' as an individual centre of consciousness serves to weaken the collateral emphasis on the divine immanence. The nature of the human person itself provides us with a corrective to any such tendency, for it affords a clue, a sign pointing to a clearing in the mist, of the direction in which, as created human beings, we might look for illumination concerning this conjunction of transcendence and immanence in God. For we have seen that the human-brain-in-the-human-body, the only instance of the personal we know directly, displays a transcendence and an immanence – both created, in this case. We survey our bodies as subjects, as we do the world with which our bodies interact. Yet the 'I' who is thus transcendent over our bodies expresses its selfhood and identity only by acting in, through, and with the processes of those bodies at all levels. The transcendent, personal 'I' can only be a particular 'I' through its immanent activity in the body.[8] In the human person there is a kind fusion, without loss of distinction, between the transcendent 'I', the self-conscious personhood, and the immanent 'I' expressed in and through the body.

Now we have had to recognize that the meanings that God wishes to unveil in the created order, his self-communications to and for man, cannot but be the more partial, broken and incomplete the more the level of creation under consideration departs from the human, and so the personal, in which the transcendence of the 'I' is experienced as immanent in our bodies. Thus, although God is, in some sense, supra-personal, we may well expect[9] in the personal – that is, in persons, in history, in personal experience, in personal encounter – to find meanings of God unveiled in a way not possibly communicated by the meanings God has written into non-human, impersonal levels of existence. The level of the personal (with all its uniqueness, new language, non-reducible concepts, new modes of experiencing, etc.) allows expression of new aspects of the meaning and purpose God is expressing in creation which could only be incompletely expressed, if at all, through the non-personal, and historically earlier, levels. The more personal and self-conscious is the entity in which God is immanent, the more capable is it of expressing God's supra-personal characteristics and the more God can be immanent personally in that entity.

In humanity, the processes within creation become aware of themselves and seek their own meaning – that is, the processes (expressing the immanence of the Creator God) acquire a dimension of self-transcendence, that of the 'I', which we have just been considering. This raises the possibility (and so hope) that the immanence of God in the world might display, in humanity at least, a hint of, some kind of reflection of, the transcendence/immanence of God. The transcendence-in-immanence of human experience raises the hope and conjecture that in humanity immanence might be able to display a transcendent dimension to a degree which would unveil, without distortion, the transcendent-Creator-who-is-immanent in a uniquely new emergent manner – that is, that in humanity (in a human being, or in human beings), the presence of God the Creator might be unveiled with a clarity, in a glory, not hitherto perceived. Might it not be possible for a human being so to reflect God, to be so wholly open to God, that God's presence was clearly unveiled to the rest of humanity in a new, emergent and unexpected manner? If that were to be so, would it not then be accurate to say that, in such a person, the immanence of God had displayed a transcendent dimension to such a degree that the presence of God in and to the actual psychosomatic unity of that person required and requires new non-reducible concepts and language to express its character and uniqueness? The mere posing of such a question cannot but raise our hope for the lifting of at least the corner of the veil that shrouds the mystery of God in an act or process initiated by God within the nexus of the history of persons. Whether or not we have been given this is a matter for further inquiry.[10]

It is at this stage of an inquiry into the relation of natural to divine being and becoming that one cannot but become acutely aware of the inadequacy of all 'God-talk'. We see very darkly through the glass of nature and experience, and the ultimate mystery of God's Being and Becoming, what God 'is' and 'is becoming', must in principle continue to remain partly hidden. One is compelled to continue to attempt to formulate the least misleading, the least inaccurate, the most illuminating and insightful ways of talking about God without whom none of us – author, reader, book – would be at all. Yet all words, metaphors, models, analogies continue to be inadequate to express that ultimate Reality – and this is scarcely surprising since there is an inalienable mystery even concerning the being and becoming of any single entity in the world, and most of all of any individual person. This mystery is not that of a problem yet to be formulated and resolved by further inquiry but is inherent in the very nature of a person in him- or herself. And if this eludes us, how much more the nature of God's own Being and Becoming, God's own selfhood?

It is related that one of the greatest theologians of the Christian era, St Thomas Aquinas, suspended work on the third part of his great *Summa theologica*, telling his secretary that, after an experience while saying Mass in December 1273, he would write no more for, he said, 'All that I have written seems to me like so much straw compared with what I have seen and with what has been revealed to me.'[11] Theology that is not fed by and consummated in prayer and worship is indeed sterile and can deteriorate into a merely intellectual exercise. Who, writing on the profundity that is God, cannot but feel with St Thomas that the bricks of his constructions are made only of straw? Nevertheless, we are commanded to love God with our minds and so such an enterprise as this is worthwhile if its limitations are recognized – that talk about God, theo-logy, is but ancillary to prayer and worship. But to pray and to worship we need supportable and believable models and images of the One to whom prayer and worship are alone to be directed. This volume is offered as a necessarily inadequate contribution to that pressing and perennial task of refurbishing our images of God.

NOTES

Other works by Arthur Peacocke cited in the notes are abbreviated as follows:

SCE   *Science and the Christian Experiment* (Oxford University Press, London, 1971)
CWS   *Creation and the World of Science* (Clarendon Press, Oxford, 1979)
IR   *Intimations of Reality: Critical Realism in Science and Religion* (University of Notre Dame Press, Indiana, 1984)
PCBO   *An Introduction to the Physical Chemistry of Biological Organization* (Clarendon Press, Oxford, 1983; repr. as pbk, with supplementary references, 1989)
GNB   *God and the New Biology* (Dent, London, 1986)

INTRODUCTION: THE THEOLOGICAL AND SCIENTIFIC ENTERPRISES

1 B. Martin and R. Pluck, *Young People's Beliefs* (General Synod of the Board of Education of the Church of England, 1977), pp. 22, 24, 59.
2 Lesslie Newbigin, *Foolishness to the Greeks* (World Council of Churches, Geneva, and Wm B. Eerdmans, Grand Rapids, Michigan, 1986), *passim.*
3 Thomas Sprat, *The History of the Royal Society of London for the Improving of Natural Knowledge* (London, 1702, 2nd edn), pp. 370–2.
4 See, for example, John Durant, 'Darwinism and divinity: a century of debate', in *Darwinism and Divinity*, ed. John Durant (Basil Blackwell, Oxford, 1985), pp. 18–23, and references therein.
5 For it has been claimed that the Judeo-Christian milieu of Western Christendom, through its belief that the natural world had a contingent order, afforded a congenial matrix, to say the least, for the rise of modern science – though a direct causality is less easily established and is probably, in any case, unprovable. For a critique of the widely held belief in this supposed historical causal relation, see Rolf Gruner, 'Science, Nature and Christianity', *Journal of Theological Studies*, 26 (1975), pp. 55–81.

6 For a careful account of the meaning of this term (which in English can be misleadingly translated as 'human sciences') and its history, see W. Pannenberg, *Theology and the Philosophy of Science*, trans. F. McDonagh (Darton, Longman and Todd, London, and Westminster Press, Philadelphia, 1976), pp. 72ff.

7 What we are to mean by 'God' can only transpire later. But I refer here to those experiences, to use the phraseology of Alister Hardy and the Centre named after him, of an 'awareness of a benevolent non-physical power which appears to be partly or wholly beyond, and far greater than, the individual self' (see Alister Hardy, *The Spiritual Nature of Man*, Clarendon Press, Oxford, 1979, p. 1). 'Religious experience', of course covers a far wider range than this, as reference to the literature of that same Centre reveals.

8 John Passmore, *Science and its Critics* (Duckworth, London, 1978), p. 57.

9 ibid., p. 96.

10 H. Harris, 'Rationality in science', in *Scientific Explanations*, ed. A. F. Heath (Clarendon Press, Oxford, 1981), p. 40.

11 Taking this in the broad sense, see n. 7.

12 See *IR* and references therein; A. R. Peacocke, 'Science and theology today: a critical realist perspective', *Religion and Intellectual Life*, 5 (1988), pp. 45–58. A helpful account of critical realism as a philosophy of science and an analysis of, and apologia for, its significance for systematic theology has been given by W. van Huysteen in *Theology and the Justification of Faith* (Wm B. Eerdmans, Grand Rapids, Michigan, 1989), ch. 9. See also Michael Banner, *The Justification of Science and the Rationality of Religious Belief* (Clarendon Press, Oxford, 1990).

13 J. Leplin, 'Introduction', in *Scientific Realism*, ed. J. Leplin (University of California Press, 1984), p. 1.

14 ibid., p. 2.

15 Ernan McMullin, 'The case for scientific realism', in Leplin, *Scientific Realism*, p. 26.

16 ibid., p. 30.

17 Janet Martin Soskice, *Metaphor and Religious Language* (Clarendon Press, Oxford, 1984), ch. 7.

18 W. H. Newton-Smith, *The Rationality of Science* (Routledge and Kegan Paul, London, 1981), pp. 164–74.

19 Soskice, *Metaphor*, p. 159.

20 Ian Barbour, *Issues in Science and Religion* (Harper and Row, New York, 1971, pbk edn), p. 158.

21 See *IR*, p. 30, for further discussion and references.

22 See n. 12 above.

23 See, for example, B. G. Mitchell, *The Justification of Religious Belief* (Macmillan, London, 1973); D. Pailin, 'Can the theologian legitimately try to answer the question: is the Christian faith true?', *Expository*

Times, 84 (1973), pp. 321–9; J. R. Carnes, *Axiomatics and Dogmatics* (Christian Journals, Belfast, 1982), ch. 5 (his criteria are: coherence, economy, adequacy and existential relevance – these overlap those cited in the text); and Banner, *Justification of Science*.

24 ibid.

25 I cannot trace the reference.

26 Hans Kung in an unpublished lecture, 'Paradigm change in theology', given at the University of Chicago in 1981; published in a different form in *Paradigm Change in Theology* ed. Hans Kung and David Tracy (T. & T. Clark, Edinburgh, 1989), pp. 3–33.

27 cf. D. C. MacIntosh, 'Experimental realism in religion', in *Religious Realism*, ed. D. C. MacIntosh (Macmillan, New York, 1931).

28 I cannot avoid here betraying my conviction that the traditional reliance of the Anglican communion *inter alia* on a judicious use of the resources of scripture and tradition, viewed in the light of reason based on experience (the 'three-legged stool'), affords the most viable way of developing a defensible and believable expression of Christian faith. Such a faith might unite Christians and convince the post-Enlightenment, 'post-modern' world of its truth – that is, that it genuinely depicts realities (or, rather, *the* Reality that is God in Christ through the Holy Spirit). It is the weaving of this threefold cord (Scripture, tradition and reason based on experience) in a church in which authority is dispersed, collegial and non-coercive, essentially dialogical, that alone, I would submit, can provide any long-term future for Christian faith in a not unjustifiably sceptical world.

29 See chs. 2–4.

30 John Bowker, *Licensed Insanities* (Darton, Longman and Todd, London, 1987), p. 13.

31 See *IR*, pp. 18–22, for references.

32 See *IR*; van Huysteen, *Theology*; Banner, *Justification of Science*; McMullin, 'The case for scientific realism'.

33 A. R. Peacocke, 'Introduction', in *The Sciences and Theology in the Twentieth Century*, ed. A. R. Peacocke (Oriel Press, Stocksfield and London, and University of Notre Dame Press, Notre Dame, Indiana, 1981), pp. ix–xviii.

34 R. J. Russell, '*A critical appraisal of Peacocke's thought on religion and science*', *Religion and Intellectual Life*, 2 (1985), pp. 48–58.

35 ibid., p. 50.

36 Ernan McMullin, 'Realism in theology and science: a response to Peacocke', *Religion and Intellectual Life*, 2 (1985), pp. 39–47.

37 See *CWS*, ch. 1 and references therein.

38 See also *GNB*, chs. 1, 2.

39 See ch. 8 and the Postscript.

40 See the useful discussion of these ideas by Eric T. Juengst, 'Response: carving nature at the joints', *Religion and Intellectual Life*, 5 (1988), pp. 70–8.

41   And in relation to the person of Jesus the Christ, as it will transpire in a subsequent development of this work, in preparation (A. R. Peacocke, *Theology for a Scientific Age*, Part III, *Human Being and Becoming*).
42   If the referent of theology is, then, to that which is 'The Transcendent-in-the-Immanent', could not its relation to other disciplines be regarded as that of a highly democratized constitutional monarchy, something like the 'Queen-in-Parliament' of the constitution of the United Kingdom?

CHAPTER 1   INTRODUCTION

1   Herbert Butterfield, *The Origins of Modern Science* (Bell, London, 1968), p. vii.
2   ibid., pp. vii, viii.
3   Introduction, n. 10.

CHAPTER 2   WHAT'S THERE?

1   Stephen Hawking, 'The direction of time', *New Scientist*, 115 (9 July 1987), pp. 46–9; *A Brief History of Time* (Bantam and Transworld, London, 1988), p. 14.
2   See, for example, Hawking, *Brief History of Time*, n. 1; Steven Weinberg, *The First Three Minutes* (André Deutsch, London, 1977); Paul Davies, *The Runaway Universe* (Dent, London, 1978); and the account in *SCE*, ch. 2.
3   H. K. Schilling, *The New Consciousness in Science and Religion* (SCM Press, London, 1973), p. 126.
4   I refer to such books as: Peter Atkins, *The Creation* (Freeman, Oxford and San Francisco, 1981); Adam Ford, *Universe: God, Man and Science* (Hodder and Stoughton, London, 1986); and *SCE*, chs. 2 and 3.
5   F. H. C. Crick, *Of Molecules and Man* (University of Washington Press, Seattle and London, 1966), p. 10.
6   See *GNB*, for a fuller discussion of this whole matter.
7   James P. Crutchfield, J. Doyne Farmer, Norman H. Packard and Robert S. Shaw, 'Chaos', *Scientific American*, Dec. 1986, pp. 38–49.
8   J. S. Bell, 'On the Einstein-Podolsky-Rosen Paradox', *Physics* 1 (1964), pp. 95–200; J. F. Clauser and A. Shimony, 'Bell's theorem; experimental tests and implications', *Reports on Progress in Physics*, 41 (1978), pp. 1881–1927; Bernard d'Espagnat, 'The Quantum Theory and reality', *Scientific American*, 241 (Nov. 1979), pp. 128–40; Abner Shimony, 'The reality of the Quantum World', *Scientific American*, 258 (Jan. 1988), pp. 46–53.

CHAPTER 3   WHAT'S GOING ON?

1   R. Harré, *The Principles of Scientific Thinking* (Macmillan, London, 1970), ch. 4.

2   e.g., see Henri Poincaré, *Science and Method*, tr. F. Maitland (Thomas Nelson, London, 1914), p. 68.

3   Michael Berry, 'Breaking the paradigms of classical physics from within', 1983 Cercy Symposium, *Logique et theorie des catastrophes*.

4   ibid.; James P. Crutchfield, J. Doyne Farmer, Norman H. Packard and Robert S. Shaw, 'Chaos', *Scientific A,. erican*, Dec. 1986, p. 38.

5   See Crutchfield et al., 'Chaos'; *PCBO*, chs. 2, 4, 5; and Paul Davies, *The Cosmic Blueprint* (Heinemann, London, 1987), chs. 3–6.

6   So the plots that mathematicians customarily use to depict changes in the state of a system (diagrams in phase-space) keep on revealing complexities and sequences of states at every level of magnification. In other words, they look like the pictures illustrating 'fractals' with which Mandelbrot has familiarized us. Indeed, mathematically the regions in the phase-space to which the systems gravitate (the states they tend to take up in ordinary language) can be proved to be fractals, having non-integer dimensions and revealing more detail as they are progressively magnified. The line depicting the state of the system continuously folds back on itself, going through states close to, but never identical with, previous ones – like dough, containing a drop of dye, that is kneaded by a baker. Such systems possess what is provokingly called a 'strange attractor' to distinguish it from the more ordinary 'attractors', the points, lines or regions in phase-space towards which non-linear systems may move in time. This 'fractal' character of the mathematical representation of these particular non-linear systems is another way of expressing that special feature of their exquisite sensitivity to the values of their distinctive parameters which makes very close states in time lead to widely different results. In other words, small fluctuations in the system can lead to very large effects (the 'butterfly effect' again), with loss of all predictive power.

7   See *inter alia*, Ilya Prigogine, *From Being to Becoming* (W. H. Freeman, San Francisco, 1980); Ilya Prigogine and Isabelle Stengers, *Order Out Of Chaos* (Heinemann, London, 1984); and *PCBO*, ch. 2.

8   Crutchfield et al., 'Chaos', p. 48.

9   Donald T. Campbell, '"Downward causation" in hierarchically organised systems', in *Studies in the Philosophy of Biology: Reduction and Related Problems*, ed. F. J. Ayala and T. Dobzhansky (Macmillan, London, 1974), pp. 179–86.

10   Roger W. Sperry, *Science and Moral Priority* (Blackwell, Oxford, 1983), ch. 6.

11   Another example from another area of science, a computer programmed to rearrange its own circuitry through a robot that it itself

controls, has been proposed by Paul Davies (*The Cosmic Blueprint*, Heinemann, London, 1987, pp. 172–4 and fig. 32) as an instance of what he called 'downward causation'. In this hypothetical (but not at all impossible) system, changes in the information encoded in the computer's software (usually taken as the 'higher' level) downwardly cause modifications in the computer's hardware (the 'lower' level) – an example of software–hardware feedback.

12 Michael A. Arbib and Mary B. Hesse, *The Construction of Reality* (Cambridge University Press, Cambridge, 1986), p. 64.

13 F. J. Ayala, 'Introduction' in Ayala and Dobzhansky, *Studies in the Philosophy of Biology*, p. ix.

14 Arbib and Hesse, *Construction of Reality*, p. 65.

15 ibid., p. 66.

16 Sperry, *Science and Moral Priority*, pp. 88, 90–6.

17 Arbib and Hesse, *Construction of Reality*, p. 64.

18 See *PCBO*, ch. 5.

19 M. Eigen, 'The self-organization of matter and the evolution of biological macromolecules', *Naturwissenschaften*, 58 (1971), p. 519.

20 F. Jacob, *The Logic of Living Systems* (Allen Lane, London, 1974), p. 13.

21 Campbell, 'Downward causation', pp. 181–2.

22 Elisabeth Vrba, 'Patterns in the fossil record and evolutionary processes', in *Beyond Darwinism*, ed. M. W. Ho and P. T. Saunders (Academic Press, London, 1984), p. 121.

23 ibid., pp. 121–2, see for further references and discussion.

24 R. C. Lewontin, 'Gene, organism and environment', in *Evolution from Molecules to Men*, ed. D. S. Bendall (Cambridge University Press, Cambridge, 1983), pp. 273–85.

25 Sir Alister Hardy, *The Living Stream* (Collins, London, 1985), pp. 161ff., 189ff.

26 Section 2(b), above.

27 D. M. Mackay, 'The interdependence of mind and brain', *Neuroscience*, 5 (1980), pp. 1389–91.

28 J. Searle, *Minds, Brains and Science* (Harvard University Press, Cambridge, Mass., 1984), p. 26.

29 Sperry, *Science and Moral Priority*, pp. 93–6; and by Donald Mackay, see 'Interdependence of mind and brain' for brief statement, with full references.

30 *SCE*, chs. 2, 3; *CWS*, ch. II; Holmes Rolston III, *Science and Religion: A Critical Survey* (Random House, New York, 1987), chs. 2, 3.

31 The depiction of this process as 'nature, red in tooth and claw' (a phrase of Tennyson's that actually pre-dates Darwin's proposal of evolution through natural selection) is a caricature for, as many biologists have pointed out (e.g., G. G. Simpson in *The Meaning of Evolution*, Bantam Books and Yale University Press, New Haven, 1971 edn, p. 201), natural selection is not even in a figurative sense the outcome of

struggle, as such. Natural selection involves many factors that include better integration with the ecological environment, more efficient utilization of available food, better care of the young, more cooperative social organization – and better capacity of surviving such 'struggles' as do occur (remembering that it is in the interest of any predator that their prey survive as a species).

32   For a fuller discussion of this, see *GNB*, Appendix.

33   Section 2(b), above.

34   R. Winkler and M. Eigen, *Laws of the Game* (Knopf, New York, 1981, and Allen Lane, London, 1982).

35   See *CWS*, ch. III; D. J. Bartholomew, *God of Chance* (SCM Press, London, 1984).

36   J. Wicken, *Journal of Theoretical Biology*, 72 (1978), pp. 191–204; *GNB*, Appendix, pp. 141–2.

37   Karl Popper, at the World Philosophy Congress, Brighton, August 1988, reported in *The Guardian*, 29 August 1988.

38   W. McCoy, *Journal of Theoretical Biology*, 68 (1977), p. 457.

39   J. Maynard Smith, in *Towards a Theoretical Biology, 2. Sketches*, ed. C. H. Waddington (Edinburgh University Press, Edinburgh, 1969), pp. 88–9.

40   P. T. Saunders and M. W. Ho, *Journal of Theoretical Biology*, 63 (1976), pp. 375–84); 90 (1981), pp. 515–30; W. McCoy, ibid.; C. Castrodeza, *Journal of Theoretical Biology*, 71 (1978), pp. 469–71.

41   For fuller discussion, see *GNB*, Appendix; and *PCBO*, ch. 6.

42   H. A. Simon, 'The architecture of complexity', *Proceedings of the American Philosophical Society*, 106 (1962), pp. 467–82.

43   E. g., G. G. Simpson, *The Meaning of Evolution* (Bantam Books, Yale University Press, New Haven, 1971 edn), p. 256.

44   Holmes Rolston (ibid.) has developed this characteristic of biological evolution in what he calls 'cruciform naturalism' (pp. 289ff.). Sentience, he argues, evolves with a capacity to separate the 'helps' from the 'hurts' of the world: with sentience there appears caring (p. 287). With the appearance of life, organisms can now view events as 'pro-' or 'anti-life' and values and 'dis-values' appear – the world becomes a 'theatre of meanings' and nature may be variously judged as 'hostile', 'indifferent' and 'hospitable' (p. 244). 'The step up that brings more drama brings more suffering' (p. 288). But 'pain is an energizing force' so that 'where pain fits into evolutionary theory, it must have, on statistical average, high survival value, with this selected for, and with a selecting against counterproductive pain' (p. 288). 'Suffering ... moves us to action' and 'all advances come in contexts of problem solving, with a central problem in sentient life the prospect of hurt. In the evolution of caring, the organism is quickened to its needs' (p. 288). 'Suffering is a key to the whole, not intrinsically, not as an end in itself, but as a transformative principle, transvalued into its opposite' (p. 288).

45   C. Isham, 'Creation of the universe as a quantum tunnelling process', in

Physics, Philosophy and Theology: A Common Quest for Understanding, ed. R. J. Russell, W. R. Stoeger and G. V. Coyne (Vatican Observatory Publication, Vatican State, 1988), p. 397.

46   J. B. Hartle and S. W. Hawking, *Physical Reviews*, D28 (1983), p. 2960; see Isham's account, 'Creation of the universe', and Stephen Hawking, *A Brief History of Time* (Bantam and Transworld, London, 1988) ch. 8.

47   Isham, 'Creation of the universe', p. 400.

48   For a fuller discussion, see *CWS*, ch. VIII; and J. Polkinghorne, *Science and Creation* (SPCK, London, 1988), pp. 64ff.

49   Freeman Dyson, *Disturbing the Universe* (Pan Books, London, 1981).

CHAPTER 4   WHO'S THERE?

1   For further accounts, see *SCE*, pp. 99–106; *CWS*, pp. 72–4; and Holmes Rolston III, *Science and Religion: A Critical Survey* (Random House, New York, 1987), chs. 4, 5.

2   For a recent survey, from scientific, philosophical and theological viewpoints, of a wide range of conceptions of the human person and of what constitutes personality – in various combinations of naturalism, reductionism, existentialism, dualism and theism – see *Persons and Personality*, ed. Arthur Peacocke and Grant Gillett (Blackwell, Oxford, 1987); see also the magisterial survey of John Macquarrie, *In Search of Humanity: A Theological and Philosophical Approach* (SCM Press, London, 1982).

3   For an account of these ideas on evolutionary epistemology and their philosophical import, see Peter Munz, *Our Knowledge of the Growth of Knowledge* (Routledge and Kegan Paul, London, 1985).

4   Such a mutually defined account of (a) the relation of consciousness to brain activity and (b) the evolution of consciousness, so defined, has recently been given by Michael A. Arbib and Mary B. Hesse, (*The Construction of Reality*, Cambridge University Press, Cambridge, 1986, pp. 76–7) in terms of schema theory. In that theory a 'schema' is a unit of representation of reality and it views 'language as metaphorical, having its meaning within the open schema networks of the participants in a discourse' (p. 67).

5   Richard Tur, 'The "person" in law', in Peacocke and Gillett, *Persons and Personality*, pp. 116–29.

6   Konrad Lorenz, *Behind the Mirror: A Search for a Natural History of Human Knowledge* (Methuen, London, 1977, English trans.) p. 113.

7   I. T. Ramsey, 'Human personality', in *Personality and Science*, ed. I. T. Ramsey and Ruth Porter (Churchill Livingstone, Edinburgh and London, 1971), p. 128.

8   John Barrow and Frank Tipler, *The Anthropic Cosmological Principle* (Clarendon Press, Oxford, 1986), p. 16.

9 J. H. Crook, *The Evolution of Human Consciousness* (Clarendon Press, Oxford, 1980), p. 35.
10 ibid., p. 36.
11 Lorenz, *Behind the Mirror*, p. 6.

CHAPTER 5 WHAT DOES IT ALL MEAN?

1 F. Hoyle, *The Nature of the Universe* (Blackwell, Oxford, 1960), p. 103.
2 See *PCBO*, ch. 6.
3 A. Einstein, *Out of My Later Years* (repr. Greenwood Press, Westpo·ˑ, Conn., 1970), p. 61.
4 H. K. Schilling, *The New Consciousness in Science and Religion* (SCM Press, London, 1973).
5 Victor Weisskopf, *Knowledge and Wonder* (Doubleda, Garden City, NY, 1962), p. 100.

CHAPTER 6 ASKING 'WHY?': THE SEARCH FOR INTELLIGIBILITY AND MEANING

1 Introduction, section 3.
2 J. J. Shepherd, *Experience, Inference and God* (Macmillan, London, 1975), p. 76.
3 M. K. Munitz, *The Mystery of Existence* (Appleton-Century-Crofts, New York, 1965).
4 Keith Ward, *The Turn of the Tide* (BBC Publications, London, 1986), ch. 3.
5 Keith Ward, *The Concept of God* (Blackwell, Oxford, 1974), p. 148.
6 Introduction, section 1.
7 Ch. 4, section 2.

CHAPTER 7 'GOD' AS RESPONSE TO THE SEARCH FOR INTELLIGIBILITY AND MEANING

1 Keith Ward, *The Turn of the Tide* (BBC Publications, London, 1986), p. 67.
2 Introduction, section 3.
3 See Introduction, n. 23.
4 John R. Carnes, *Axiomatics and Dogmatics* (Christian Journals, Belfast, 1982), ch. 5.
5 ibid.
6 ibid.
7 Richard Swinburne, *The Coherence of Theism* (Clarendon Press, Ox-

ford, 1977); *The Existence of God* (Clarendon Press, Oxford, 1979); *Faith and Reason* (Clarendon Press, 1981); Ward, *Turn of the Tide*; Alvin Plantinga, 'Reason and belief in God', in *Faith and Rationality*, ed. A. Plantinga and N. Wolsterstorff (University of Notre Dame Press, Notre Dame, Indiana, 1983), pp. 16–93.

8 Anthony Kenny, *The God of the Philosophers* (Clarendon Press, Oxford, 1979); J. L. Mackie, *The Miracle of Theism* (Clarendon Press, Oxford, 1982).

9 Mackie, *Miracle of Theism*; Richard Swinburne, 'Mackie, induction, and God', *Religious Studies*, 19 (1983), pp. 385–91.

10 Swinburne, ibid., p. 385.

11 Swinburne, *Existence of God*, p. 8.

12 Here, and in the phrases that follow, the wording of Swinburne (ibid., p. 8) is followed, denoted by quotation marks.

13 Swinburne, *Existence of God*, p. 8, n. 1. Here I would prefer to regard God as 'personal', or as 'at least personal', rather than as 'a person', since to call God 'a person' seems to me to indicate a greater insight into the mystery of the ultimate Reality that is God than is warrantable. One is trying to express the experience believers have that God relates to them personally and that God is 'something like' (see the quotation from E. McMullin, Introduction p. 12 and n. 15) a personal agent in their lives and, it will be argued, in the world. Theological language, as was stressed in the Introduction, is inevitably metaphorical so that qualifying adjectives ('at least personal') and adverbs ('personally') are preferable, in my view, to unqualified nouns ('a person') in referring to God.

14 Swinburne, p. 92.

15 ibid., p. 93.

16 Swinburne, 'Mackie, induction and God', p. 385.

17 Swinburne, *Existence of God*, p. 32.

18 Swinburne, 'Mackie, induction and God', p. 391.

19 *The Concept of God*, ed. Thomas V. Morris (Oxford University Press, Oxford, 1987).

20 ibid., pp. 6, 7.

21 *Believing in the Church – The Corporate Nature of Faith*, a report by the Doctrine Commission of the Church of England (SPCK, London, 1981).

22 *We Believe in God*, a report by the Doctrine Commission of the Church of England (Church House Publishing, London, 1987).

CHAPTER 8   THE CONCEPT OF GOD: IMPLICATIONS OF SCIENTIFIC PERSPECTIVES

1 See the Postscript for a further discussion of this distinction.

2 Ch. 7, section 1.

3 See Part I, above, and references therein; see also John Polkinghorne,

One World (SPCK, London, 1986), pp. 22ff., 44ff.

4 Ch. 2, sections 1 and 2.

5 Ch. 2, section 4.

6 Ch. 2, section 3.

7 Ch. 5, nn. 1, 3.

8 Ch. 3, sections 1(d), 3(a).

9 Ch. 2, section 1.

10 *Summa Theologicae* I.2.3.

11 Ch. 2, section 1.

12 ibid.

13 Using (*faute de mieux*), here and elsewhere, the traditional male pronoun in English, but not thereby intending to exclude feminine aspects of God.

14 Ch. 3, section 3.

15 This chapter, section 2.

16 Ch. 7, section 1.

17 e.g., Richard Swinburne, *The Existence of God* (Clarendon Press, Oxford, 1979), p. 8 and *passim*.

18 Ch. 7, section 2.

19 Ch. 4, section 2.

20 P. W. Atkins, *The Creation*, (W. H. Freeman, Oxford and San Francisco, 1981).

21 D. J. Bartholomew, *God of Chance* (SCM Press, London, 1984), pp. 64–5.

22 H. Montefiore, *The Probability of God* (SCM Press, London, 1985); John Polkinghorne, *Science and Creation* (SPCK, London, 1988).

23 See for example, the discussion of J. Leslie, 'How to draw conclusions from a fine-tuned universe', in *Physics, Philosophy and Theology: A Common Quest for Understanding* (Vatican Observatory publication, Vatican City State, 1988, distributed by University of Notre Dame Press), pp. 297–311; see also his *Universes* (Routledge and Kegan Paul, London and New York, 1989).

24 Montefiore, *Probability of God*; Polkinghorne, *Science and Creation*.

25 *CWS*, pp. 67–72.

26 ibid., pp. 70–1.

27 Ch. 4, section 1.

28 A. N. Whitehead, *Science and the Modern World* (Mentor Books edn, New York, 1949), p. 56.

29 John Durant, on 'Is there a role for theology in an age of secular science?', in *One World: Changing Perspectives on Reality*, ed. J. Fennema and I. Paul (University of Twente and Kluwer Academic Press, 1990), pp. 161–72.

30 Ch. 4, section 1 and *CWS*, pp. 70–1.

31 See ch. 2, section 3.

32 Here following *CWS*, pp. 72–3.

33 G. E. Pugh, *The Biological Origins of Human Values* (Basic Books, New York, 1977); see *CWS*, p. 154, n. 13, for more details.

34 See R. Trigg, *The Shaping of Man* (Blackwell, Oxford, 1982).

35   Ch. 3.
36   Ch. 2, section 2, and ch. 3, section 3(a).
37   Ch. 8, section 1.
38   C. Darwin, *The Origin of Species* (Thinkers Library, Watts London, 6th edn), p. 408.
39   Genesis 1:31.
40   *CWS*, pp. 108–11.
41   Manfred Eigen and Ruthild Winkler, *The Laws of the Game* (Knopf, New York, 1981 and Allen Lane, London, 1982).
42   Ch. 3, section 1.
43   See for example, Ilya Prigogine and Isabelle Stengers, *Order Out Of Chaos* (Heinemann, London, 1984); and *PCBO* for other references.
44   Ch. 3, section 2(a).
45   See ch. 3, section 1(b).
46   Ch. 3, section 2(b).
47   Jacques Monod, *Chance and Necessity* (Collins, London, 1972).
48   Bartholomew, *God of Chance.*
49   A. R. Peacocke, 'Chance, potentiality and God', *The Modern Churchman*, 17 (n.s. 1973), pp. 13–23; and in *Beyond Chance and Necessity*, ed. J. Lewis (Garnstone Press, 1974), pp. 13–25; 'Chaos or cosmos', *New Scientist*, 63 (1974), pp. 386–9; *CWS*, ch. 3.
50   *CWS*, p. 94.
51   Ilya Prigogine, *From Being to Becoming* (W. H. Freeman, San Francisco, 1980); Prigogine and Stengers, *Order Out Of Chaos*. For some recent accounts of the scientific work of the Brussels school and its significance, see *GNB*, appendix on 'Thermodynamics and Life', pp. 133–60, and *PCBO*, esp. ch. 2.
52   Eigen and Winkler, *Laws of the Game*; M. Eigen and P. Schuster, *The Hypercycle* (Springer-Verlag, Berlin, 1979); see also *PCBO*, ch. 5.
53   Richard Dawkins, *The Blind Watchmaker* (Longmans, Harlow, 1986).
54   *CWS*, pp. 105–6.
55   ibid., pp. 108–11.
56   ibid., p. 95.
57   Bartholomew, *God of Chance*, p. 97.
58   ibid.
59   ibid., p. 98.
60   ibid.
61   ibid., p. 102.
62   Ch. 8, section 1.
63   Ch. 3, sections 1 and 2.
64   Ch. 7, section 1.
65   Jürgen Moltmann, *The Crucified God* (SCM Press, London, 1974); W. H. Vanstone, *Love's Endeavour, Love's Expense* (Darton, Longman and Todd, London, 1977).
66   Bartholomew, *God of Chance*, p. 138. Some of the things, he argues (pp. 139ff.), which one might expect a creative God to wish to do are: to act

in 'the springs of creative thought in the human mind'; to be involved in, a party to, human decision making; to be at work at those junctures where man makes mistakes, or threatens to do so; to be active on the side of reconciliation between warring factions; to communicate his presence in critical circumstances; and, perhaps, to engineer coincidences in 'very special circumstances'. All of these concern the problem of the nature of God's interaction with the world and will have to be discussed, and not necessarily accepted, later.

67 This chapter, section 1(g).

68 The whole question of 'moral evil' in the world that results from human dispositions ('sin') and actions ('sins') will arise in the context of subsequent consideration of 'Human being and becoming' (in a successor to this work).

69 Ch. 3, section 3; *CWS*, pp. 198–202, 213–14, 229–30.

70 Paul S. Fiddes, *The Creative Suffering of God* (Clarendon Press, Oxford, 1988) p. 3 (italics in original).

71 ibid., p. 45 (see also ch. 2 *passim*).

72 I hint here at my broad acceptance of John Hick's 'Irenaean' theodicy in relation to 'natural' evil (see 'An Irenaean theodicy', in *Encountering Evil*, ed. Stephen T. Davis (T. & T. Clark, Edinburgh, 1981), pp. 39–52; and his earlier *Evil and the God of Love* (Macmillan, London, 1966), especially chs 15 and 16) and the position outlined by Brian Hebblethwaite in ch. 5, 'Physical suffering and the nature of the physical world', of his *Evil, Suffering and Religion* (Sheldon Press, London, 1976).

73 cf. this chapter, section 1, *passim*.

74 For both his personhood and his ability to act in the world, see J. R. Lucas, *A Treatise on Time and Space* (Methuen, London, 1973), chs 55, 56; Nelson Pike, *God and Timelessness* (Routledge and Kegan Paul, London, 1970); Keith Ward, *Rational Theology and the Creativity of God* (Blackwell, Oxford, 1982).

75 See Lucas, *Treatise on Time and Space*, chs 55, 56; Pike, *God and Timelessness*; Ward, *Rational Theology*; P. T. Geach, 'The future', *New Blackfriars*, 54 (1973), p. 208.

76 This chapter, section 1(e).

77 Lucas, *Treatise on Time and Space*, ch. 17, *passim*.

78 Ward, *Rational Theology*, p. 151–2.

79 John Polkinghorne, *Science and Providence* (SPCK, London, 1989) p. 82.

80 ibid.

81 'It is therefore true to say that when you [God] had not made anything there was no time, because time itself was of your making', *Confessions* xi.14, trans. R. S. Pine-Coffin (Penguin Classics edn, Harmondsworth, London, 1961), p. 263.

82 Ward, *Rational Theology*, p. 160.

83 See discussion in this chapter, pp. 121–3 and above, and ch. 7, section 1.

84 H. K. Schilling, *The New Consciousness in Science and Religion* (SCM

Press, London, 1973), p. 126.

85 cf. R. Swinburne, *The Coherence of Theism* (Clarendon Press, Oxford, 1977), p. 175, where he develops an account of omniscience not as knowledge of everything true but as knowledge of everything true it is logically possible to know. He suggests the following understanding of omniscience: 'A person *P* is omniscient at a time *t* if and only if he knows of every true proposition about *t* or an earlier time that it is true *and* also he knows of every true proposition about a time later than *t*, such that what it reports is physically necessary by some cause at *t* or earlier, that it is true. On this understanding of omniscience, *P* is omniscient if he knows about everything except those future states and their consequences which are not physically necessitated by anything in the past; and if he knows that he does not know about those future states.'

86 See above, ch. 7, section 1, where the phraseology of R. Swinburne, in *The Coherence of Theism* and *The Existence of God* (p. 8), is reproduced.

87 For a philosophically more thorough exposition of an understanding of God's relation to time very close to that in the text, see Ward, *Rational Theology*, ch. 7. This section in the text is much indebted to the expositions of both Keith Ward and John Lucas.

88 As R. Swinburne *inter alia* has argued (in *The Coherence of Theism*, pp. 211–15).

89 *We Believe in God*, a report by the Doctrine Commission of the Church of England (Church House Publishing, London, 1987), p. 160.

90 ibid., pp. 159–60.

91 Ch. 3, section 3(b); Stephen Hawking, *A Brief History of Time* (Bantam and Transworld, London, 1988), ch. 8; J. B. Hartle and S. W. Hawking, *Physical Reviews*, D28 (1983), p. 2960.

92 Hawking, *Brief History of Time*, pp. 134–6.

93 ibid., p. 135.

94 ibid., p. 136.

95 ibid., p. 174.

CHAPTER 9 GOD'S INTERACTION WITH THE WORLD

1 Michael J. Langford, *Providence* (SCM Press, London, 1981), p. 6.

2 John Macquarrie, *Principles of Christian Theology* (SCM Press, London, 1966), p. 219.

3 Christoph Schwöbel, 'Divine agency and Providence', *Modern Theology*, 3 (1987), pp. 225–44, esp. p. 241.

4 ibid., p. 241.

5 Vernon White, *The Fall of a Sparrow*, (Paternoster Press, Exeter, 1985), pp. 54–5.

6 Langford, *Providence*, p. 41.

7　ibid., p. 42.

8　Thomas F. Tracy, *God, Action and Embodiment* (Eerdmans, Publishing Co., Grand Rapids, 1984), p. xii.

9　ibid.

10　Langdon Gilkey, 'Cosmology, ontology, and the travail of Biblical language', *Journal of Religion*, 41 (1961), pp. 194–205; rep. in *God's Activity in the World*, ed. Owen C. Thomas (Scholars Press, Chico, Cal., 1983; page numbers refer to this edn), p. 37. Italics added.

11　ibid., pp. 42–3.

12　David Brown, *The Divine Trinity* (Duckworth, London, 1985), pp. 5, 33. In this context, theology might well take a hint from philosophical discussions of the mind–body problem, in which some authors (e.g. Donald Davidson, 'Mental events', in *Experience and Theory*, ed. L. Foster and J. W. Swanson, University of Massachusetts Press, 1970) speak of mental events as 'supervenient' upon the neuronal activities of the brain, rather than 'intervening' in them – meaning by this that mental events can at least be affirmed to have a controlling, directing, supervisory influence on brain events without entailing reducibility to, or in any way being disruptive or interruptive of, them. To be fair to Brown's position, it should be noted that in the Introduction (p. xv) to *The Divine Trinity* he says that intervention as 'part of the normal pattern of divine activity' is what he is aiming to establish. He has subsequently further clarified his position in an article, 'God and Symbolic Action' (in *Divine Action: Studies Inspired by the Philosophical Theology of Austin Farrer*, ed. B. Hebblethwaite and E. Henderson, T. & T. Clark, Edinburgh, 1990), where he concedes that his position might be better described as 'interactionist', for he is chiefly concerned to allow God at least the same power and dignity of action as we are prepared to ascribe to ourselves in relation to others.

13　William P. Alston, 'God's action in the world', in *Evolution and Creation*, ed. Ernan McMullin, University of Notre Dame Press, Notre Dame, Indiana, 1985, pp. 197–220.

14　ibid., pp. 213–14.

15　ibid., p. 217.

16　Far from all; see also Alston, ibid., pp. 210–14.

17　David E. Jenkins, *God, Miracle and the Church of England* (SCM Press, London, 1987), p. 64.

18　ibid., pp. 63–4.

19　Schubert M. Ogden, 'What sense does it make to say, "God Acts in History"?', ch. VI of *The Reality of God and Other Essays* (Harper and Row, New York, 1963; repr. in O. C. Thomas, *God's Activity*, pp. 77–100).

20　Gordon D. Kaufman, *God the Problem* (Harvard University Press, Cambridge, Mass., 1972).

21　Such criticisms of Ogden's position were made by James Wm. McClendon, in 'Can there be talk about God-and-the-world?', (*Harvard Theological Review*, 62 (1969), pp. 33–49), and by David H.

Kelsey, in 'Can God be an agent without a body?' (*Interpretation*, 27 (1973), pp. 358–62). The former remarks (n. 12) that 'in making the distinction, which modern philosophy owes to Descartes, between "inner" and "outer", Ogden opens the door to a host of troubles'; and the latter (p. 359) 'that Ogden seems to have a dualistic view of "person".... It sometimes seems to come to expression in a mind/brain dualism.' There have been criticisms on a similar score of Kaufman's position, calling it 'residual Cartesianism' (E. Michael McLain, 'On theological models', *Harvard Theological Review*, 62 (1969), pp. 155–87), to which Kaufman has replied in the preface to *God the Problem* (n. 17).

22   Tracy, *God, Action and Embodiment*, pp. xv, xvi.

23   See, for example, the illuminating and thorough article by R. Ellis, 'God and "Action"', *Religious Studies*, 24 (1989), pp. 463–82. (I am grateful to Dr Ellis and Cambridge University Press for permission to reproduce the quotation below.) Ellis usefully identifies and enumerates (pp. 475–6) fifteen theses concerning human action that emerge from current philosophical analysis. He goes on – pertinently to our present purposes – to relate these analogically to the notion of God's 'action'. Since this analysis is presupposed in the discussion here I cannot do better than to summarize it in his own words (pp. 478–81; the bracketed small Roman numerals refer to the fifteen theses, as he enumerated them):

> ... for God to be said to *act* in the fullest sense ... he should have (i) an intention for a particular state of affairs. God's act (ii) is his intention for an event ... God is able (iii) to think about his acts far more rationally and with much greater vision than we. God's intention has (iv) future reference i.e. (xv) it is directed to a specifically desired state of affairs: he intends this, not that. God (v) is conscious of his intention, and (vi) statements of his intentions are the way of giving answers to questions 'why?' asked of certain events. (vii) All God's intended acts are voluntary ... The only ways in which God's acts can be considered involuntary are perhaps (a) because of states of affairs in the world which God wishes were not so, and which he must 'take into account' in acting ... (b) if the best for a given situation which God is able to intend for it will still bring inevitably discord and suffering ...
>
> God is responsible (x) for all events which occur according to his intention for them and as a result of his intention for them. Such an act is *his* act ... He is also responsible for effects which he could reasonably have been expected to have prevented from occurring, i.e. if they were not beyond his control ... For an act to be God's act he must have intention for it and have made it what it was.
>
> ... (xi) the distinction between basic and complex actions.

God's basic actions are the simple offerings of himself to his creatures in love, in which he may offer (though it will not often be acknowledged consciously) his intention and influence. God acts in this basic way on every existing thing at every instant... Such would be the content of much of our talk about providence... But God also acts in a complex way, involving the realising of his intention through other free agents... we are here talking of 'Double Agency'. God can act (xiv) through the free agency of another, and yet we may still say that it is properly and mostly *his* act...

We must recall what was said concerning the nature of complex actions: they bring with them the increasing possibility of failure (viii, xiii)...

... when we propound a theory of God's complex action in history, using a variety of free agents, then the task seems to demand our recognition that as acts get more complex, they also get more 'risky'... it may be useless to attempt a conception of God's agency unless we envisage this agency as operative among other autonomous agents...

God's basic actions cannot fail, but his complex actions are inevitably more precarious. We suggest then, that 'action' may well include within it the notion of possible failure...

God's aim and intentions are constant, and he is always acting (basic) and seeking to act (complex) according to his constant love.

24 Richard Swinburne appears to be unusual among contemporary philosophical theologians in arguing for a dualistic interpretation of the mind/body problem (in *The Evolution of the Soul* (Clarendon Press, Oxford, 1986), in which the 'soul' is regarded as a distinct entity, but not naturally immortal) and this shapes very directly his understanding of God's action in the world.

25 D. J. Bartholomew, *God of Chance* (SCM Press, London, 1984), p. 123; and see above, ch. 3(b).

26 Thomas, *God's Activity*, pp. 234–5.

27 ibid., pp. 235–6.

28 The approach which regards accounts in scientific and theistic languages as simply two alternative perspectives, equally valid in their respective 'language games'. The weakness of this approach is that, if one takes the critical-realist view of both scientific and theological affirmations, one cannot ignore the relation of what the two languages are asserting about the one actual, real world.

29 Thomas, *God's Activity*, ch. 14.

30 Thus no general attempt will be made here to classify authors according to their different approaches.

31 See nn. 19 and 20, above.

32 G. D. Kaufman, *God the Problem* (Harvard University Press, Cam-

bridge, Mass., 1972).

33   The response of process theologians to 'how?' questions C and D ('To what effect?' and 'To what extent?') is more a part of their account of God's purposes than of how they envisage God as involved in actual processes.

34   Maurice Wiles, 'Religious authority and divine action', *Religious Studies*, 7 (1971), pp. 1–12: reproduced in Thomas, *God's Activity*, pp. 181–94.

35   It is true that Wiles (n. 37, below,) does distance himself from those who view the world as 'a closed deterministically ordered system' (*God's Action in the World*, p. 65) and from 'extreme dualists' in their 'understanding of the human person' (p. 30). He attributes, by analogy, mentalistic properties, such as 'intentions' and 'purposes', to God as manifest in God's one, continuous, act of creation. Even so, he does not elaborate the kind of causality that operates when human ('mentalistic') intentions manifest themselves as actions in a physical world. This is crucial for making the analogy of God's agency to that of persons plausible with respect to the nexus of physical events in the world. Moreover the unpredictability of many macroscopic systems (see ch. 3, section 1) is not taken into account by Wiles or any of the other authors, even while some (it appears) do accept the widely acknowledged indeterminacy of the physical world at the quantum level.

36   Kaufman, *God the Problem*, p. 137.

37   Maurice Wiles, *God's Action in the World* (SCM Press, London, 1986), pp. 20, 28–9, 93.

38   Austin Farrer, *Faith and Speculation* (A. & C. Black, London, 1967).

39   Kaufman, *Problem of God*, preface; Brian L. Hebblethwaite 'Providence and divine action', *Religious Studies*, 14 (1978), pp. 223–36; David Galilee, 'The Remaking defended', *Theology*, 78 (1975), pp. 554–5.

40   Farrer, *Faith and Speculation*, p. 159.

41   Brian Hebblethwaite has called Farrer's analogy 'the paradox of double agency, the hidden hand of God making the creature make itself, in and through the interaction of each created energy, at each level of complexity, thus realising specific divine purposes in the evolution of man, in the history of our salvation, and in men's lives as they open themselves up to the will of God, and become the vehicles of God's action to each other' 'Providence and divine action' n. 34, p. 229).

42   Farrer, *Faith and Speculation*, p. 66.

43   Maurice Wiles, 'Farrer's concept of divine agency', *Theology*, 84 (1981), p. 248.

44   Langford, *Providence*, p. 76.

45   ibid.

46   ibid., p. 87.

47 ibid.
48 ibid., p. 89.
49 See also this chapter, section 3b.
50 Langford, *Providence*, p. 90.
51 ibid.
52 White, *Fall of a Sparrow*, p. 108.
53 The resort of Vernon White (ibid., pp. 104–5), and indeed of D. J. Bartholomew (*God of Chance*, p. 142), to the ill-established claims that 'psychokinetic' phenomena occur, can only be regarded as a counsel of despair, if not as an outright aberration.
54 Vincent Brummer, *What Are We Doing When We Pray?* (SCM Press, London, 1984).
55 ibid., p. 90.
56 See ch. 3, section 1.
57 For a discussion of the irreducible unpredictability of non-linear dynamical systems at the macroscopic level, see pp. 50–3.
58 John Polkinghorne, *Science and Providence* (SPCK, London, 1989), p. 31.
59 John V. Taylor, *The Go-between God* (SCM Press), 1972, p. 28.
60 Polkinghorne, *Science and Providence*, p. 31.
61 ibid., p. 32.
62 I, too, with both Taylor and Polkinghorne, wish to stress emphatically that God interacts continuously with the world to implement his purposes, but I suggest that his influence on events is by means of a continuous top-down causative input on the world as a whole in the way elaborated later in this section. I agree with John Polkinghorne that this 'input', in my approach regarded as into the system as a whole, may best be conceived of as that of information, but am less certain than he that *no* energy is required for such an input (as we saw, Hawking has also argued that there can be no storage of information without expenditure of energy (ch. 2, section 1 and n. 1)). Even 'the bead at the top of a vertical smooth U-shaped wire' (Polkinghorne, *Science and Providence*, p. 32) cannot require less than one quantum of energy to make it go to one side rather than the other. One can never escape entirely the conundrum of the 'causal joint'! Although the *concept* of information is clearly distinguishable from that of energy, in the real world we seem to know of no transfers of information that do not involve exchanges of matter/energy, however small relatively to the scale of the systems in question.
63 Ch. 8, section 2.
64 For the reasons why the majority of physicists reject the existence of 'hidden variables' underlying the probabilistic predictions of quantum theory which would make the theory deterministic, see J. C. Polkinghorne, *The Quantum World* (Penguin Books, Harmondsworth, 1986), chs. 5 and 7. See also our earlier discussion on divine knowledge (ch.

8, section 2(c)) for what such 'self-limitation' of God's knowledge might mean.
65   Ch. 3, section 1.
66   Ch. 8, section 2(c).
67   Ch. 3, section 3(a).
68   Karl Popper, lecture to the World Philosophy Congress, Brighton, August 1988; reported in *The Guardian*, 29 August 1988.
69   Bartholomew, *God of Chance*, p. 138.
70   Ch. 8, section 2(b).
71   Ch. 3, sections 1 and 2.
72   Ch. 3, section 1(d).
73   Ch. 3, section 2(b).
74   Ch. 3, section 2(c).
75   e.g., the present author in *CWS*, pp. 45, 141, 201, 207, 352, where this way of speaking is denoted as 'pan-*en*-theism'. This term is defined (*Oxford Dictionary of the Christian Church*, 2nd edn, revised, ed. F. L. Cross and E. A. Livingstone, Oxford University Press, Oxford, 1983, p. 1027) as 'The belief that the Being of God includes and penetrates the whole universe, so that every part of it exists in Him but (as against pantheism) that His Being is more than, and is not exhausted by, the universe.' Since it was first defined by K. C. F. Krause (1781–1832) it seems to have incurred some disfavour for reasons not readily apparent. In our century it has been particularly espoused by process theologians. However, the basic concept, as defined in this text and by the definition in the *Oxford Dictionary of the Christian Church*, seems to me to be not at all dependent on that particular metaphysical system and to be entirely consistent with Christian theism as a useful spatial model.

It does not, in my usage at least, have any implication (cf. John Polkinghorne, *Science and Creation*, SPCK, London, 1988, p. 53) that the world is in some sense a *part* of God, that is, of the same kind of being as God. This would indeed deny the ultimate otherness of God from that which he has created and imply that the world was of the same stuff or 'substance' as God himself. But this does not follow from the definition of the term which allows there to be an ontological gap in mode of being between God and the world while at the same time stressing two essential features of that relation – the accessibility of all-that-is to God and God's ultimate ontological 'beyondness', expressed by a spatial metaphor in the model. Because of misconceptions surrounding the word 'pan-en-theism', I shall, as far as possible, avoid its use, but not the idea itself, as defined above.

David Pailin in his *God and the Processes of Reality* (Routledge, London and New York, 1989, ch. 5) has given a useful exposition of the idea of 'panentheism' following mainly the expositions of Charles Hartshorne. They both contrast it with 'classical pantheism' and with 'classical (immured) theism'. For classical pantheism, 'the divine being is constituted by the sum total of all that truly is' (ibid., p. 77), the divine is totally receptive of all events in the world, and it also 'involves a denial of God's genuine independence of the world' (p. 77). For classical theism, 'God and the constituents of the world have each an appropriate degree of autonomy and the nature of the divine is such that no significant reciprocity is possible between them' (p. 78); it denies any dependence of God on the world. This God of 'classical theism', as both Hartshorne and Pailin denote it, is necessary, absolute and perfect – like the God of some philosophers. Neither of these theisms corresponds to the God of Christian belief, as we inferred earlier (ch. 7, section 2, and ch. 8), and I share their desire to affirm both that God is causally independent of the world, that the world has a derivative existence, and is thereby dependent on God, *and* that God interacts continuously with the world. So 'panentheism is not a new position but a new appreciation of the proper conceptual structure of a dominant tradition of religious faith in God' (p. 81). The technical term 'panentheism' for Christian theism, awkward though it is, at least expresses an overt desire to hold together both the transcendence and the immanence of God in relation to the world. Moreover Pailin, in concord with Hartshorne, regards their 'dipolar panentheism' as a 'concept of God as Eternal-Temporal Consciousness, Knowing and including the World (ETCKW)' (p. 84).

Some or all of these attributes of God have been variously deduced by others (e.g., by R. Swinburne; see ch. 7, section 1) on grounds, it should be noted, that do not invoke the metaphysics of 'process thought', with which the term 'panentheism' has, in my view, been unfortunately too closely tied. I think process theology has tended to over-emphasize God's *total* receptivity to all events in the world in a way that seems to allow God little discrimination. In my own past usage of the term 'panentheism', I have not wanted to imply an equally direct involvement of God in all events nor that all events equally and in the same sense affect God – as often appears to be an implication of process theology.

76 *Acts*, 17:28 (AV).

77 *Confessions*, VII.7, trans. E. B. Pusey (from *Great Books of the Western World*, vol. 18, ed. R. M. Hutchins, Encyclopaedia Brittanica, Inc., Chicago, 1952, p. 45).

78 See, *inter alia*, C. Blakemore, *The Mechanics of the Mind* (Cambridge University Press, Cambridge, 1976); the articles assembled in the *Scientific American* publication *The Brain*, (W. H. Freeman, San Francisco and Oxford, 1979); and the comprehensive information in *The Oxford Companion to the Mind*, ed. Richard L. Gregory (Oxford University Press, Oxford, 1987).

79 cf. the earlier quotation from I. T. Ramsey, a Christian philosopher of religion, ch. 4, section 1, and n. 7.

80 A. R. Peacocke, *CWS*, pp. 119–22, 128–31; idem, 'A Christian

materialism?', in *How We Know*, ed. M. Shafto (Harper and Row, San Francisco, 1985), pp. 146–68.

81   ibid., pp. 147–9, 163–4.
82   Ch. 3, section 2(c).
83   p. 61.
84   This chapter, section 4.
85   Kaufman, *God the Problem*; Wiles, *God's Action in the World*.
86   Hugh Montefiore, *The Probability of God* (SCM Press, London, 1985), p. 98.
87   e.g. in *CWS*, pp. 104ff., 210, *passim*.
88   In *GNB*, pp. 97ff.
89   However, this response did not satisfy David Pailin (in *God and the Processes of Reality*, Routledge, London and New York, 1989), who considered that an emphasis on the inherent creativity of natural processes still cannot avoid implying 'that while God initially established the potentialities of the constituents of that [evolutionary] process, *it develops automatically*.... this way of understanding divine creativity suggests that God does not affect what particular forms of being emerge in the natural order.... God on this view seems to have neither direct nor even indirect influence on what happens – until, perhaps, human beings... appear' (p. 136, italics added).

But if, as I am here suggesting, God is interacting with the whole world system in a top-down causative action on the whole, then this divine action: (a) would be discernible by us only through the actualizations of the potentialities of the fundamental entities of the universe and of the natural processes they undergo, as, manifest in their inbuilt propensities towards complexity, sensitivity and open-endedness (and so towards consciousness and freedom); and (b), at the same time, could be the means whereby God effected his purposes by steering events towards particular instantiations of these selfsame potentialities, and as particular manifestations of their inbuilt propensities – yet without any 'intervention by God' occurring at any level lower than that of the whole, that is, at any of the lower levels analysed by the particular sciences appropriate to them.

I would suggest that this 'top-down' causal interpretation of God's continuous interaction with the world as a whole provides a coherent way of combining a strong emphasis on the immanence of God in and the transcendence of God over the world and its processes, both of which I have previously argued (in *CWS* and *GNB*) must be held together for a satisfactory conception of God's relation to the world. This combination of the ideas of immanence and top-down causation (and of the other considerations in the main text) seems to me to be more coherent with the ability of the natural sciences to interpret the processes of the natural world at many observable levels than is the postulate of process theology that there is some kind of direct divine influence on *all* particular natural events (often called a 'lure', as if all events had a mental component).

On the view proposed here, God's general interaction with the world as a whole can, but not must, have particular consequences, if God wills them in accord with his general purposes for the universe and its creatures, without any intervening (or 'giving an aim', or 'luring', in process terminology) at the level in the whole system of natural processes at which the particular event to be influenced occurs.

90 See p. 145, above.
91 See n. 62 above.
92 David Galilee and Brian Hebblethwaite, 'Farrer's concept of double agency: a reply', *Theology*, 35 (1982), pp. 7–10.
93 ibid., p. 9.
94 ibid.
95 Ch. 8, sections 1 and 2.
96 John Macquarrie, 'God and the World', *Theology*, 75 (1972), pp. 394–403.
97 ibid., p. 394.
98 ibid., pp. 394–5.
99 See Sallie McFague, *Models of God* (SCM Press, London, 1987), pp. 63ff. For McFague the patriarchal associations of the monarchical models rule them out of consideration, but I think this dismissal is unwarranted. For these models incorporate a sense of the personal transcendence of God over the world that is essential to the concept of God, even when any false notion of 'maleness' in the Godhead is, quite rightly, expunged.
100 *We Believe in God*, report of the Doctrine Commission of the Church of England (Church House Publishing, London, 1987), pp. 148ff.
101 ibid., p. 149.
102 ibid.
103 McFague, *Models of God, passim*.
104 e.g., the present author in *CWS* (pp. 141ff.), in which I point out that if in some sense the world is 'within' God (a spatial metaphor), God is 'more than' the world and God is creator *of* the world, then a natural analogy is that of a mother bearing a child within her, with the obvious limiting ('is not') feature of this metaphor, namely that God is the source of being of that which God creates within 'herself', whereas a human mother is not the *creator* of the growing embryo she carries within her.
105 *We Believe in God*, p. 154.
106 For fuller expositions see *IR* (ch. 1) and A. R. Peacocke, 'Science and theology today: a critical realist perspective', *Religion and Intellectual Life*, 5 (1988), pp. 45–58 and references therein; also Janet Martin Soskice, *Metaphor and Religious Language* (Clarendon Press, Oxford, 1985) and McFague, *Models of God*.

107 McFague, *Models of God*, pp. 69–78; Grace Jantzen, *God's World, God's Body* (Darton, Longman and Todd, London, 1984).

108 According to Julius Lipner, it could also, if taken seriously by Christians, be of great value in dialogue with Hinduism, in the light of the theology of Ramanuja, an eleventh- to twelfth- century (CE) Tamil Brahmin (J. J. Lipner, 'The world as God's 'body': in pursuit of dialogue with Ramanuja', *Religious Studies*, 20 (1984), pp. 145–61.

109 Our stress is on models of the *creative* activity of God in the world. But, of course, these do not exhaust the range of metaphors that have been employed to represent God's general activity in the world. I. T. Ramsey, for example, in *Models for Divine Activity* (SCM Press, London, 1973), demonstrates how 'Spirit' (= 'wind' or 'breath') has been developed and grown in the Judeo-Christian tradition as a model of God's activity. '*Spirit is a noun* whose logical tradition is more reliably a verb: *being active, God-active*. It tells of a becoming, not a *being*' (p. 14). He also shows how the model of 'economy' (with its senses of administration, provision for need and discipline) was once used widely by Christian theologians as a model for God's activity, but has fallen into desuetude. Finally, he develops the model of God's ubiquity or omnipresence that is provided by talk of God's locatable presence, which may be impersonal or personal – and the latter connotation, of God's personal presence, has been employed by M. Wiles (*Faith and the Mystery of God*, SCM Press, London, 1982, pp. 122ff.) to express God's action in the world in relation to both prayer and to the concept of 'spirit' and, following G. W. H. Lampe (*God as Spirit*, Oxford University Press, 1977), in relation to the Incarnation.

110 Macquarrie, *Principles*, pp. 200–9.

111 ibid.

112 Stephen Hobhouse, *The Selected Mystical Writings of William Law* (C. W. Daniel & Co., London, 1938), p. 250.

113 From William Law, *An Appeal* (1740), reproduced in Hobhouse, *Selected Mystical Writings*, p. 36.

114 Macquarrie, *Principles*, pp. 200–9.

115 e.g. Macquarrie, *Principles*, p. 202; and, more recently, this model has been endorsed as helpful and suggestive in *We Believe in God*, n. 77, pp. 151ff.

116 Dorothy Sayers, *The Mind of the Maker* (Methuen, London, 1941), p. 23.

117 ibid., p. 97.

118 ibid., p. 28. She stresses that 'Idea' in this quotation is not used in the traditional philosopher's sense but in the sense in which it is used by a writer when he says 'I have an idea for a book'; and 'energy' and 'power' are similarly used in their everyday, non-physicist's, sense.

119 ibid., p. 42.

120 Austin Farrer, *A Science of God?* (Geoffrey Bles, London, 1966), p. 76.

121 Wiles, *God's Action*, p. 37.

122   *We Believe in God*, p. 151.
123   Sayers, *Mind of the Maker*, pp. 45–7.
124   Quoted by Karl Popper in his 'intellectual autobiography', *Unended Quest* (Fontana/Collins, London, 1976), p. 59; see p. 206, n. 59 for details.
125   ibid.
126   See *CWS*, pp. 82–4.
127   Ch. 3, section 3(a).
128   cf. *CWS*, pp. 105–6.
129   This and the preceding follow closely paragraphs in *IR*, pp. 72–3.
130   The fascinating nature of music has also provided Colin Gunton with concepts useful in interpreting the Christian doctrine of the Incarnation (in *Yesterday and Today: A Study of Continuities in Christology*, Darton, Longman and Todd, London, 1983, pp. 115ff.); and it has proved to be a rich quarry for M. Eigen and R. Winkler in explicating aspects of modern biology and other sciences (*Laws of the Game*, Knopf, New York, 1981, and Allen Lane, London, 1982), as well as many otherwise baffling features of modern physical concepts of the world (see also A. R. Peacocke, 'The theory of relativity and our world view', in *Einstein: The First Hundred Years*, ed. M. Goldsmith, A. Mackay and J. Woudhuysen, Pergamon Press, Oxford and London, 1980, esp. pp. 87–9, where reference is made to the use of musical imagery by M. Capek, *The Philosophical Impact of Contemporary Physics*, Van Nostrand, Princeton, 1961, pp. 371ff.).
131   T. S. Eliot, 'The Dry Salvages', *The Four Quartets*, 11. 210–12.
132   For an earlier exposition of this suggestion, see *SCE*, pp. 194–6; and *CWS*, ch. 7, esp. pp. 304–11.
133   I am indebted to Sir David Lumsden, for his helpful contributions to my thinking in this paragraph and, indeed, this whole section on musical creativity.
134   Some of the ideas in this section were originally presented in *CWS*.
135   Psalm 33 v. 6.
136   See ch. 3, section 2; ch. 9, section 2(b), (c).
137   John Macquarrie, 'God and the world: one reality or two?', *Theology*, 75 (1972), pp. 394–403.
138   ibid., p. 400–1.
139   ibid., p. 401.
140   Ch. 3, section 1.
141   C. E. Raven, *Natural Religion and Christian Theology*, Gifford lectures, 2nd series, 1952, *Experience and Interpretation*, (Cambridge University Press, Cambridge, 1953), II, p. 157.
142   cf. *CWS*, pp. 208–9.
143   Grace M. Jantzen, *God's World, God's Body* (Darton, Longman, and Todd, 1984), p. 98.
144   Ch. 8, section 2(c).
145   See above, p. 135.

146 Langford, *Providence*, pp. 13–24; Macquarrie, *Principles*, ch. XI.
147 Langford, *Providence*, p. 17.
148 ibid., p. 18.
149 ibid., p. 19.
150 This chapter, section 1.

POSTSCRIPT

1 John Macquarrie, *Principles of Christian Theology* (SCM Press, London, 1966), p. 101.
2 'Lets-be' in the terminology of Macquarrie, ibid.
3 For an interesting exposition and analysis of these terms in the context of the theologies of Charles Hartshorne and Karl Barth, see Colin E. Gunton, *Being and Becoming* (Oxford University Press, Oxford, 1978).
4 See David A. Pailin, *God and the Processes of Reality* (Routledge, London and New York, 1989), esp. ch. 7. Pailin takes a stronger line than is adopted here, namely, that God is *necessarily* creative: '..."If God, then creator" seems a necessary entailment (for a being which is not the creative ground of all reality would not satisfy the definition of what it is to be 'God'); and "If creator, then continually and universally involved in events" seems a plausible implication (for a God who initiated the creative process and then carelessly abandoned it to its own devices ... is hardly a proper object of worship).... To cast doubt ... on the possibility of talking significantly about God as creator is to cast doubt on the significance of theistic understanding' (p. 123). 'As personal ... the divine must be held to be related to what is other than Godself, since it is only possible to be personal in relation to others. Similarly, it may be argued that as ultimate in value God must be considered to be loving ... and that to be loving requires objects for its expression.... God cannot be coherently considered to be without a world and so must be regarded as necessarily creative' (p. 126).
5 A. Louth in *The Origin of the Christian Mystical Tradition* (Clarendon Press, Oxford, 1981, p. 91) quotes Gregory of Nyssa: 'for he is invisible by nature, but becomes visible in His energies, for He may be contemplated in the things that are referred to Him' (*Hom.* VI, 12690, in H. Graef's translation). Louth goes on to make the point that, for Gregory of Nyssa, to know God is to possess him not to be informed about him. The soul is a mirror reflecting the divine image and therefore contemplates God by contemplating the divine image present within itself. 'In the darkness of unknowability the soul contemplates God in the mirror that it is' (Louth, *loc.cit.*).
6 According to Rowan Williams, *The Wound of Knowledge*, (Darton, Longman and Todd, London, 1979), pp. 54–5.
7 ibid., p. 54.

8 cf. *CWS*, pp. 131ff.

9 cf. *CWS*, pp. 212–13.

10 A. R. Peacocke, *Theology for a Scientific Age (Part III): Human Being and Becoming,* in preparation.

11 Related by F. C. Copleston, *Aquinas* (Penguin Books, London, 1955), p. 10.

INDEX

(of the main text and of extended notes)